NYSTCE® STUDENTS WITH DISABILITIES (060)

Ken Springer, Ph.D.
Southern Methodist University
Dallas, Texas

Michelle Chamblin, Ed.D.
Molloy College
Rockville Centre, New York

Ann Monroe-Baillargeon, Ph.D.
Alfred University
Alfred, New York

Research & Education Association

Research & Education Association
61 Ethel Road West
Piscataway, New Jersey 08854
E-mail: info@rea.com

**NYSTCE® Students with Disabilities (060)
with Online Practice Tests**

Printed in the United States of America

Library of Congress Control Number 2015954888

ISBN-13: 978-0-7386-1145-7
ISBN-10: 0-7386-1145-X

The competencies presented in this book were created and implemented by the New York
State Department of Education. For further information visit *www.ny.nesinc.com*.

Cover image: © iStockphoto.com/Peopleimages

All trademarks cited in this publication are the property of their respective owners.

REA® is a registered trademark of
Research & Education Association, Inc.

Contents

CONTENTS

CONTENTS

About Our Authors

Dr. Ken Springer is a faculty member at Southern Methodist University. After receiving his Ph.D. from Cornell University in 1990, he joined SMU's Psychology Department. In 2002, he moved to the Department of Teaching and Learning, where he teaches graduate classes in methodology and conducts research in the area of academic achievement.

Michelle Chamblin earned her Ed.D. from Teachers College, Columbia University in New York. She has worked as a special education teacher for The New York City Board of Education and a resource room teacher and administrator for the Elmont School District also located in New York. Michelle has worked with children and families both in the United States and abroad on matters pertaining to education. She currently works as an Associate Professor at Molloy College located in Rockville Centre, New York. Above all, she is a fearless mother of triplets!

Ann Monroe-Baillargeon, Ph.D., is the chair and professor of Education at Alfred University, in Alfred, New York. Dr. Monroe-Baillargeon received her B.A. degree in Special Education from The University of Wisconsin-Milwaukee, her M.S. degree in Educational Leadership from the University of Southern Maine, and her Ph.D. in Teaching and Curriculum from Syracuse University. She teaches courses in special education, inclusive education, literacy practices, research methodologies, and advanced trends in education. Her research focuses on inclusive education and teacher education and literacy. Her work in teacher education is deeply informed by her sister Lisa, a woman with mental retardation for whom she is a legal guardian and advocate, and her 15 years of K-12 teaching and leadership in special education.

About REA

Founded in 1959, Research & Education Association (REA) is dedicated to publishing the finest and most effective educational materials—including study guides and test preps—for students in middle school, high school, college, graduate school, and beyond.

Today, REA's wide-ranging catalog is a leading resource for students, teachers, and other professionals. Visit *www.rea.com* to see a complete listing of all our titles.

Acknowledgments

We would like to thank Pam Weston, Publisher, for setting the quality standards for production integrity and managing the publication to completion; John Cording, Vice President, Technology, for coordinating the design and development of the REA Study Center; Larry B. Kling, Vice President, Editorial, for supervision of revisions and overall direction; Diane Goldschmidt, Managing Editor, for coordinating development of this edition; Kathy Caratozzolo of Caragraphics for typesetting this edition; Linda Robbian for copyediting; Ellen Gong for proofreading; and Eve Grinnell, Graphic Artist, for page design.

CHAPTER 1

Passing the NYSTCE Students with Disabilities Test

Congratulations! By taking the NYSTCE Students with Disabilities test, you are on your way to a rewarding teaching career. Our book and the online tools that come with it give you what you need to succeed on this important exam, bringing you one step closer to being certified to teach in New York.

Our NYSTCE Students with Disabilities Book + Online Prep package includes:

- Complete overview of the NYSTCE Students with Disabilities examination

- Comprehensive review of all competencies

- Two full-length practice tests (in the book and online) with powerful diagnostic tools to help you pinpoint your strengths and weaknesses and focus your study

- Detailed answer explanations

There are many different ways to prepare for the NYSTCE Students with Disabilities test. What's best for you depends on how much time you have to study and how comfortable you are with the subject matter. Our book and online tests give you the tools you need to customize your prep so you can make the most of your study time.

How to Use this Book + Online Prep

About the Review

The review chapters in this book are designed to help you sharpen your command of all the skills you'll need to pass the NYSTCE Students with Disabilities test. Whether you're a recent graduate of a traditional teacher education program or you've gone the alternate route, our review will reinforce what you have learned and show you how to relate the information you have acquired to the specific competencies on the exam.

Our targeted review covers what you need to know to succeed on the exam. After studying our review, you will have an excellent grasp of the subject matter and a solid foundation for passing the exam.

About the REA Study Center

We know your time is valuable and you want an efficient study experience. At the online REA Study Center (*www.rea.com/studycenter*), you will get diagnostic feedback right from the start on what you know and what you don't know.

Here's what you'll find at the Study Center:

- **2 Full-Length Practice Tests**—Simulate the computer-based format of the acutal NYSTCE test and give you the most complete picture of your strengths and weaknesses.

- **Automatic Scoring**—Find out how you did on your test, instantly.

- **Diagnostic Score Reports**—Get a specific score tied to each competency, so you can focus on the areas that challenge you the most.

- **On-screen Detailed Answer Explanations**—See why the correct response option is right, and learn why the other answer choices are incorrect.

- **Timed Testing**—Learn to manage your time as you practice, so you'll feel confident on test day.

If you are studying and don't have Internet access, you can take the printed tests in the book. These are the same practice tests offered at the REA Study Center, but without the added benefits of timed testing conditions and diagnostic score reports. Remember, the more you practice, the more comfortable you will be with the format of the NYSTCE Students with Disabilities test—and that will help you score higher!

Getting Started

Before you work through this book, we strongly recommend that you visit the New York State Teacher Certification Examinations website at *www.nystce.nesinc.com*. There you'll find the most current information on the exam, including registration information, testing sites, testing format, test-day advice, registration cost, and other available test preparation materials.

An Overview of the Test

Who Takes the Test, and What Is It Used for?

The NYSTCE Students with Disabilities test is used by the State of New York to assess knowledge of teacher certification candidates. If you do not achieve a passing score on the test, don't panic. You can take the test again, so you can work on improving your score in preparation for your next administration.

About Computer-Based Testing

The NYSTCE Students with Disabilities test is offered only on computer at flexible times and locations throughout the year. In computer-based testing, examinees complete the test by selecting answers on-screen to multiple-choice questions and typing responses to constructed-response assignments. The NYSTCE Students with Disabilities test contains one constructed-response item.

When Should the NYSTCE Students with Disabilities Test Be Taken?

The test is usually taken immediately before the completion of a teacher certification program at a college or university. This gives candidates enough time to retake the test if necessary. Our practice tests will familiarize you with the format of the exam so that you do not have to go through the anxiety of learning about the NYSTCE Students with Disabilities test during the actual exam.

When and Where Is the Test Given?

The NYSTCE Students with Disabilities test is administered at various times and locations in New York State and in select cities nationwide. The exam can be taken year-round, Monday through Saturday by appointment. To find a testing center near you, visit the official website: *www.nystce.nesinc.com*.

Is There a Registration Fee?

Yes, you must pay a fee to take the NYSTCE Students with Disabilities test. Payment must be made at the time of registration using a credit card (VISA or MasterCard only).

Why should I take the NYSTCE Students with Disabilities Test?

The New York State Certification Examinations (NYSTCE) includes among its components a set of Content Specialty Tests. Teachers in New York must achieve passing scores on the Content Specialty Test in their subject area. A passing score on this exam is among the requirements for several different certificates. Whether you are a student, a graduate from an approved teacher preparation program in New York State, or an educator who has received certification in another state, you should carefully read the requirements for working with students with disabilities provided on the New York State Education Department website.

What Is Assessed on the NYSTCE Students with Disabilities Test?

The NYSTCE Students with Disabilities exam tests seven broad competencies along with the performance indicators aligned to each competency. Listed on the next page are the competencies used as the basis for the Students with Disabilities examination, as well as the approximate percentage of the total exam that each competency covers. These competencies represent the knowledge that teams of teachers, administrators, subject area specialists, and others have determined to be important for beginning teachers who work with students with disabilities.

Each chapter in this book reviews the competencies one by one. The review material is organized within each chapter by the performance indicators that the New York State Education Department lists for each competency.

The following chart shows the approximate percentages devoted to each subject covered on the exam:

Competency	Approximate Percentage of Questions on the Exam
0001 Foundations of Special Education	10%
0002 Knowledge of Students with Disabilities	10%
0003 Assessment and Individual Program Planning	20%
0004 Strategies for Planning and Managing the Learning Environment and for Providing Behavioral Interventions	10%
0005 Instructional Planning and Delivery to Promote Students' Success in the General Curriculum	20%
0006 Strategies for Teaching Communication Skills, Social Skills, and Functional Living Skills	10%
0007 Analysis, Synthesis and Application (1 constructed-response question)	20%

Scoring the NYSTCE Students with Disabilities Test

How is the Test Scored?

The Students with Disabilities exam consists of 90 selected-response questions and 1 constructed-response question. You will have 195 minutes to complete the exam. It is suggested that you spend approximately 60 minutes completing the selected-response section and 135 minutes responding to the constructed-response question. You will not lose points for incorrect answers to the selected-response questions; therefore, you should not leave any of these questions unanswered. However, you must respond to the constructed-response question. If you do not respond, or if your response is otherwise unscorable, you will not pass.

Responses to the 91 items are scaled so that scores on the Students with Disabilities test range from 100 to 300. A score of 220 is considered passing.

When Will I Receive my Score Report?

Scores for the Students with Disabilities test are available roughly one month after the exam date. The exact dates of availability are specified on the NYSTCE website.

Study Schedule

Although our study plan is designed to be used in the six weeks before your exam, if necessary, it can be condensed to three weeks by combining each two-week period into one. Be sure to set aside enough time—at least two hours each day—to study. The more time you spend studying, the more prepared and relaxed you will feel on the day of the exam.

When you take the practice tests, be sure to simulate the conditions of the test as closely as possible. Turn off all electronic devices and sit down at a table free from distraction. Read each question carefully, consider all answer choices, and pace yourself.

As you complete each practice test, review the detailed explanations for the questions you answered incorrectly. Concentrate on one problem area at a time by reading the question and explanation, and by studying our review until you are confident that you have mastered the material. Give extra attention to the review chapters that cover your areas of difficulty, as this will build your skills in those areas.

Week	Activity
1–3	Study review chapters 1 through 8. Useful study techniques include highlighting key terms and information and taking notes as you read the review. Learn all the competencies by making flashcards to help you study.
4	Take online Practice Test 1.* Review your score report, and identify topics where you need more review.
5	Take online Practice Test 2.* Review your score report and restudy the appropriate review section(s) until you are confident you understand the material.
6	With your score report in hand, use the time remaining before the actual test to restudy any topics you missed. If time allows retake the Practice Tests and see how much your score has improved.

*If you do not have Internet access, take the printed versions of the tests in the book. These are the same practice tests offered online, but without the added benefits of timed testing conditions, automatic scoring and diagnostic score reports.

Test-Taking Tips to Boost Your Score

Although you have probably taken standardized tests before, you may still experience some anxiety about the Students with Disabilities test. This is perfectly normal, and there are several ways to help alleviate test-day nervousness. Here are some tips to help you raise your score.

1. Guess Away

One of the most frequently asked questions about the Students with Disabilities test is: Can I guess? The answer: absolutely! There is no penalty for guessing. That means that if you guess incorrectly, you will not lose any points, but if you guess correctly, you will gain points. While it's fine to guess, it's important to guess smartly, or use the process of elimination (see Strategy No. 2). Your score is based strictly on the number of correct answers. So answer all questions and take your best guess when you don't know the answer.

2. Process of Elimination

Process of elimination is one of the most important test-taking strategies at your disposal. Process of elimination means looking at the given answer choices and eliminating the ones you know are wrong, including answers that are partially wrong. Your odds of getting the right answer increase when you're able to disregard a wrong choice.

3. All in

Review all the response options. Just because you believe you've found the correct answer—or, in some cases, answers—look at each choice so you don't mistakenly jump to any conclusions. If you are asked to choose the *best* answer, be sure your first answer is really the best one.

4. Letter Choice of the Day

What if you are truly stumped and can't use the process of elimination? It's time to pick a fallback answer. On the day of the test, choose the letter choice (i.e., A, B, C, or D) that you will pick for any question you cannot guess. According to the laws of probability, you have a higher chance of getting an answer right if you stick to one answer choice when you have to guess an answer instead of randomly picking one.

5. Use Choices to Confirm Your Answer

The great thing about multiple-choice questions is that the answer has to be staring back at you. Have an answer in mind and use the choices to *confirm* it.

6. Watch the Clock

Among the most vital point-saving skills is active time management. Keep an eye on the timer on your computer screen. Make sure you stay on top of how much time you have left and never spend too much time on any one question. Remember, most multiple-choice questions are worth one raw point. Treat each one as if it's the one that will put you over the top. (You never know, it just might.) For the constructed-response question, make sure you have enough time to write a well-organized essay. The last thing you want on test day is to lose easy points because you ran out of time and focused too much on difficult questions.

7. Read, Read, Read

It's important to read through all the multiple-choice options. Even if you believe answer choice A is correct, you can misread a question or response option if you're rushing to get through the test. Slow down, calm down, read all the choices. Verify that your choice is the best one, and click on it.

8. Isolate Limiters

Pay attention to any limiters in a multiple-choice question stem. These are words such as *initial, best, most* (as in *most appropriate* or *most likely*), *not, least, except, required,* or *necessary*. Especially watch for negative words, such as "Choose the answer that is *not* true." When you select your answer, double-check yourself by asking how the response fits the limitations established by the stem. Think of the stem as a puzzle piece that perfectly fits only the response option(s) that contain the correct answer. Let it guide you.

9. It's Not a Race

Ignore other test-takers. Don't compare yourself to anyone else in the room. Focus on the items in front of you and the time you have left. If someone finishes the test 30 minutes early, it does not necessarily mean that person answered more questions correctly than you did. Stay calm and focus on *your* test. It's the only one that matters.

10. Confirm Your Click

In the digital age, many of us are used to rapid-clicking, be it in the course of emailing or gaming. Look at the screen to be sure to see that your mouse-click is acknowledged. If your answer doesn't register, you won't get credit. However, if you want to mark it for review so you can return later, that's your call. Before you click "Submit," use the test's review screen to see whether you inadvertently skipped any questions.

11. Creature of Habit? No Worries.

We are all creatures of habit. It's therefore best to follow a familiar pattern of study. Do what's comfortable for you. Set a time and place each day to study for this test. Whether it is 30 minutes at the library or an hour in a secluded corner of your local coffee shop, commit yourself as best you can to this schedule every day. Find quiet places where it is less crowded, as constant background noise can distract you. Don't study one subject for too long, either. Take an occasional breather and treat yourself to a healthy snack or some quick exercise. After your short break—5 or 10 minutes can do the trick—return to what you were studying or start a new section.

12. Knowledge is Power

Purchasing this book gave you an edge on passing the Students with Disabilities test. Make the most of this edge. Review the sections on how the test is structured, what the directions look like, what types of questions will be asked, and so on. Take our practice tests to familiarize yourself with what the test looks and feels like. Most test anxiety occurs because people feel unprepared when they are taking the test, and they psych themselves out. You can whittle away at anxiety by learning the format of the test and by knowing what to expect. Fully simulating the test even once will boost your chances of getting the score you need. Meanwhile, the knowledge you've gained will also will save you the valuable time that would have been eaten up puzzling through what the directions are asking As an added benefit, previewing the test will free up your brain's resources so you can focus on racking up as many points as you can.

13. B-r-e-a-t-h-e

What's the worst that can happen when you take a test? You may have an off day, and despite your best efforts, you may not pass. Well, the good news is that a test can be retaken. In fact, you may already be doing this—this book is every bit for you as it is for first-timers. Fortunately, the Students with Disabilities test is something you can study and prepare for, and in some ways to a greater extent than other tests you've taken throughout your academic career. Yes, there will be questions you won't know, but neither your teacher education program nor state licensing board (which sets its own cut scores) expects you to know everything.

When unfamiliar vocabulary appears, don't despair: Use context clues, process of elimination, or your letter of the day to make your choice, and then press ahead. If you have time left, you can always come back to the question later. If not, relax. It is only one question on a test filled with many. Take a deep breath and then exhale. You know this information. Now you're going to show it.

The Day of the Test

Before the Test

On the day of the test, you should wake up early after a good night's rest. Have a good breakfast and dress in layers that can be removed or added as the conditions in the testing center require. Arrive at the testing center 30 minutes before your scheduled testing time. This will allow you to collect your thoughts before the test, and will also spare you the anguish that comes with being late. As an added incentive to make sure that you arrive early, keep in mind that if you arrive more than 15 minutes late to your test appointment, you may not be admitted.

Before you leave for the testing site, make sure that you have your proper identification. Proper identification must be current, government-issued, printed in English, show the name in which you registered for the exam, and have your photograph and signature.

Acceptable forms of identification include:

- Driver's license with photograph and signature
- Passport with photograph and signature

- State identification with photograph and signature

- National identification with photograph and signature

- Military identification with photograph and signature

- Alien Registration Card

Be sure to check the NYSTCE website close to the date of your test in case there are any changes to these requirements.

There are also very strict rules about what you may not bring to the testing site. You may not bring watches of any kind, cell phones or any other electronic communication devices. Scrap paper, written notes, books, and any printed material is prohibited. Smoking, eating, or drinking are not allowed, so do not bring any food or drinks, including water, to the site. Finally, weapons of any kind are banned, as are any visitors, including relatives.

Once you enter the test center, follow all the rules and instructions given by your test supervisor. Failure to do so may result in your dismissal from the testing center. You may also have your scores canceled.

Good luck on the exam! You are well on your way to certification.

CHAPTER 2

COMPETENCY 0001
Foundations of Special Education

This chapter introduces some of the legal, professional, historical, and scientific foundations of the education of students with disabilities, including special education in the New York State public school system.

Performance Indicator* (a): Historical and philosophical foundations of the field of special education and of contemporary issues, trends, and research

This section briefly touches on the historical and philosophical foundations of special education.

Historical Changes

By the early 20th century, compulsory education had been established in every state in the United States. Children with disabilities were often excluded from public schools. Most states had laws allowing schools to refuse to admit children who could be considered "uneducable." The parents of these children had few options other than to keep their children at home, pay for expensive private schools, or place the children in an institution.

Following World War II, parent-based organizations began to advocate for the educational rights of children with disabilities. These grassroots movements fueled government actions ranging from the Panel on Mental Retardation, created by President John F. Kennedy in 1961, to the creation of the Elementary and Secondary Education Act in 1965. These social and political changes in turn paved the way for the most important piece of legislation affecting the education of students with disabilities: Public Law 94-143, the Education for All Handicapped Children Act (EHA), passed in 1975 and later reauthorized as the Individuals with Disabilities Education Act (IDEA).

---

* "PI" is used throughout this text as an abbreviation for Performance Indicator.

IDEA is grounded in a number of concepts that were innovative at the time of its initial passage, including the granting of children with disabilities the right to a free, appropriate public education in the least restrictive environment (LRE). This requirement of IDEA is commonly referred to as **inclusion**, and as the term suggests, it distinguishes the contemporary treatment of children with disabilities from older approaches in which they were routinely excluded from public school settings.

Broadly, inclusion refers to the practice of educating students with disabilities in the general education classroom, so that they may participate in day-to-day routines alongside students without disabilities to the greatest extent possible. IDEA does not guarantee inclusive education to students with disabilities; rather, it ensures that inclusion is a default, or normative scenario, for which there may be exceptions. IDEA requires that students with disabilities be included in the general education classroom and only removed and/or provided with special services if the classroom environment cannot be modified to adequately support their educational progress. Thus, inclusion can be contrasted with the practice of **mainstreaming**, in which students with disabilities were included in the general education classroom only when their achievement would be near grade level without substantial support. The main difference between inclusion and mainstreaming is that inclusion treats the general education classroom as the student's primary placement, along with the general education teacher as the student's primary instructor. Educational practices that require a student with disabilities to spend time outside the general classroom, or to be instructed by other experts, are considered supplementary.

PI (b): Relevant laws, regulations, state policies, and ethical guidelines (e.g., related to referral, assessment, eligibility, placement within a continuum of services, behavior management planning and implementation, mandated reporting, maintaining confidentiality)

In this section, you will find information about some of the federal and state laws, regulations, policies, and guidelines that impact the education of students with disabilities.

The focus of this section will be on IDEA, as it is the federal legislation with the strongest and most direct impact on special education.

IDEA

The **Individuals with Disabilities Education Improvement Act (IDEIA)** is the federal law that governs the education of children with disabilities. This law was first introduced in 1975 as the Education for All Handicapped Children Act, and then revised, renamed, and reauthorized several times, most recently in 2004.

IDEIA is often simply referred to as the **Individuals with Disabilities Education Act (IDEA)**, which was the name of the law immediately prior to its reauthorization in 2004. You will also see reference to the law as IDEA 2004. All material in this chapter pertains to the current version of the law.

An Overview of IDEA

Through IDEA, the federal government provides states with funding for special education. In turn, the states must comply with numerous requirements that pertain to children ranging from birth to age 21. Some of the more important requirements are summarized as follows:

- States must conduct **Child Find** activities to identify and evaluate children who may have disabilities. Students who may have a disability must be evaluated, at no cost to parents, for their eligibility for special education services. Parents must be involved in the evaluation process. (Throughout this book, the term "parents" will be used as shorthand for "parent(s) or guardian(s).") Either parents or a school professional such as a teacher may request an evaluation, but parental consent is required before evaluation of an individual student can take place.

- Students with disabilities are entitled to the same types of educational experiences as their peers without disabilities. Schools must provide each child with a disability an educational experience that is appropriate to his/her age and abilities at no cost to the parents. This requirement of IDEA is referred to as a **Free Appropriate Public Education (FAPE)**.

- Students with disabilities are to be educated in the **least restrictive environment (LRE)**, meaning that their educational experiences must be as similar as possible to those of children who do not have disabilities. The goal of the LRE requirement is for students with disabilities to remain in the general education classroom to the greatest extent possible, with the fewest possible changes to day-to-day routines, and to be removed from regular classes and/or provided with special services only when the severity of their disability requires doing so in order for them to be educated appropriately. Participation in general education activities is not an all-or-nothing opportunity for students with disabilities; rather, schools must provide a **continuum of services** that allow these students to participate to the greatest extent possible. Along with the FAPE requirement discussed above, the LRE requirement is the foundation of inclusion.

- Between ages 3 and 21, each student with a disability must have an **Individualized Education Program** (also called an individualized education plan or **IEP**). The IEP describes the child's present level of progress and learning capacity, the short- and long-term educational goals for the child, and the accommodations and services which will be provided in order to achieve those goals. (Prior to age 3, each child who shows signs of developmental delay must have an **Individualized Family Service Plan [IFSP]**, a written document similar to the IEP that focuses on the family and the child's natural environment.) The IEP is a written document created by a team typically consisting of the child's parents, a special education professional, a general education teacher, a representative of the school, and others. The educational objectives described in the IEP must be aligned with state curriculum standards for general education. When the student reaches age 16, the IEP must include a description of the student's goals following graduation as well as the transition services needed to achieve those goals.

- The rights and interests of parents and their children with disabilities must be protected through confidentiality with respect to children's educational records, nondiscriminatory practices in the assessments used to determine disability status, the provision of information about parents' and children's rights to the parents in the form of procedural safeguards, and the opportunity for parents to express dissatisfaction with their children's educational experience through due process hearings and other means.

More detail about these and other requirements will be provided throughout this chapter. Further information about IDEA is available at the U.S. Department of Education website at *www.ed.gov*. In addition, the New York State Education Department website contains information about IDEA as well as state laws, policies, and resources pertaining to special education and students with disabilities (see the Office of Special Education pages at *www.nysed.gov*).

Other Legislation

Along with IDEA, other federal legislation impacts the education of students with disabilities. For example:

- The **Vocational Rehabilitation Act** and the **Americans with Disabilities Act (ADA)** forbid discrimination against individuals with disabilities.

- The **Family Educational Rights and Privacy Act (FERPA)** helps ensure the privacy of educational records such as IEPs.

- The **No Child Left Behind Act (NCLB)** increases the accountability of schools with respect to the academic progress of students with disabilities.

Special education in New York is also regulated by state- and city-level legislation. These laws and rules are consistent with, and extend the, provisions of IDEA and other federal legislation.

Referrals

IDEA, as well as New York State regulations, specify a process for referrals. First, in order to determine whether a child has a disability and requires special education services, a referral for evaluation must be made. A referral can be made by parents, school staff, and/or school administrators. Other individuals, such as physicians, judicial officers, and students themselves (if over age 18), can make a request for an initial referral too. In New York State, the multidisciplinary team that receives referrals is called the **Committee on Special Education (CSE)**. (For children between the ages of 3 and 5, this team is called the **Committee on Preschool Special Education [CPSE]**.) The responsibilities of the CSE, which are described in further detail in later chapters (particularly Chapter 4), include the following:

- making arrangements for the evaluation of a student who has been referred

- determining on the basis of evaluation results whether the student is eligible for special education services

- developing and implementing an appropriate IEP

- reviewing the IEP on an annual basis and modifying it as needed

- developing a transition plan

Once a referral has been made, parents will receive a notice that describes their rights and includes contact information for someone who can answer pertinent questions. Parents will also be asked to meet with a social worker and/or other educational professional from the school, at which time their rights will be explained in their preferred language or mode of communication. Parents whose children have not previously received special education services will be asked to sign a consent form permitting evaluation. In the case of an initial referral, parental consent is required in order for evaluation to proceed. However, school officials may attempt to obtain authority to conduct an evaluation by means of mediation or an impartial hearing.

■ Assessment

The assessment of students with disabilities is governed by IDEA, NCLB, the ADA, and other federal, and New York State laws and regulations. The following are requirements that IDEA specifies with respect to the assessment of students who have, or who are suspected to have, disabilities:

- School officials must notify parents prior to any assessments over and above those that are routinely administered to all students. Parental permission is required prior to beginning these assessments.

- The assessments must be conducted by an interdisciplinary team that includes at least one teacher or educational professional who is knowledgeable about the student's suspected disability.

- Assessments must be carried out on an individual basis.

- Assessments must consist of more than one test or criterion for determining eligibility for special education services, and for determining placement.

- Assessment materials must be nondiscriminatory with respect to the student's racial and cultural background, and the assessments must be administered in the student's primary language or mode of communication.

- Assessments must be empirically validated for the purpose for which they are used and must be administered by individuals trained in their administration.

- Test protocols must be adhered to unless it is necessary to make accommodations for a particular student.

- For children between birth and three years of age, assessment must take place in "natural" environments such as the home or day care center.

Further details on assessment and evaluation are provided in Chapter 4.

Confidentiality

Together with the FERPA, IDEA provides for the confidentiality of education records that are created and maintained for children with disabilities. Confidentiality must be maintained with respect to information that might unnecessarily identify a student as having a disability. Parents must be informed of this requirement and must give consent in order for personally identifiable information to be shared outside of the school district. Parents must also have access to all such information maintained by the school.

The IEP is an education record created specifically for children with disabilities. As such, the contents of the IEP must be kept confidential, except when school staff has a legitimate need to be aware of the contents. The amount of information a teacher, for example, may have about a particular child's IEP will vary from student to student. Parents may request that teachers have access to information in the IEP.

> **PI (c): The rights and responsibilities of students with disabilities, parents/guardians, teachers, other professionals, and schools**

Some of the rights and responsibilities of the stakeholders involved in special education were discussed in the previous section. This section provides further information about procedural safeguards and due process.

Procedural Safeguards

Procedural safeguards consist of a set of rules and procedures designed to protect the rights and interests of parents and their children with disabilities. IDEA requires that schools give parents of children with disabilities an explanation of the procedural safeguards, also known as parents' rights, when their children are evaluated or re-evaluated, (a) when the parents are invited to CSE or CPSE committee meetings, (b) when the parents file a complaint, and (c) when they request the procedural safeguards. The following are examples of information conveyed in the procedural safeguards:

- Parents must receive notice in advance of any meetings, evaluations, services, placements, or other activities involving the child. Parents can choose the language or mode of communication for such notices.

- Parental consent is required prior to any actions pertaining to the child and prior to the sharing of any information about the child outside of the school district. Parents can give consent to none, some, or all of the services recommended.

- Parents are entitled to see their children's educational records and to receive explanations and interpretations of the records from the school district.

- Mediation will be provided to parents who have complaints or who cannot agree with the CSE or CPSE team on planning or services for their children. If mediation is unsuccessful, a due process hearing will allow parents' complaints to be addressed by an impartial, outside expert appointed by the Board of Education.

Due Process

In general, **due process** refers to principles that attempt to guarantee the rights of citizens. The rights and responsibilities that IDEA accords to parents, children, and schools are complex, and there are many potential sources of conflict. Parents may disagree with the decision of the CSE or CPSE as to whether their child has a disability or with the team's view of the nature of that disability. Parents may disagree with the school's placement of the child in or out of the general education classroom. They may disagree with other elements of the school's approach to educating the child, or they may feel that the quality of the educational experience is inconsistent or lacking. Owing to these and other conflicts that arise, **due process hearings** allow the parents to bring their complaints before an impartial, experienced individual from outside the school district. IDEA requires states to create a mechanism for due process hearings while allowing the states some latitude in procedural details. The hearings are conducted at no cost to parents, although parents are ordinarily responsible for their attorney's fees. Due process hearings can also be requested by schools, as happens sometimes, for example, when parents refuse to allow a child to be evaluated for the presence of a disability.

Age of Majority

The **age of majority** is the age that a person becomes a legal adult. In many states, including New York, the age of majority is 18. Once a student with a disability has reached the age of majority, the student must receive notice of IEP meetings, consent to evaluations and other IEP content, and otherwise function as their parents once did prior to the student reaching the age of majority.

> **PI (d): Culturally responsive strategies that promote effective communication and partnerships with students with disabilities and their parents/guardians to help students with disabilities achieve desired learning outcomes**

This section discusses culturally responsive strategies for promoting effective communication and collaboration among the stakeholders in special education.

Culture refers to shared values, beliefs, and practices that can be transmitted from one generation to the next. Some of these values, beliefs, and practices will be present across cultures, while others will be distinctive to a particular culture. However, even within a particular culture, not all individuals will share the same values. Moreover, culture is constantly changing. Effective communication between educational professionals and the families they serve can be challenging even when all parties have the same cultural backgrounds. When cultural backgrounds differ, teachers and other educational professionals will need to use culturally responsive strategies to facilitate effective communication.

Effective communication across cultures begins with the understanding that there are surface and underlying cultural differences. Differences in clothing, eating habits, and language all reflect surface differences. Below the surface are ideas and assumptions that may have a substantial impact on behavior even if not explicitly articulated. For example, there are cultural differences in what constitutes polite and impolite behavior. A student may avoid eye contact with the teacher because his culture teaches that meeting the gaze of certain adults is considered rude. Another student might use language that the teacher considers inappropriate (or the teacher may use language that offends the student) owing to cultural differences in what constitutes polite speech. Culturally responsive communication not only takes into account surface differences (e.g., differences in language) but also those deeper differences than may strongly impact student attitudes and behavior.

Culturally Responsive Strategies

Listed below are some culturally responsive strategies that promote communication and partnerships among students and families from all backgrounds:

- Teachers should strive to get to know students and their families. Making a personal connection helps students and families feel more comfortable, encourages them to express their needs to the teacher, helps the teacher identify areas of need and interest, and provides opportunities for the teacher to share resources.

- Teachers should recognize how the cultural backgrounds of individual students and families influences their behavior and speech, including their interactions with those of other cultures, and to adapt their communication whenever possible to meet the needs and interests of each student and family.

- Teachers should proactively encourage student-led discourse whenever appropriate, as well as student and parent involvement in classroom and school activities.

- Teachers should respond promptly and appropriately to culturally insensitive speech expressed by students, as well as to any prejudicial or discriminatory behavior that is observed.

> **PI (e): Effective strategies for communicating and collaborating with general education teachers, school staff members, paraprofessionals, related services providers, medical personnel, volunteers, and representatives of community agencies to help students with disabilities achieve desired learning outcomes**

In this section, you will read about methods of communication, consultation, and collaboration involving the many people who are involved in the education of students who have, or who are suspected to have, a disability.

The Team Approach

A team approach to the identification and support of students who have or who may have a disability is required by IDEA. Depending on the state, one or more teams may be formed in order to carry out and/or oversee activities such as prereferral, assessment, and IEP design and implementation. In the state of New York, the CSE or CPSE serves as the team that manages these activities.

Prereferral

The purpose of **prereferral** is to help students who are struggling in the general education setting before referring them for special education assessment. Through prereferral, the team obtains information about the student's strengths and weakness, designs and oversees the implementation of interventions, and evaluates the results of the interventions. If the interventions are successful, referral may not be needed, and the student may be able to function in the general education classroom with the support of teachers who provide some extent of differentiation. If the interventions are not successful, referral for special education assessment will be made.

In some states, including New York, **Response to Intervention (RTI)** is used as the prereferral process. RTI is a school-level process that involves screening, monitoring, and responding appropriately to individual students based on their academic progress. All students receive high-quality instruction. Over time, students who struggle academically are provided increasingly intensive and individualized instruction. If a student reaches the final "tier" or level of individualized instruction and continues to struggle, the student will be referred for special education assessment.

Assessment and IEPs

Assessments are carried out to evaluate each referral, i.e., to determine whether a student has a disability and is eligible for special education services. IDEA requires that a team be responsible for designing, implementing, and summarizing the results of the assessment. The assessment team takes the lead in determining whether the student has a disability and, if so, what educational supports are needed. IDEA also requires that a multidisciplinary team use the results of assessment and other information to create, implement, monitor, and periodically review the effectiveness of an IEP for the student. In New York State, the CSE or CPSE serves these various functions. (See Chapter 4 for additional information about assessment and IEPs.)

Team Characteristics

The team or teams that serve children who have or who may have a disability reflect a number of distinct characteristics. Each of these characteristics can be observed in the CSE or CPSE committees:

- The team is composed of individuals from a variety of backgrounds who each contribute an important perspective on the student's needs. The team(s) are multidisciplinary and are composed of general and special educators as well as other professionals. Parents and students are included as appropriate.

- The team serves multiple purposes. In particular, information-seeking, planning, implementing, monitoring, and evaluating are part of the activities carried out by the team(s).

- Because the team is multidisciplinary and multipurpose, open communication and a collaborative spirit is critical to its effectiveness.

Communication is necessary not only within teams but also between teams and school administrators, such as principals, as well as parents.

PI (f): Strategies for engaging in self-reflection and ongoing professional development activities to enhance effectiveness as an educator of students with disabilities

---

This section discusses self-reflection and professional development, two partially overlapping activities that are critical to the effectiveness of all educators, including those who work with students who have disabilities.

Self-Reflection

Self-reflection refers to the process of becoming aware of and analyzing one's own thoughts, feelings, and behaviors. Below are some examples of how self-reflection can benefit the special education professional:

- Through self-reflection, a teacher can examine his/her own assumptions about particular students or groups of students and identify problematic biases. For example, the teacher may have very low expectations for the academic progress of a mentally challenged student in her class, owing to her underestimation of the student's capacity to learn. Or, the teacher may assume that a particular student with attention difficulties is a "bad" kid when, in fact, the student wishes to exhibit better classroom behavior but is easily distracted and has poor impulse control. Identifying such biases through self-reflection is the first step toward correcting them.

- Through self-reflection, a teacher can examine his/her own feelings about particular students or groups of students and note how those feelings affect his/her interactions with them. For example, the teacher may notice in himself a feeling of repugnance toward students with severe medical conditions, or a feeling of apprehension toward students who are severely autistic. Although these feelings may be natural, they can interfere with the teacher's ability to interact with the students effectively. Self-reflection can help the teacher identify such feelings and address them in a productive manner.

- Through self-reflection, a teacher can examine his/her own behavior in classroom settings and identify both effective and problematic behaviors. For example, the teacher might notice that she pays too little, or too much, attention to a student with dyslexia who cannot keep up with peers during whole-class activities that require reading. Reflecting on such behaviors will help the teacher develop more positive and productive classroom behaviors.

- Through self-reflection, a teacher can develop a proactive attitude toward instruction and professional development. The teacher can become more aware of his/her own strengths and limitations as an educator, as well as be more knowledgeable about the strategies that maximize the strengths, overcome the limitations, and otherwise contribute to professional development.

Professional Development

Professional development opportunities are available to special education teachers through their own schools; local agencies; outside workshops; media, such as books and websites; and professional organizations, such as those described in section PI (h). Through professional development activities, teachers are exposed to basic concepts, advanced strategies, and cutting-edge trends with respect to topics such as the following:

- the causes, etiologies, and effects of specific disabilities

- strategies and resources for working with children who have specific disabilities

- strategies for instruction and classroom management

- federal, state, and local laws and policies in special education

- methods of assessment and alternative testing

- identification and referral of at-risk students

- IEP planning, implementation, and review

- transition planning

- advocacy for students with disabilities

PI (g): Strategies and information sources for remaining current regarding research-validated practice in the field of special education

The No Child Left Behind Act (NCLB) of 2001 requires that instructional practices be predicated on scientifically based research. That is, educational theories, informal anecdotes about teaching and learning, and common sense, are not considered to be sufficient bases for instructional practice. IDEA is closely aligned with NCLB with respect to the role of scientifically based research in special education. In this section, you will read about the meaning of the phrase "scientifically based research" and how to keep up with research of this sort that has implications for special education.

Characteristics of Scientifically Based Research

Scientifically based research (SBR) is distinguished by a number of characteristics:

- SBR relies on systematic, empirical methods. The word "empirical" means "based on observation." SBR can be distinguished from theorizing, speculation, traditional beliefs, and anecdotal evidence.

- SBR relies on rigorous data analysis that justifies the conclusions that are drawn. That is, SBR consists of more than just casual observation. Data must be collected, carefully analyzed, and interpreted.

- SBR relies on methods that yield consistent data across measures and studies. SBR is grounded in replication, which means that results should not be trusted or applied in educational settings until they have been demonstrated more than once across different approaches to measurement and different investigations.

- SBR relies on clear, detailed reports of studies in peer-reviewed journals, books, and other sources, or reports that are approved by panels of independent experts. Because replication is critical, clear and detailed reportage is important as well.

Preferred Research Designs

Although many types of designs are used in scientific research, NCLB and IDEA indicate a preference for experimental or quasi-experimental research designs. An **experimental design** is an approach to gathering data that reflects several characteristics:

- Participants are randomly assigned to groups. For example, a researcher who wishes to know whether the use of a new self-monitoring strategy improves children's reading fluency may randomly assign some children to receive training in the new self-monitoring strategy. These children are referred to as the experimental group (or the intervention group). Through random assignment other children may be chosen to receive literacy instruction as usual. These children are referred to as the control group (or the comparison group).

- Pre-test and post-test data are collected. In the example given above, reading fluency would be measured among both groups before and after the experimental group receives training in the new strategy. If the reading fluency of the experimental group improves more than the reading fluency of the control group from pre-test to post-test, we can conclude that use of the new self-monitoring strategy positively impacts children's fluency.

A **quasi-experimental** design is like an experimental design except that there is no random assignment to groups. Rather, existing groups are used. In the previous example, a quasi-experimental design would be represented by the use of one classroom as the experimental group and another classroom as the control group. Although the researcher might randomly select these classrooms, the children who are part of each classroom cannot be randomly chosen. Rather, each classroom constitutes an existing group.

Reliable Sources of Scientifically Based Research

Reliable sources of scientifically based research that can influence instructional practice include the following:

- peer-reviewed books and journals

- the websites of state education agencies, such the New York State Education Department website

- the websites of the U.S. Department of Education

- other websites sponsored by the U.S. government (which can be identified by means of the *.gov* suffix in their addresses)

- the websites of organizations whose mission it is to serve children with disabilities and their families (see section PI (h) for descriptions of some of these organizations)

The **What Works Clearinghouse (WWC)** is an example of a U.S. government website that provides information about scientifically based research of relevance to instructional practice. The WWC is part of the Institute of Education Sciences, which is the research arm of the U.S. Department of Education. The goal of the WWC website is to provide educators with instructional techniques and strategies that have been shown to be effective through scientifically based research (as defined above).

PI (h): Local, state, and national services, resources, and organizations serving students with disabilities and providing program support

This section provides information about a few of the many organizations that provide information, materials, and other resources of interest to parents, educators, administrators, researchers, and others who are involved either personally and/or professionally in the education of students with disabilities.

National Organizations

- The **U.S. Department of Education (ED)** maintains a website devoted exclusively to IDEA. This website includes the full text of IDEA, summaries of IDEA and cross-references to other pertinent legislation, discussions of recent trends in research and practice, training materials, resources for schools, and a variety of other information of relevance to families, educators, administrators, and researchers.

- The U.S. Department of Education's **Office of Special Education and Rehabilitative Services (OSERS)** offers programs, services, and a variety of resources that promote inclusion, equity, and opportunity for students with disabilities. The OSERS website contains information of relevance to families, educators, administrators, and researchers.

- The **National Dissemination Center for Children with Disabilities** provides the full text of IDEA and information about this law, as well as information about other legislation that pertains to students with disabilities, about the characteristics and management of specific disabilities; about research-based best practices in special education; and about other topics of relevance to families, educators, administrators, and researchers.

- The **Council for Exceptional Children (CEC)** provides information pertaining to the education of students with disabilities; special education legislation and advocacy; careers and professional development opportunities in special education; scientific and professional trends; and other topics of relevance to families, educators, administrators, and researchers.

- The **American Educational Research Association (AERA)** is one of the largest professional and scientific organizations that supports research pertaining to children with disabilities. Within the AERA, the Special Education Research Special Interest Group (SER-SIG) promotes and disseminates research on children with disabilities and issues related to their education.

- The **National Association of Special Education Teachers (NASET)** is an example of a professional organization with a focus on the education of children with disabilities. NASET provides special education professionals with information about policy and research, professional development and career opportunities, and other resources.

Local Organizations

- IDEA requires that every state maintain a **Parent Training and Information (PTI)** center, which provides information to parents and those who work with them about IDEA, special education services, parent organizations, and other local groups of interest.

- Parents may also receive information from the **Child Find coordinator** working within a particular school district or county. As noted earlier in the chapter, Child Find provisions in IDEA require that children who may have disabilities be identified and evaluated.

Organizations in New York

- The New York State **Office of Special Education**, housed within the State Education Department's Office of P-12 Education, maintains a website with resources for families, educators, administrators, and researchers.

- **Quality assurance regional offices**, which are also part of the Office of Special Education, oversee special education in New York State and provide a variety of resources to families, educators, administrators and researchers. There are currently 7 offices located around the state.

- **Special education parent centers** provide information, resources, and strategies to parents of children with disabilities. Currently, there are 13 centers in New York State.

- **The Advocacy Center** is the Parent Training and Information Center in New York State, which promotes advocacy through information, workshops, services, outreach, and many other activities.

PI (i): The teacher's responsibility to advocate for the interests of students with disabilities

This section briefly discusses some of the strategies teachers should use to advocate for the interests of students with disabilities. These strategies include the following:

- Teachers should familiarize themselves with relevant federal, state, and local laws and school policies pertaining to students with disabilities. Knowledge of how students with disabilities must be served, according to the law, is the first step in ensuring that students receive those services.

- Teachers should become as knowledgeable as possible about the backgrounds, strengths, and weaknesses of individual students with disabilities. IEPs should be examined carefully, for example, and people with knowledge of the students, including parents and colleagues, should be consulted. At the same time, teachers should learn as much background information as possible about the disabilities of individual students, including disability-related needs and effective strategies for meeting these needs. The teacher may need to engage in informal, student-specific assessments and to tailor instructional strategies for students on the basis of those assessments. By knowing more about individual students and their areas of strength and need, teachers can advocate more effectively for those students.

- Teachers should maintain open communication with other educators, CSE members, experts, and parents about students who have or who are suspected to have a disability. Factual information about students should be shared whenever relevant and appropriate. If the teacher suspects that a student has a disability, the teacher should not make a diagnosis, but rather refer the student for evaluation. Monitoring students, as well as sharing pertinent information with other educators and parents, can help promote the interests of students. Providing parents with information and resources of relevance to their students is a particularly important form of advocacy.

- Teachers should maintain open, effective communication with their principals and other administrative staff and be cognizant of the roles and responsibilities of the administration. Student needs should be described clearly and objectively, in a positive manner, and supported by teacher notes and other documentation.

Practice Questions

1. The least restrictive environment requirement of IDEA is closely associated with

    A. assessment.

    B. mainstreaming.

C. inclusion.

D. procedural safeguards.

2. A due process hearing might be most appropriate for which of the following situations?

A. A general education teacher has become frustrated with a student who has ADHD and poor impulse control, and the teacher seeks an outlet for the student's frustration.

B. A principal is concerned that a parent brings her child to school late several mornings per week and has not responded to a note from the teacher.

C. A special education teacher and a general education teacher disagree about the best approach for helping a mentally challenged student progress in reading.

D. A parent disagrees with an assessment team's conclusion that her son has dyslexia, but after meeting with the team and a mediator, no resolution is achieved.

3. In New York, which of the following groups would be responsible for establishing, implementing, and monitoring progress toward annual goals for a sixth grade student with disabilities?

A. CEC

B. CPSE

C. CSE

D. NYSTCE

4. Information about a 20-month-old's language delay and steps that will be taken to provide support would be found in an

    A. Individualized Family Service Plan.

    B. Individualized Education Plan.

    C. Infant Assessment Plan.

    D. Inter-agency Enrichment Plan.

5. Each of the following would be a reliable source of scientifically based research, EXCEPT for

    A. a peer-reviewed academic journal.

    B. a nationally renowned newspaper.

    C. the What Works Clearinghouse.

    D. a pamphlet created by the U.S. Department of Education.

Answers to Practice Questions

1. C.

    Although the least restrictive environment (LRE) of IDEA does not guarantee inclusion, it fosters an inclusive environment, and thus, Choice C is the correct answer. Choices A and D are incorrect because neither assessment nor procedural safeguards have any particular relationship to the LRE. Choice B is incorrect because the LRE prohibits mainstreaming as a general strategy for dealing with students with disabilities.

2. D.

    Due process hearings are generally a last resort after disagreements involving school personnel and parents cannot be resolved through other means. Thus, Choice D is the correct answer. Choices A and B are incorrect because in these scenarios, disagreements between school personnel and parents are not clearly evident. Choice C is incorrect because the disagreement does not involve a parent.

3.   C.

Choice C is correct because one of the primary roles of the Committee on Special Education (CSE) is to develop, implement, and oversee Individualized Education Plan (IEP) goals. Choice B is incorrect because the Committee on Preschool Education (CPSE) would only handle IEPs for children between the ages of 3 and 5. Choices A and D are incorrect because they refer to the Council on Exceptional Children and the New York State Teacher Certification Examinations, respectively.

4.   A.

Choice A is correct because Individualized Family Service Plans are appropriate for infants. Choice B is incorrect because Individualized Education Plans are not formulated until after the child is 3 years old. Choice C is incorrect because it pertains to assessment and would probably not include a discussion of steps that will be taken to provide support. Choice D is incorrect because this phrase is not standard.

5.   B.

Choice B is correct because a newspaper would not be a reliable source of scientifically based research, unlike the other options.

CHAPTER 3

COMPETENCY 0002
Knowledge of Students with Disabilities

This chapter provides information about the types of disabilities classified in the Individuals with Disabilities Education Act (IDEA) and describes how these disabilities are distinguished from typical characteristics and patterns of development.

PI (a): Typical and atypical human growth and development in various domains (e.g., cognitive, linguistic, social, emotional, physical, sensory)

Human development is a complicated process that involves change within numerous specific domains, such as cognition, language, and socioemotional functioning. Each domain is complex, as are the processes of typical and atypical development within the domain. In this section, the domains of language and literacy are used to illustrate the complexity of development. Information is provided about the components of each domain and about patterns of growth and change.

Receptive vs. Expressive Language

The information presented in this section is informed by a fundamental distinction between **receptive language** (the ability to understand language) and **expressive language** (the ability to express oneself using language).

Receptive language, or comprehension, includes the ability to understand speech, written text, and/or the elements of a sign language. Expressive language, or production, includes the ability to speak, write, and/or sign.

Receptive and expressive language rely on independent skills. As a result, a child may have impairments in either type of skill without necessarily experiencing difficulties with both. For example, children who stutter have an expressive language impairment, but their receptive language may be normal. In contrast, children with hearing impairments have a receptive language impairment yet may not experience difficulties expressing themselves. A child who is deaf, however, may experience impairments in receptive and expressive language.

Throughout normal development, receptive language tends to be superior to expressive language. That is, at any given age, children's ability to understand language is superior to their ability to express themselves. Children understand more vocabulary, grammar, and pragmatic rules than may be evident in their speaking and writing.

■ Components of Language

Language consists of a number of components, or systems, that play an essential role in communication. The components discussed here include phonology, semantics, grammar, pragmatics, and orthography.

Phonology

Phonology refers to speech sounds. Each **phoneme** in a language consists of a distinct sound used to distinguish spoken words in the language. For example, the word "sick" consists of three phonemes—/s/, /i/, and /k/. The word "six" consists of four phonemes—/s/, /i/, /k/, and /s/. The English language contains about 45 phonemes. Although infants with normal hearing are competent from an early age at discriminating between phonemes, children initially find it challenging to analyze and explicitly identify such differences (as discussed under the topic of phonological awareness later in this chapter). Thus, phonological development in oral language consists of the growing ability to analyze and identify language sounds, as well as improvement in the production of these sounds.

Semantics

Semantics refers to the meanings of parts of words, words, sentences, and larger units. Vocabulary acquisition is an important part of semantic development involving changes in both expressive and receptive language. Over time, children learn new words as well as gaining a deeper understanding of the words they already know, including the knowledge of how a word's meaning may shift to a greater or lesser extent from context to context.

Grammar

Grammar refers to the rules that govern the structure of language. Grammar can be further divided into two systems of rules: syntax and morphology.

- **Syntax** pertains to rules governing the placement of words in phrases, clauses, and sentences. Native speakers of a language understand many syntactic rules. In English, for example, when a boy enters the classroom, it is acceptable to say "Steve is here now" or "Steve is now here," but it is incorrect to say "Steve here is now." When a person says "In my hand there is a miniscule....," the listener knows that the word that comes next must be a noun. If the listener does not know what the word "miniscule" means, once the speaker has completed the sentence, the listener will at least understand that miniscule is an adjective describing a characteristic of the object in the speaker's hand.

- **Morphology** refers to rules governing the use of **morphemes**, or the smallest parts of words that contribute to meaning. In English, for example, the verb "learn" takes on somewhat different meanings depending on whether we refer to someone as "relearning," "unlearning," "learning," or "having learned," because the prefixes "re-" and "un-" and the suffixes "-ing" and "-ed" each modify the basic meaning of the verb. These prefixes and suffixes are morphemes. Other examples of morphemes include the letter "s" (e.g., when placed at the end of a word to create a plural) and the word "book" (as used in words such as "bookmark" and "bookshelf").

Grammatical development is reflected in increasing mastery of the rules of syntax as well as morphology. As with semantic development, the acquisition of grammar is reflected in changes in expressive and receptive vocabulary.

Pragmatics

Pragmatics can be defined as whatever contributes to meaning over and above the literal meanings of the words that are used. Many different kinds of pragmatic cues contribute to meaning. Following are a few examples:

- Contextual information often provides important clues to meaning. For example, in the sentence "Jackson searched for the bug," the word "bug" will be interpreted differently depending on whether Jackson has been previously described as afraid of insects or as a professional spy.

- Differing tones of voice often convey important differences in meaning. For example, the sentence "Why don't you visit me?" can be construed as an invitation or a complaint depending on the speaker's tone and phrasing.

- When language is used in a figurative way, as in the case of metaphor or analogy, the intended meaning of a phrase differs from the literal meaning. For example, the sentence "This classroom is like a jungle!" does not mean that the classroom literally resembles a jungle in the sense of being filled with trees and wild animals. Rather, the speaker intends to call attention to the messiness of the classroom, the chaotic behavior of the students, or some other detail.

- There are many conventions governing word choice in communicative contexts, such as how much information to convey or what level of formality is needed. For example, students are expected to address their teachers somewhat differently from the way they speak with each other. The casual style in which they speak with each other may be inappropriate when addressing a teacher, just as the comparatively polite language used to address a teacher may seem stilted when talking with a peer.

As with semantic and grammatical development, children's growing knowledge of pragmatics is reflected in both expressive and reflective language changes.

Orthography

Orthography refers to the system of representing oral language in writing. Rules of orthography pertain to spelling, punctuation, capitalization, and use of hyphens. In English, for example, children must learn the Roman alphabet and then the many rules governing letter-sound correspondences. As children learn these rules (and their many exceptions), their reading and writing develop, and changes can be observed in both expressive and receptive language skills.

The Sequence of Language Development

Normal development of expressive and receptive language proceeds somewhat predictably. Although there is much variation among children in rate of development, language- and communication-related disabilities may be indicated when a particular child lags far behind peers in rate of acquisition.

To illustrate those aspects of language development that are predictable, the following is a short list of a few of the milestones of receptive and expressive language development that can be observed from birth through age 3:

Age	Receptive	Expressive
Birth to 3 months	Turns head toward sounds; responds to familiar voices	Coos; gurgles; smiles; produces different cries for tiredness, hunger, pain
4–7 months	Responds to own name; distinguishes among people	Laughs; babbles; expresses emotion vocally
8 months–1 year	Understands simple words, commands, gestures	Imitates speech sounds; uses gestures such as pointing; may begin to talk
1 year–2 years	Understands growing number of words	Talks in one- and then two-word phrases; produces growing number of words
2 years–3 years	Participates more actively in conversations	Speaks intelligibly; expresses a range of emotions, desires, comments, questions

The more extreme the deviation from this typical timeframe of development, the more likely the child has a disability that is related to language and communication. Atypical development is possible with respect to one, some, or all components of language described earlier (phonology, semantics, grammar, pragmatics, orthography). However, children vary widely in rate of development, and thus, some extent of delay in the emergence of these abilities and behaviors is not necessarily indicative of a problem.

Reading

Reading is an extension of language development that plays a central role in children's academic performance. This section reviews the typical progression in the development of reading. Incorporated into this review are definitions of the key components of reading development.

As children acquire reading skills, their development can be divided into stages. The following is one of many approaches to describing the stages:

Pre-reading

Long before children know how to read, they acquire skills and experiences that will contribute to later reading development. They enjoy listening to and retelling stories, for example, and they gradually realize that certain marks in their environment convey stories and other kinds of information. Children see the marks (i.e., words) on signs, in books, and in other places, and they recognize that these printed marks are meaningful to others, even though they do not understand yet how the marks represent spoken words. Thus, young children gradually acquire **concepts of print**, such as the concept that the words in a picture book convey stories, and the concept that these words are printed in an orderly, linear way (such that people read from top to bottom and from left to right).

Learning to Read

In order to enter the "learning to read" stage, children must acquire **alphabet knowledge**, or the ability to name the letters of the alphabet and recognize these letters in print. Also critical to the emergence of reading is the **alphabetic principle**, the understanding that letters represent sounds in systematic and predictable ways. Children's understanding of the alphabetic principle is accompanied by increases in **phonological awareness**, or the ability to consciously recognize, discriminate among, and manipulate language sounds such as phonemes and syllables. Put simply, knowledge of the relationship between spoken and written words (alphabetic principle) supports and is supported by awareness that spoken words are composed of units of sound (phonological awareness).

As children begin to read simple texts, most of their efforts will be devoted to **decoding**, or the sounding out of words. At the same time, high-frequency words (e.g., "you," "the," "and") will start to be recognized automatically and become part of children's growing set of **sight words**. At this stage, reading requires much support from more experienced individuals such as parents and teachers. Support will be essential for progress in decoding, comprehension, and **fluency** (i.e., the ability to read quickly, effortlessly, accurately, and expressively).

Transitional Reading

Once children have mastered the alphabet and many of the rules linking letters and letter combinations to sounds, they can read more fluently and with greater comprehension. During this transitional period, decoding skills become more advanced, and the number of sight words that children automatically recognize continues to grow. These changes allow children to read aloud with greater fluency and to focus more on the meaning of what they read. Improvements in reading comprehension can now be seen in children's ability to infer meaning from context, make predictions about what will happen next in a story, and discuss what they have read. Most children still need support in all aspects of reading but can proceed with less dependence on teachers or other experienced individuals.

Reading to Learn

The "reading to learn" stage is marked by improvements in children's decoding skills, increases in the number of sight words they automatically recognize, and a deeper understanding of the reading process and the properties of texts. These changes allow age-appropriate materials to be readily understood. Although children are not yet reading with the same fluency or comprehension as adults, reading skills have progressed to the point that more attention can be paid to content than to the mechanics of reading. The abilities that are well-developed but continue to progress during this stage include the ability to

- apply knowledge of letter-sound correspondences to difficult words
- infer meaning from context
- make predictions about what will happen in a story
- identify text structures
- read critically
- shift between close reading and skimming
- read with fluency

- self-correct during reading

- read independently

Reading Development: The Example of Decoding

The stages described above constitute a general way of summarizing reading development. Other approaches describe the stages of specific reading-related skills. These approaches can be helpful in identifying students with reading-related disabilities; again, the greater the extent of divergence between a particular student's development and the age-related shifts generally observed, the greater the need to evaluate the student carefully for a disability, and the greater the likelihood that one will be observed.

To illustrate the developmental stages of a specific reading skill, this section focuses on decoding. Among early readers, decoding is the primary method of word recognition. According to a prominent analysis, the development of decoding skills reflects four phases: pre-alphabetic, partial-alphabetic, full-alphabetic, and consolidated.

Pre-alphabetic

In the **pre-alphabetic** phase, children can identify words, but they do so by treating words as visual objects, rather than by applying letter-sound associations. Examples would be a child who can read the word "look" because she remembers that it has two "eyeballs" inside it, or the child who can read the word "stop" on a stop sign owing to the sign's distinctive color and shape. As these examples illustrate, pre-alphabetic children do not yet think of a word as composed of letters, such that individual letters contribute to the pronunciation of the word. These children are "pre-alphabetic" in the sense of not knowing—or not making use of—alphabet knowledge.

Partial-alphabetic

In the **partial-alphabetic** phase, children know some letters and letter-sound associations and can use them, along with contextual cues such as the visual appearance of words, to engage in decoding. This phase is called "partial-alphabetic" because children use alphabet knowledge only for decoding some words or letters in words. An example would be the child who can read the word "bat" because she knows how "b" and "t" sound and remembers that when they are separated by one roundish-looking letter, the word is "bat." However, the same child might not be able to read the word "ball," because she does not know how the last letters sound, or because she mispronounces the "a."

Full-alphabetic

In the **full-alphabetic** phase, children apply alphabet knowledge systematically when decoding, and they often decode words letter by letter. Decoding is consequently more accurate than before. An example would be the child who reads the sentence "We hope to find gold" as "We hop to find gold." In this example, the child reads each word letter by letter and accurately decodes the first word and the last three words. Moreover, when misreading the word "hope," the child does not come up with a nonsense word, as earlier readers might, but rather a real word that is grammatically appropriate and not entirely unrelated to the semantic context of the sentence.

Consolidated-alphabetic

In the **consolidated-alphabetic** phase, recurring letter patterns become consolidated. Rather than sounding out words letter by letter, children recognize that certain groups of letters function as units. An example would be the child who recognizes that the rime "ight," the prefix "ex-," and the suffix "-tion" are always pronounced the same way, as in the words "light," "exit," and "nation." Children in the consolidated-alphabetic phase are able to read more quickly and acquire more sight words as they increasingly consolidate letter patterns. Some of the letter groups, or phonological units, that young readers now recognize are as follows:

- **Digraphs** are pairs of letters that represent a single sound, such as "sh" and "oo."

- **Consonant clusters** are pairs of consonants that appear together in a syllable. Unlike digraphs, they do not represent a single sound. Thus, in the word "charts," the "ch" is a digraph, while the "ts" is a consonant cluster.

- **Syllables** are units of pronunciation containing one vowel sound. Some syllables contain consonants, while others do not. For example, the word "uneaten" consists of three syllables—one containing a vowel sound and a consonant ("un"), one containing a vowel sound but no consonant ("ea"), and one containing a vowel sound and two consonants ("ten").

- **Rimes** are the parts of syllables consisting of the vowel and any consonant that follows. Examples of rimes include "og" in the word "dog" and "ank" in the word "bank." (**Onsets** are the parts of syllables that precede the vowel. In the preceding examples, the onsets are "d" and "b," respectively.)

- **Morphemes**, as discussed earlier, are the smallest units of words that contribute to meaning. Although some morphemes consist of individual letters (e.g., the "s" that makes a word plural), many others consist of letter groups.

Reading Difficulties

As with language more generally, a reading-related disability is likely to the extent that children lag behind their peers in the sequence of changes described above. Experts have not reached a consensus as to how to classify different types of reading difficulties. One point on which all would agree is that there is much variability in reading difficulties from child to child (and that it is more important to identify the reading skills for which a particular child needs extra support than it is to agree on how to label the child). Among children who are labeled as dyslexic, for example, there is much variability in both the nature and the severity of the symptoms.

Dyslexia is considered a learning disability that primarily affects reading. Individuals with dyslexia read at a level much lower than would be expected, given that their intelligence is at least normal. Dyslexia that can be observed in early childhood is called **developmental dyslexia**, while dyslexia that is acquired as the result of disease or injury to the brain is called **alexia**.

Below are some of the symptoms associated with dyslexia. A particular child with dyslexia is likely to exhibit some, but not all, of these symptoms.

- Difficulty recognizing familiar words

- Inability to decode unfamiliar words

- Difficulty segmenting words into phonemes

- Difficulty identifying or creating rhymes

- Seeing letters or words in reverse

- Seeing letters move or blur

- Dysfluency when reading out loud

- Difficulty following a sequence of instructions

- Poor spelling

- Difficulty learning a foreign language

Along with the symptoms described above, dyslexic children often exhibit characteristics such as a reluctance to read, a high rate of guessing when encountering unfamiliar words in a text, and low academic self-efficacy. These characteristics can be understood in light of the fact that reading is especially effortful and frustrating for these children.

PI (b): Characteristics, identification criteria, etiologies, and medical aspects of various types of disabilities (e.g., learning disability, intellectual disability, autism, multiple disabilities)

Using the framework provided by IDEA, this section discusses the characteristics, identification, etiologies, and medical aspects of disabilities.

IDEA identifies numerous categories of disability as well as providing definitions and examples of each category. A fundamental distinction is made between infants and toddlers, on the one hand, and older children on the other.

Infants and Toddlers with Disabilities

IDEA defines "infants and toddlers with disabilities" as children between birth and age 3 who are experiencing developmental delays in one or more of the following areas:

- cognitive development

- physical development

- social or emotional development

- communication development

- adaptive development

The category of infants and toddlers with disabilities also includes children between birth and age 3 who have been diagnosed with a condition that is highly likely to produce one or more types of developmental delay. Finally, states and local education agencies have the option of using the term "developmental delay" for a child between the ages of 3 and 9, if the child exhibits delays in one of the aforementioned areas, and as a result of the delay, the child needs special education and related services.

Children with Disabilities

For the age range 3 to 21 years, IDEA lists 13 categories of disability, described below in alphabetical order:

- **Autism** refers to a developmental disability, generally detectable before age 3, that affects communication, social interaction, and learning. The child with autism may show language delays, unusual speech patterns, aversion to eye contact and touch, repetitive behaviors, and resistance to change in daily routines.

- **Deaf-blindness** refers to simultaneous hearing and visual impairments that are so severe the student cannot benefit sufficiently from programs and services that are designed for exclusively deaf or exclusively blind children. Deaf-blindness is usually **congenital** (i.e., present at birth) but may be **adventitious** (i.e., acquired through illness or injury).

- **Deafness** refers to an extreme hearing impairment that adversely impacts the student's educational performance. Deafness may be congenital or adventitious.

- **Emotional disturbance** refers to a condition that reflects at least one of the following characteristics over an extended period of time: an inability to learn that cannot be attributed to other factors, such as intellectual or sensory deficits, or health problems; an inability to build or sustain satisfactory personal relationships with others; feelings or behaviors that are ordinarily inappropriate; pervasive unhappiness or depression; and a tendency to develop physical symptoms or fears related to personal problems or problems at school. Schizophrenia, anxiety disorders, and depression are among the many examples.

- **Hearing impairment** refers to an impairment in hearing that undermines the student's educational performance but is not severe enough to be classified as deafness. Hearing impairments may be congenital or adventitious. Children with hearing difficulties are only classified as hearing impaired if the difficulties persist even after corrections (e.g., surgery and/or use of hearing aids).

- **Intellectual disability** refers to general intellectual ability that is significantly below average, combined with limitations in adaptive behavior, which adversely impacts the student's educational performance. The primary example would be mental retardation, which is often congenital but may be adventitious. The phrase "adaptive behavior" in the definition indicates that mental retardation involves not only much lower than average intelligence, but also impairments in the extent of the child's social competence and independence.

- **Multiple disabilities** refer to a combination of disabilities that is so severe the student cannot benefit sufficiently from programs and services that are designed for any one of those disabilities.

- **Orthopedic impairment** refers to musculoskeletal problems, congenital or adventitious, that adversely influence the student's educational performance. Examples include cerebral palsy, polio, and amputations.

- **Other health impairment** refers to health problems affecting strength, energy, or alertness to a degree that adversely impacts the student's educational performance. Among the many examples would be leukemia, epilepsy, diabetes, asthma, lupus, and sickle cell anemia.

- **Specific learning disability** refers to problems with the ability to comprehend or produce information when performing academic tasks. Dyslexia, dyscalculia, and minimal brain dysfunction are among the many examples. Such learning disabilities are usually congenital, but may be adventitious. The term "specific" indicates that this disability is restricted to particular school subjects or tasks. A student with a specific learning disability may perform well in some subjects or tasks, and perform poorly on others. These students are not impaired in general learning ability, but rather in some specific skill or skills.

- **Speech or language impairment** refers to communication disorders that adversely impact the student's educational performance. Examples include articulation disorders, stuttering, and mutism. Such learning disabilities are usually congenital, but may be adventitious.

- **Traumatic brain injury** refers to any acquired injury to the brain that undermines the student's educational performance. Such injuries may result from accidents involving motor vehicles, sports, and other causes. Children with traumatic brain injury may have impairments in physical, behavioral, cognitive, social, and/or emotional functioning, depending on the nature and severity of the injury.

- **Visual impairment** refers to visual problems that adversely influence the student's educational performance. Visual impairments are usually congenital but may be adventitious. Children with visual difficulties are only classified as visually impaired if the difficulties persist even after corrections (e.g., surgery and/or use of corrective lenses).

PI (c): Similarities and differences among students with and without disabilities

This section touches on some of the important implications of the similarities and differences among students with and without disabilities.

The impact of a disability may be very specific, as in the example of a student who stutters but who has no other impairment, or relatively broad, as in the example of a severely retarded student whose ability to think, learn, and communicate is impaired regardless of topic. Teachers must remember that students with disabilities are not simply "different" from their peers, and that in fact their similarities with peers may be vastly greater than the differences among them. At the same time, each student is unique. A disability is one of many characteristics that distinguishes students from each other. The student who stutters may be a visual learner who enjoys math but dislikes social studies, for example. He may be a talented athlete whose parents are going through a divorce. In short, his stuttering is just one of many distinguishing features about him. Each of these features will impact multiple aspects of functioning. If a student dislikes social studies, he may be more prone to frustration or bad behavior in his social studies class. If his parents are going through a divorce, his mood and interest in school may fluctuate from day to day. And, because he stutters, he may experience teasing and social rejection by peers, and he may feel frustrated or depressed about his difficulties with speech.

Because a disability is only one of the many distinguishing characteristics of a student, the feelings, beliefs, and behaviors that students exhibit may or may not be related to the disability. When a student appears to be depressed and disengaged, what could be the problem? Does the student dislike the material being taught? Is one of the student's family members extremely ill? Does the student feel discouraged about a personal limitation? Or is there some other issue yet to be understood by the teacher? If the student has a disability, the sadness and disengagement that the student exhibits may or may not be related to the disability.

Finally, owing to similarities between students with and without disabilities, concerns have been raised about the possibility of misclassifications involving the latter. Students who have been diagnosed with mild intellectual or learning disabilities, for example, may simply be low achievers. This possibility points to the broader issue that there is a continuum of functioning rather than a clear distinction between having or not having a disability. Although this distinction must be made when determining eligibility for special education services, teachers will encounter students who reflect different points on the continuum. Over time a teacher may work with students who have severe dyslexia; students with mild dyslexia; general education students whose reading achievement is low; average readers; and students whose reading is above average.

PI (d): How the characteristics of various disabilities can influence an individual's education and life

This section briefly discusses the impacts of disabilities on students.

Depending on the nature and severity of a student's disability, the student may have needs in one or more of the following areas:

- academic functioning (e.g., a student with a learning disability is unable to master the general education curriculum at the same rate as peers without additional support)

- behavioral functioning (e.g., a student with a traumatic brain injury that affects impulse control is unable to sit quietly in class or concentrate on individual work without additional support)

- social functioning (e.g., a student with autism is unable to interact effectively with teacher or peers without additional support)

- physical functioning (e.g., a student with visual and auditory impairments is unable to participate in physical activities with peers without additional support)

As noted in the previous section, a disability may affect a student's functioning in one specific area, such that the similarities between the student and peers are much greater than the differences among them. In some cases, however, the student's disability affects functioning in multiple areas, and any combination of types and severity of effects is possible. For example, a student with an intellectual disability might experience academic difficulties and impaired social functioning (because he struggles to understand conversations and activities initiated by peers) yet have no particular difficulties with behavioral or physical functioning. A student with an emotional disturbance might experience no difficulties with academic or physical functioning yet find it challenging to behave appropriately in the classroom and when interacting with peers. A student with diabetes will have physical challenges but may never experience difficulties in other areas of functioning (or experience only temporary difficulties when blood sugar levels are unusually low or high). Teachers who work with students who have disabilities must keep in mind that each student has a unique combination of strengths, challenges, needs, and interests depending on the nature and severity of the disability and on other characteristics, such as the student's age and cultural background.

> **PI (e): How students with disabilities learn, including students from culturally and linguistically diverse backgrounds, and developmentally and age-appropriate strategies for addressing those differences**

This section discusses learning and instruction involving students with disabilities, including those from diverse backgrounds.

Learning and Instructional Strategies

According to IDEA, a student with a disability will be eligible for special education services if the disability interferes with the student's learning. However, learning can be impaired in a variety of ways, depending on the nature and severity of the disability.

Identifying students with disabilities as early as possible and developing appropriate instructional and curricular modifications is desirable. With respect to instructional and classroom management strategies, best practices in the general education classroom tend to be desirable for the education of students with disabilities. Some examples of best practices include the following:

- maintaining an academic focus in the classroom

- holding high expectations for students' academic performance and behavior

- making students accountable for their work and classroom behavior

- creating a positive, cooperative classroom atmosphere

- differentiating instruction according to individual student characteristics

- monitoring student behavior and engagement

(Chapter 6 focuses extensively on best practices in instruction for all students, including students with disabilities.)

Cultural and Linguistic Differences

Students and families from culturally and/or linguistically diverse backgrounds may face challenges in the process of adjusting to the educational system. These challenges can magnify the existing challenges that students with disabilities and their families confront. For example:

- The terms and jargon used in special education may be difficult to understand for individuals who are not completely fluent in English.

- Individuals from other cultures may have culturally specific concepts of disabilities that differ from those reflected in American educational practice.

- A sense of being "different" sometimes experienced by students with disabilities and their families can be magnified by cultural and/or linguistic differences.

- Negative stereotyping may be perpetrated more frequently against students with disabilities who exhibit cultural and/or linguistic differences.

Teachers can address these challenges by means of culturally-responsive teaching, which contains elements such as:

- Teachers should learn about cultural differences, speak positively about these differences and about diversity, and make use of opportunities to incorporate different cultural beliefs and practices into instruction as well as into the materials present in the classroom.

- Teachers should acknowledge differences among students in a positive way, and treat those differences as opportunities for whole-class learning.

- Teachers should individualize instruction as much as possible based on the backgrounds of individual students. Differentiating instruction in this way includes modifications to instructional strategies and content in light of students' particular strengths and areas of need, as well as the use of culturally specific content as appropriate.

- Teachers should encourage student and family involvement in planning and other activities. Doing so helps students and families feel that their backgrounds and perspectives are valued.

PI (f): Factors that affect development, learning, and daily living in students with disabilities (e.g., roles of families and communities; effects of medications, sensory impairments, and medical conditions)

The impact of factors such as sensory impairments and medical conditions on students with disabilities is discussed above in sections PI (b) and PI (c). This section touches on two additional factors that affect the development, learning, and daily functioning of these students.

Social Support

The extent of support that a student with disabilities receives from family, community, and school can affect any or all aspects of the student's development and functioning. For example, involved and well-informed parents may recognize signs of a disability when the child is very young, request evaluation from a medical or school professional, and provide consistent and effective support. In such cases, the severity of the disability may be lessened, and the student's ability to learn and function will be enhanced, because the parents help their child adjust to both the academic and the social climate of school, as well as life outside school. In contrast, learning and daily functioning may be adversely affected if parents are relatively uninvolved, slow to recognize a potential problem or to seek help, and/or resistant to working with medical or school personnel on strategies for supporting their child.

Medication

The medication that a student takes to help manage a disability is likely to improve the student's ability to learn and function. At the same time, many medications have temporary or ongoing side effects that interfere with learning and daily life. For example, drugs that prevent seizures, alleviate pain, and reduce the severity of anxiety or depression have all been associated with diminished attention and memory. When a student is taking medicine for a disability, the teacher should keep in mind:

- Medication is likely to be just one of many kinds of support that the student needs. Other areas of support should not be neglected.

- Medication is intended to benefit the student in specific ways. The teacher should understand what benefits can or cannot be expected from the medication.

- Medication may have side effects. The teacher should learn what side effects are possible and then work with the student on strategies for minimizing or compensating for the side effects.

- The teacher should monitor changes in student performance and functioning that may be medication-related. The teacher should respond appropriately to signs that the benefits are declining or the side effects are increasing.

Practice Questions

1. In the word "breaking" what is the "ing"?

   A. A phoneme.

   B. A morpheme.

   C. A consonant.

   D. A digraph.

2. When a child with a learning disability struggles to learn "The Alphabet Song" (a song in which the letters of the alphabet are sung in order), the underlying limitation reflects which of the following?

   A. Alphabetic principle.

   B. Alphabet knowledge.

   C. Phonological awareness.

   D. Phonemic awareness.

3. Which of the following observed in a fourth grader would be most suggestive of dyslexia?

   A. Impaired hearing and difficulty segmenting words into phonemes.

   B. Good attentional skills and limited vocabulary.

   C. Normal intelligence and difficulty with decoding.

   D. Traumatic brain injury and difficulty following instructions.

4. Which of the following characteristics is described as one of the symptoms of autism?

   A. Difficulty paying attention in social settings.

   B. Resistance to change in daily routines.

   C. Lack of interest in mechanical objects.

   D. Excessive verbalization with others.

5. Maria is a 10th grade student who takes anti-seizure medication and experiences side effects such as occasional disorientation and drowsiness. Maria's teacher notices that for several days, Maria has been especially lethargic and "out of touch." What is happening to Maria?

   A. Maria's depression is becoming worse.

   B. Maria is having an adverse reaction to her medication.

   C. Maria is developing a physical illness.

   D. It is impossible to tell without further information.

Answers to Practice Questions

1. B.

   Choice B is correct because a morpheme is the smallest unit of meaning in a word. In this case, "ing" indicates present active tense. Choice A is incorrect because "ing" consists of three phonemes. Choice C is incorrect because "ing" contains two consonants. Choice D is incorrect because a digraph consists of pairs of letters that constitute a single sound.

2. B.

As "The Alphabet Song" only teaches children the names and sequence of the letters in the alphabet, choice B is the correct answer. Choice A is incorrect because the alphabetic principle consists of knowledge that letters represent sounds in systematic ways. Choice C is incorrect because phonological awareness pertains to the ability to discriminate among and manipulate language sounds. Likewise, choice D is incorrect because phonemic awareness pertains to the ability to discriminate among and manipulate phonemes.

3. C.

In the absence of further information, dyslexia could not be ruled out for any of the options. Among these options, however, normal intelligence combined with a reading-specific limitation is most suggestive of dyslexia, and thus, choice C is the correct answer.

Choice A is incorrect because the difficulty with segmentation could be attributed to the hearing problem. Choices B and D do not clearly indicate a reading-specific problem.

4. B.

Choice B is correct because resistance to change in familiar routines is a common symptom among autistic children. Choice A is incorrect because although autistic children may not be attentive enough in certain situations, difficulty paying attention is not a symptom distinctive to autism per se. Choice C is incorrect because some autistic children show particular interest in mechanical objects. Choice D is incorrect because many autistic children exhibit impaired communication with others.

5. D.

Maria's symptoms could be reflective of worsening depression, adverse side effects of a medicine, a physical illness, or some other problem. Thus, choice D is the correct answer. The problems described in choices A, B, and C cannot be definitively concluded.

CHAPTER 4

COMPETENCY 0003
Assessment and Individual Program Planning

This chapter pertains to the selection, use, and interpretation of assessments used with students who have, or who are suspected to have, a disability. The chapter also reviews how Individualized Education Programs (IEPs) are developed, implemented, and monitored through collaboration among educational professionals.

PI (a): Basic and specialized terminology used in the assessment of students with disabilities

This section introduces some key terminological distinctions used in the practice of assessment.

In educational settings, **assessment** is the systematic gathering and analysis of information about students in order to make decisions that may benefit their educational experience. The term "assessment" can be used in at least two different but related senses:

- The specific tool used to gather information can be referred to as an assessment. For example, a vision screening, a test of reading fluency, and a state-mandated achievement test are each a type of assessment.

- The process of gathering information can be referred to as assessment. For example, the administration of a state-mandated achievement test on one particular occasion is an example of an assessment.

Throughout this chapter, basic and specialized terminology used in the assessment of students with disabilities will be introduced. In addition, a key distinction between "assessment" and "evaluation" should be noted. Although the two terms are sometimes used interchangeably, the following distinction is also made:

- Assessment is an ongoing process of monitoring student learning and identifying areas of strength and weakness. The ultimate goal of assessment is to improve student achievement, and thus, it can be considered a formative activity.

- Evaluation is the determination of what students have already achieved. The goal of evaluation is to judge the extent of student achievement, and thus, it can be considered a summative activity.

To illustrate the distinction described above, the assessment of a particular student's spelling ability could be carried out by examining the student's essays, homework assignments, spelling tests, and other written work created throughout the semester in order to determine whether the student is progressing as expected. Evaluation would be illustrated by the assigning of a grade to a spelling test at the end of the semester. As this example illustrates, assessment and evaluation are closely intertwined.

PI (b): The characteristics, uses, and limitations of various types of formal and informal assessments

In this section, you will read about the uses, types, characteristics, and limitations of formal and informal assessments.

Assessment is carried out to answer the following questions:

- What is the extent of a student's progress in particular areas?

- Which students need extra support?

- In what areas do particular students need extra support?

- Which approaches to providing extra support are likely to benefit a particular student?

- Is the extra support being provided to a particular student effective?

- Is a particular student eligible for special education services?

- Are the special education services being provided to a particular student effective?

Assessment data is gathered to address one or more of these questions. In order to properly evaluate the data, teachers must consider the timing and purpose of the assessment, the appropriate interpretation of assessment results, and the nature of what is measured by the assessment. These considerations are discussed further in this section as well as later in the chapter.

Types of Assessment

A distinction can be made among five types of assessments in terms of when they are administered and what use they serve (i.e., what kinds of information they are intended to provide about students):

- **Screening assessments** are administered to all students in a particular group, such as a grade or a school. Screening is typically carried out at the beginning of the school year, as in the example of a vision screening administered to all incoming kindergarten students. The goal of screening is to identify, as early as possible, students who may need extra academic support. Screening may also be carried out on an individual basis, as when a teacher observes the classroom behavior of a student who may be experiencing an emotional disturbance.

- **Prereferral assessments** are administered to individual students in some states before formally referring them for special education. Such assessments typically provide more information than what can be obtained through screening. When a student is struggling in some respect, prereferral assessments can be used to determine which instructional modifications are likely to help the student, and whether these modifications are successful (thereby allowing a formal referral for special education to be avoided in some cases). Prereferral assessment can also be used to document the need for formal referral for special education and may then become part of the student's IEP.

- **Diagnostic assessments** are administered to individual students who may need extra support. In some cases, diagnostic assessments are used because screening has suggested the presence of a disability (in which case the diagnostic assessment may function as a prereferral assessment). In other cases, the diagnostic assessment is used because the student has already been referred for special education and more information is needed. Diagnostic assessments provide a more in-depth understanding of a child's skills and instructional needs than screening assessments do. The goal of a diagnostic assessment is to determine areas of strength and weakness for a particular student. In some cases, the assessment is also designed to identify the nature of the student's disability. The assessment used may be a standardized test, but significant decisions about the student (e.g., determination of eligibility for special education services) will consist of information gathered from several sources. For example, a student who is suspected of having a receptive language limitation may be administered the Peabody Picture Vocabulary Test, a standardized test of receptive vocabulary. In addition, school records, teacher observations, parent interviews, and other sources of information may be considered in determining to what extent, if any, the student has a receptive language impairment.

- **Progress monitoring assessments** are used to determine whether an individual student's progress is adequate. Progress monitoring is conducted frequently over some finite period of time, and it often focuses on one specific academic area (e.g., reading fluency) or behavioral dimension (e.g., impulse control). The actual assessments used could be informal or formal and administered either before or after participation in special education services. Examples of progress monitoring include the curriculum-based measurement approaches discussed at length later in this chapter.

- **Outcome assessments** are used to determine the extent of student achievement at the end of the school year or other significant time period. Outcome assessments thus fall under the heading of evaluation, as defined earlier in this chapter. A well-known example of outcome assessment would be the state-mandated achievement tests that students of certain grade levels must take in specified content areas at the end of the academic year.

Assessment information must be interpreted in light of whether screening, prereferral, diagnosis, progress monitoring, or outcome evaluation was the original purpose of the assessment. Each type of assessment tends to yield a different type of information that is used for a somewhat different purpose.

Alternative Assessments

Alternative assessments are not standardized, norm-referenced, or based on multiple-choice response formats. Rather, they tend to be defined in terms of student expression, in the sense that they are based on behaviors, products, and other forms of expression that are not captured in traditional assessments.

Traditionally, educational assessments relied heavily on standardized tests such as the state-mandated group achievement tests used to determine how well students have mastered curriculum standards. Although such tests continue to be used and to provide useful information, a number of criticisms have been raised about their format and content. Criticisms of these tests include the following:

- Recall and rote learning is valued over critical reflection.

- The knowledge being tested is trivialized by reducing it to multiple-choice format.

- Test-takers are required to choose among pre-determined options rather than constructing solutions.

- Arbitrary time limits are imposed for test completion.

- The test structure implies that there is only one correct solution to each problem.

As a result of these and other criticisms, educators have shifted toward the inclusion of alternatives to group-administered achievement tests and other traditional approaches to assessment. The following are descriptions of some of these alternative assessments.

Observational Assessment

An **observational assessment** yields descriptions of student behavior in natural settings. In many cases, the goal of observational assessment is to describe behavior as objectively as possible, without making inferences about underlying thoughts, motives, feelings, and expectations. In some cases, the observer comments on the student's apparent state of mind as well. Some examples of observational assessment methods are as follows:

- **Checklists** are used to note the presence or absence of specific behaviors (e.g., talking out of turn, interrupting, leaving one's seat at inappropriate times, making unnecessary noises, and other disruptive behaviors).

- **Rating scales** are used to note the extent to which a behavior is expressed (e.g., the extent of engagement in class activities, as indicated by participation in group work and interaction with teacher and peers during class discussion).

- **Duration records** are used to note the amount of time the student spends engaged in a particular behavior (e.g., talking to another student when it is understood to be inappropriate to do so).

- **Time-sampling records** are used to note the number of times the student engages in a particular behavior during a particular time period (e.g., tapping a pencil or pen during math class in a manner that may be disruptive).

- **Anecdotal records** are used to record narrative descriptions of behavior in particular settings (e.g., the student's behavior during one class period).

Ecological Assessment

An **ecological assessment** focuses on the student's functioning in different environments. The goal of the assessment is to identify environments in which the student functions with greater or lesser difficulty, to understand what contributes to these differences in functioning, and to draw useful implications for instructional planning. An example of ecological assessment would be the observation of a mildly autistic student in class, in the cafeteria, on the playground, and in other school settings, in order to better understand the situations in which the student experiences conflict with peers.

Authentic Assessment

An **authentic assessment** provides descriptions of student performance on real-life tasks carried out in real-world settings (or simulations of real-world settings). Authentic assessment is based on the assumption that the purpose of learning is not simply to do well on tests but also to acquire knowledge and skills that can be more broadly applied to life situations. Thus, the goal of authentic assessment is to determine how well a student performs when the knowledge and skills acquired in class are applied to meaningful tasks. An example of an authentic assessment would be a description of how accurately and effectively students maintain a bank account in their mathematics class. Although an actual account is not created, the activity is "authentic" in the sense of allowing students to apply mathematical skills to the management of money in a simulated real-life context.

Authentic assessments can take on many forms. For example, students may be assessed by means of a **rubric**, or a guide to the evaluation of student work that provides definitions of different levels of performance. Whether used for authentic assessment or for some other type of assessment, rubrics have a number of advantages, including the following:

- Rubrics provide students with guidance as to what is expected of them and how their work will be evaluated.

- Rubrics can provide useful feedback to students at a variety of levels.

- The creation of rubrics push teachers to clarify their standards of evaluation.

- Use of rubrics helps assessment be more reliable, i.e., more consistent over time and across students.

Portfolio Assessment

A **portfolio** is a collection of work produced by a student over time. The goal of portfolio assessment is to gauge student effort, progress, and achievement through examination of many different kinds of work that the student has produced in a particular class or related to a specific theme. For example, in an elementary language arts class, a portfolio that will be examined at the end of the year might include materials such as:

- A list of books that the student has read along with his/her personal reactions to the books

- A collection of tests and homework assignments

- Transcripts of story retells produced by the student

- Audiotapes of the student reading selected passages out loud

- Drafts and final versions of critical reviews created by the student

- Drafts and final version of an original story created by the student

Alternative Assessment and Students with Disabilities

Alternative assessments are appropriate for use with general education students as well as with students with disabilities. Alternative assessments can supplement the evaluation of student progress through traditional forms of assessment. In some cases, alternative assessments should be used in place of traditional ones.

Most students with disabilities can participate in assessments such as the state-mandated achievement tests used for accountability purposes, given appropriate accommodations. However, some students, such as those with severe cognitive impairments, will require alternatives to traditional assessments. These students are not expected to master the state curriculum standards, and thus, the traditional achievement tests are not appropriate measures of progress.

Generally, students with disabilities who do not participate in regular assessments must be provided with alternatives. The alternative assessments should be aligned with the instruction provided to each student and should be as similar as possible to the content of state and district assessments. Documentation of student performance and how performance is evaluated should be recorded.

Alternative Assessment and State-Mandated Testing

The alternative assessments described are used in classroom settings in place of regular assessments. Alternative assessments can also be used in place of state-mandated testing.

In the New York State Testing Program, the alternative assessment is called the **New York State Alternative Assessment (NYSAA)**.

Eligibility to participate in the NYSAA is determined by the Committee on Special Education (CSE) team. The NYSAA is administered to students whom the CSE has designated as having severe cognitive disabilities. These students must be assessed by means of the NYSAA once per year, beginning at age 9 and continuing through age 14, in order to document their progress toward achieving the New York State learning standards and alternate grade-level indicators. A secondary NYSAA is administered during the school year when students turn 17 or 18 years of age.

NYSAA performance is recorded in the form of observations, interviews, parent surveys, student work, and other materials gathered over a period of several months. Performance is scored on a 4-point rating scale, with a 1 indicating that the student requires extensive scaffolding in order to participate in an activity that reflects a particular standard and alternative performance indicator, and a 4 indicating that the student can participate in the activity independently, in a variety of settings, and can evaluate his/her own performance.

PI (c): Strategies for selecting and administering nonbiased assessments for given students

Bias must be avoided in the assessment of all students who have, or who are suspected of having, a disability. This section discusses strategies for selecting and administering nonbiased assessments. As noted at the outset of this section, the risk of bias is greater for particular groups of students.

Disproportionality

The Individuals with Disabilities Education Act (IDEA) requires school districts to design policies and procedures that prevent students from certain racial and ethnic groups from being overrepresented in special education programs. IDEA contains this requirement because of ample evidence that these and other groups are disproportionately represented in special education. As explained below, disproportionality is closely related to assessment practices.

The following groups of students have been found to be overrepresented in special education programs (these groups are not completely exclusive of each other):

- students from certain racial or ethnic backgrounds (e.g., African-American and Hispanic students)

- students from low socioeconomic status backgrounds (i.e., poor students)

- students from non-majority linguistic backgrounds (e.g., students who speak a regional dialect)

- English language learners (i.e., students whose first language is not English)

The fact that these groups are overrepresented in special education programs is sometimes referred to as the disproportionality problem, or simply **disproportionality**. (Disproportionality also refers to the underrepresentation of certain groups in special education, a topic that is not discussed in this chapter.) If students with disabilities were always identified accurately, then disproportionality would constitute a problem in the sense of suggesting that certain groups (e.g., poor students) need greater academic support. However, the primary concern about disproportionality is that it represents some degree of inaccuracy in the identification of students with disabilities. That is, disproportionality is assumed to result in part from a higher rate of mislabeling students from certain groups as having disabilities. This sort of mislabeling is problematic for a number of reasons:

- Labeling a student with a disability can create social and academic stigmas for the student and for the group represented by the student.

- Once students have begun to receive special education services, they tend to remain in special education.

- Students in special education programs may have diminished opportunities for contact with peers.

- Students in special education programs may experience lower academic expectations, less rigorous curricula, and fewer opportunities both in and beyond school.

Causes of Disproportionality

Studies point to a number of reasons for the disproportionate representation of certain students in special education programs. In particular, students from non-white and/or poor backgrounds are more likely to experience one or more of the following:

- pre-educational experiences that provide less preparation for school than the experiences of middle-class peers

- poverty-related experiences that appear to increase the risk of certain kinds of disabilities

- referral for special education assessment by teachers (i.e., students from minority backgrounds are referred at higher rates than their white, middle-class peers)

- discrimination as a result of test bias

Implications of Disproportionality for Assessment

The disproportionality problem calls for caution when conducting assessments with students from non-majority backgrounds and when interpreting the results of assessments with these students, particularly when the assessments may be used as part of the process of identifying a disability or making determinations about placement. The following are some strategies that have been recommended:

- greater support for the pre-educational and early educational experiences of all children, including those who may be assessed (accurately or inaccurately) at some point with a disability

- use of approaches such as prereferral as a means of helping struggling students prior to referral for special education assessment

- use of multiple assessments, including alternative assessments, in order to prevent biased tests from serving as the primary basis for identification of disabilities

- use of assessments that are appropriate in content for each student's particular cultural and linguistic background

- use of assessments, whenever possible, for which members of the student's cultural group were included in the normative sample

- administration of assessments by individuals trained in their administration and in the assessment of culturally and linguistically diverse populations

- additional training for teachers to increase their understanding of the disproportionality problem and how to avoid it (e.g., how to identify causes of academic underperformance other than disabilities, such as limited English proficiency, and how to take into account cultural differences when conducting informal assessments)

Nonbiased Assessments

IDEA states that assessment materials must be nondiscriminatory with respect to the student's racial and cultural background. More specifically, the requirements of IDEA with respect to avoiding bias include the following:

- Assessments must be administered in the student's primary language or mode of communication.

- States must make provisions for testing accommodations (described further below).

- Test bias must be avoided in the selection of assessments.

Test bias is implicated whenever certain groups consistently score differently from other groups (e.g., when females tend to score lower than males, rural students tend to score lower than urban students, and students of one ethnicity tend to score lower than students of other ethnicities). As discussed above, disproportionality has been attributed in part to the fact that some educational assessments are biased in content, in the sense of containing items that favor students from middle-class, majority backgrounds. This form of test bias illustrates what is sometimes called "item bias."

A common example of test bias can be seen in test questions containing content that is likely to be more familiar to middle-class students, such as a question on a vocabulary test about a "yacht" or a passage in a reading comprehension test in which a family is trying to decide which of their two cars to use for the family vacation.

Assessment Accommodations

IDEA requires that the assessment of students with disabilities, like other educational activities, be carried out in the least restrictive environment (see Chapter 2 for definition). IDEA also requires that students with disabilities be included in the state-mandated assessments of achievement used for accountability purposes. If possible, students with disabilities will participate in these assessments with no change to the test protocol. When a particular student cannot do so without additional support, the school will provide **accommodations**, or adjustments to the way the assessments are administered that allow students with disabilities to participate on an equal basis with their peers. IDEA requires each state to develop guidelines for the accommodations and, to the extent feasible, to develop and administer state-mandated assessments using principles of universal design.

The purpose of accommodations is to allow students with disabilities to demonstrate their achievement without being unfairly limited owing to their disabilities. Accommodations should be as minimal as possible. New York State policy requires the following:

- Accommodations must not change the content of what a test measures or otherwise invalidate the results.

- Accommodations must not substitute for knowledge or abilities that the student has not attained, or give an unfair advantage to the student.

Accommodations can be made along the dimensions of presentation, response, setting, and/or scheduling.

Presentation Accommodations

Presentation accommodations involve changes to the format of information presented in the assessment. Below are some examples:

- increased sized of font and response bubbles

- increased spacing between items

- highlighting of key phrases in instructions

- administration of assessment through a sign language interpreter

- administration of assessment by audiotape

- administration of assessment through tactile formats (e.g., Braille)

Presentation accommodations may be needed if a student has a visual or auditory impairment, a medication-related impairment in processing written text, or a reading disability.

Response Accommodations

Response accommodations involve changes to the format by which the student provides responses to the assessment. The following are some examples:

- use of a scribe to record student responses

- use of audiotaping student responses

- provision of response forms with added cues

- allowing students to use a computer to record responses

- allowing students to take notes prior to response

- allowing students to mark answers without filling in bubbles

Response accommodations may be needed if a student has a physical or cognitive impairment that prevents the student from using a writing implement or from shifting between a test booklet to a response form.

Setting Accommodations

Setting accommodations involve changes to the location and/or conditions of the assessment. Below are some examples:

- preferential seating for a student during assessment

- administration of assessment to small groups in separate settings

- administration of assessment to individuals in separate settings

- administration of assessment under conditions of special lighting or acoustics

- administration of assessment in a location with minimal distractions

Setting accommodations may be needed if a student has a severe attentional problem, a perceptual impairment, or a tendency to engage in behaviors that are highly distracting to others.

Scheduling Accommodations

Scheduling accommodations involve changes to the timing and scheduling of assessments. Examples include the following:

- allowing the assessment to be completed on separate occasions

- allowing the assessment to be completed at a particular time of day

- allowing the order of assessment components to be varied

- allowing frequent breaks during assessment

- allowing consumption of specific foods during assessment

- allowing extended time for the assessment

Scheduling accommodations may be needed if a student has a medical condition that requires distributed testing and extreme anxiety with respect to certain kinds of test content.

Selection of Accommodations

Accommodations should be provided for assessment if they are routinely provided to the student for instructional purposes. Accommodations are not used to give students with disabilities an unfair advantage, but rather to help them express their knowledge and skills on assessments. For example, on a writing test, providing a student with a scribe would not be appropriate if the test is intended to measure handwriting skill. However, if the purpose of this particular test is to gauge a student's verbal expression, and a student has a physical impairment that makes handwriting difficult, then the provision of a scribe is appropriate and would not give the student an unfair advantage.

The preceding example illustrates the importance of considering what an assessment is intended to measure before determining what accommodations, if any, are appropriate. The most important considerations in the selection of an assessment are the student's needs and the ways in which the student's disability are likely to impact performance.

PI (d): Interpreting information from formal and informal assessments

This section introduces some of the technical concepts and categories important to the interpretation of assessment data. Discussed in this section are different types of assessments (norm-referenced, criterion-referenced, etc.) as well as the technical adequacy (i.e., validity and reliability) of assessments.

A distinction can be made between norm-referenced, criterion-referenced, individual-referenced, and performance-based assessments. These four types of assessment differ in how the results for individual students should be interpreted.

Norm-Referenced Assessment

A **norm-referenced assessment** provides results for an individual student that are understood by comparison to **norms**, or results obtained from the student's peer group. "Norming" an assessment means administering the assessment to a large sample and then recording the distributions of scores along dimensions such as age or gender. Most norm-referenced assessment results indicate the individual's performance level compared to others of the same age. An example of a prominent norm-referenced assessment would be the Wechsler Intelligence Scale for Children (WISC-IV). The screening, prereferral, and diagnosis assessments noted earlier sometimes consist in part of norm-referenced tests.

Norm-referenced assessments are **standardized**, meaning that their administration and scoring is both predetermined and consistent. Owing to standardization and norming, scores on norm-referenced tests can be expressed in a familiar format such as percentile ranking. A child whose WISC-IV score represents the 64th percentile has scored higher than 63% of children of the same age who have also taken this test.

Care is needed in the use and interpretation of norm-referenced assessments among students who have, or are suspected to have, a disability. A student's disability may prevent that student from expressing the true extent of his/her knowledge or skills, as in the example of a student with normal intelligence whose score on an intelligence test is low because of a visual impairment, dyslexia, and side effects of essential medication. In this example, the student's abilities are underestimated by the assessment results because of a disability that affects test performance but not the student's actual abilities. A different problem arises when low performance on an assessment accurately reflects the student's capabilities but misleadingly implies the presence of a disability. A student who obtains an extremely low percentile ranking on a specific assessment may simply be weak in the area being assessed. (Alternatively, the student may fail to understand the instructions, find the test format unfamiliar, or lack interest in performing well on the assessment.)

Criterion-Referenced Assessment

Whereas a norm-referenced assessment compares an individual's scores to the scores of his/her peer group, a **criterion-referenced assessment** compares the individual's performance to some predetermined standard, or criterion. Examples of prominent criterion-referenced assessments include the "high-stakes" achievement tests that all states administer in order to monitor student progress. Like norm-referenced assessments, criterion-referenced assessments are standardized in terms of how they are administered and scored.

Some criterion-referenced assessments are simply used to determine whether or not each student has met a predetermined criterion, an example being the vision screening administered at the beginning of the school year to all students. Others, such as state-mandated achievement tests, allow for more fine-grained evaluations of student performance.

Whereas the screening, prereferral, diagnostic, and progress monitoring assessments discussed earlier may or may not consist of criterion-referenced tests, outcome assessments are almost always criterion-referenced. Evidence of a disability may include falling below some criterion on a criterion-referenced assessment and/or an especially low percentile ranking on a norm-referenced assessment. However, as with norm-referenced assessments, caution is needed in the use and interpretation of criterion-referenced assessments among students who have, or who are suspected to have, a disability. A student may fail to meet some criterion owing to a disability that impairs test performance but that does not diminish the underlying ability being tested. Moreover, a student may fail to meet some criterion owing to an academic weakness, unfamiliarity with the test, and lack of motivation, rather than the presence of a disability.

Individual-Referenced Assessment

An **individual-referenced assessment** is used to compare an individual's score at one point in time with the same individual's score at some other point or points in time.

Rather than being compared to a normative sample or to some predetermined standard, the individual is compared to himself/herself. Whereas most norm-referenced and criterion-referenced assessments consist of standardized tests, individual-referenced assessments may or may not be standardized. Progress-monitoring assessments are often individual-referenced. An example of such an assessment would be the **running record** that teachers use to track the progress of students in areas like reading. A running record records a student's performance across multiple administrations of the same task. If the teacher is interested in a student's oral fluency, for example, the teacher might keep a running record of the details of the student's performance when reading a particular passage on different occasions, so that those aspects of fluency that improve, decline, or stay the same from occasion to occasion can be recorded.

Performance-Based Assessment

Norm- and criterion-referenced assessments typically require students to choose among a predetermined set of options (as in, for example, a multiple-choice test). These assessments yield objective scores, as do many individual-referenced assessments. For a **performance-based assessment**, the student must exhibit some behavior or create some product requiring integration of knowledge and skills. Although guidance may be given, students do not simply choose among preset options, and thus, their behavior or product may need to be evaluated subjectively. Examples of performance-based assessments include:

- a performance (e.g., performance of a musical piece)

- a demonstration (e.g., demonstration of a lab procedure)

- an essay (e.g., a position paper on conservation)

- a project (e.g., a collage)

- a portfolio (e.g., a collection of student work during the semester)

Performance-based assessments are becoming increasingly popular as supplements or alternatives to traditional norm- and criterion-referenced tests, and in some cases, they are particularly well suited for the assessment of students with disabilities.

Technical Adequacy of Assessment

Validity and reliability are two of the important concepts that are used in the interpretation, analysis, and application of assessment results, regardless of whether the assessments are norm-referenced, criterion-referenced, or performance-based. Validity and reliability are often referred to together as representing the "technical adequacy" of an assessment.

Validity

When using assessment information to make instructional decisions, teachers should always consider carefully what the assessment measures. There are many tests of reading, for example, but some tests focus on comprehension and higher-order thinking, others yield information about decoding skills, while still others reveal information about multiple aspects of reading ability. A teacher who is planning specialized instructional support for a student with reading difficulties must be aware of exactly what the reading assessment measures, in order to be able to examine the student's scores and identify those areas in which the student needs extra support. To the extent that this is possible, the teacher should also consider how accurately the particular assessment measured what it is intended to measure, given the content of the assessment, the testing conditions, and whether scores on the assessment are likely to be predictive of the student's performance in class. These examples illustrate the need to consider the validity of an assessment.

Validity refers to the extent to which an assessment measures what it is intended to measure. There are several types:

- **Criterion-related validity** refers to the extent to which scores on an assessment are related to some criterion measure. Depending on when the criterion measure is obtained, a further distinction can be made between two types of criterion-related validity—**concurrent validity** (the criterion measure is administered at the same time as the assessment) and **predictive validity** (the criterion measure is administered at some point in the future). Concurrent validity is important to the validation of new measures. For example, a new test and an established test may be administered to the same group of individuals in order to compare scores. The new test will be validated to the extent that the scores are similar. Predictive validity is important to the determination of whether an assessment provides useful information about future performance, including performance in educational and vocational settings.

- **Content validity** refers to the extent to which an assessment accurately measures some identifiable content, such as curriculum standards or clearly defined behaviors. Whereas criterion-related validity is often determined quantitatively, by examining the extent of correlation between measures, the determination of content validity requires expert judgment. Researchers, teachers, and/or others may need to examine the content of an assessment in order to determine the extent of its alignment with the material or skills being tested.

- **Construct validity** refers to the extent to which an assessment accurately measures some underlying construct, such as intelligence, motivation, and engagement. Whereas content validity pertains to how well an assessment measures something observable, such as the content specified in curriculum standards, construct validity is a matter of how well an assessment taps into an underlying construct that cannot be observed directly. Construct validity is especially important to consider when an assessment is used with students who have, or may have, a disability. For example, low performance on a test may indicate that some underlying ability is impaired, or it may indicate that the student has a disability that interferes with expression of that ability, as in the earlier example of a student with normal intelligence performing poorly on an intelligence test owing to a visual or reading impairment.

Each type of validity is critical to the use of assessment data in educational settings. To illustrate, here are examples of questions about validity that are often asked when an assessment is administered to general education students:

- How well do the results of the assessment predict student performance in a particular class? (This is a predictive validity question.)

- To what extent is the content of the assessment aligned with curricular and instructional objectives for a particular class? (This is a content validity question.)

- To what extent does the assessment measure aptitude for learning the sort of material that is likely to be covered in a particular class? (This is a construct validity question.)

The following are examples of questions about validity that might be asked when an assessment is administered to students who have, or who may have, a disability:

- How low must performance be on the assessment in order to constitute evidence that a student will perform poorly in a particular class? Does especially low performance on the assessment suggest that the student will need extra academic support in order to function in the class? What other assessments might be needed in order to achieve greater accuracy in developing predictions about future class performance? (These are all predictive validity questions.)

- Does the assessment primarily measure student mastery of some content area (e.g., mathematical calculation) or does it also constitute a measure of independent skills (e.g., reading comprehension) in which a student with certain disabilities (e.g., dyslexia) might be weak? To what extent does the assessment measure the content it is intended to measure rather than these other skills? Do students with certain disabilities need accommodations in order for their mastery of the content to be more accurately represented by the assessment? (These are all content validity questions.)

- How low must performance be on the assessment in order to constitute evidence of an underlying problem such as an intellectual disability? What other assessments might be needed to help discern the nature of the underlying problem, if any? Does low performance on the assessment indicate that the student is impaired with respect to the ability being assessed, or does the student have some other disability (e.g., a visual impairment) that prevents the student's assessment-related ability from being accurately expressed? Do students with certain disabilities need accommodations in order for their underlying ability to be more accurately represented by the assessment? (These are all construct validity questions.)

Reliability

When using assessment information to make instructional decisions, teachers should also consider whether the assessment is likely to yield results that are consistent over time, across settings, and so forth. Inconsistent results undermine the usefulness of an assessment as a means of monitoring student progress and identifying students who need extra support.

Reliability is the term used to refer to the consistency of assessment results. Like validity, reliability is a desirable characteristic of an assessment. Three of the many types of reliability are:

- **Test-retest reliability** refers to the extent to which results will be the same upon repeated administrations of the same assessment. Test-retest reliability must be considered regardless of who participates in an assessment, but it is a particularly important consideration when the assessment is used to monitor the progress of students for whom this form of reliability may be diminished owing to a disability. Examples include students with attentional problems as well as those with medical problems who experience intermittent fluctuations in energy. For these students, test-retest reliability may be lower than for others, and thus, the results obtained from multiple testings must be interpreted cautiously.

- **Inter-rater reliability** refers to the extent to which observers agree on assessment results. Inter-rater reliability is not usually considered when assessment responses are simple and objective (e.g., responses to a multiple-choice test). However, inter-rater reliability becomes an important concern when assessment responses are complex, ambiguous, or otherwise require subjective interpretation. For example, inter-rater reliability should be measured when judging essays created for a test of written expression, when counting the number of disruptive behaviors exhibited in a natural setting, and when determining that a musical performance reflects "proficiency." When assessment results are used as part of a strategy for diagnosing a student with a particular disability, inter-rater reliability is especially critical.

- **Equivalent-forms reliability** refers to the extent to which alternate forms of the same assessment yield the same results. Equivalent-forms reliability can only be considered when a test has multiple forms. The importance of developing multiple forms of a test is to allow repeated administrations of the test while preventing familiarity effects from influencing the results.

> **PI (e): How individual evaluation assessment and data and other assessment information is used to make eligibility, program, and placement decisions for students with disabilities; how to evaluate instruction; how to monitor progress of students with disabilities; how to make responsive, research-based, and time adjustments to instruction**

This section provides information on how the CSE and Committee on Preschool Special Education (CPSE) make use of assessments to guide and monitor the education of students with disabilities.

Eligibility for Services

In New York State, eligibility for special education services is based on the results of an assessment arranged by the CSE or CPSE. The initial assessment must include the following:

- a physical exam

- a psychological evaluation (mandatory for preschoolers; as appropriate for older students)

- a social history

- observations of the student in the current educational setting

- other assessments as appropriate (e.g., vocational assessments for students ages 12 and up)

The CSE or CPSE determines on the basis of assessment results whether a student is eligible for special education services. Children who are considered eligible for special education services must be reevaluated every three years, if not more frequently. The parents may at any time request a hearing to challenge the eligibility determination.

In general, a child is considered eligible for special education services if the CSE or CPSE concludes that the child has one of the 13 types of disability listed in Chapter 3, and the child's educational performance is adversely affected by the disability. Both conditions must be met in order for the child to be eligible for special education services. The child need not be failing in school in order to be deemed eligible. As noted in Chapter 3, each particular state may choose to also consider developmental delay, along with the resulting need for special education and related services, as sufficient criteria for eligibility.

Generally, the CSE or CPSE uses the following process to determine eligibility:

- review the referral

- review background information

- develop an evaluation plan indicating what tests and other forms of assessment will be used to evaluate the child

- share the evaluation plan with parents and obtain consent

- arrange for the student to be assessed

- evaluate the results of assessments, along with other available information, to determine whether the student has a disability, and if so, what special education and related services he/she needs

- generate a written report of findings

- meet with parents and determine eligibility

The tests and other assessments that are used to determine eligibility must meet a number of criteria. The following are some key examples:

- The assessments must not be racially or culturally biased.

- The assessments must be administered in the student's native language and/or in some other suitable medium (e.g., sign language).

- The assessments must have good validity and reliability.

- The assessments must be administered by trained individuals in the way that was intended by the creators of the assessments.

IDEA specifies that eligibility for special education and related services cannot be based on the results of a single test or any other single form of assessment. The CSE or CPSE must always consider multiple assessments and other sources of information before making a decision about whether the student has a disability and is eligible for special education and related services.

If the parents disagree with the results of the evaluation, they may request an **Individual Educational Evaluation (IEE)** that is paid for by the school. Mediation and due process hearings are also options if parents cannot resolve their differences with the CSE or CPSE concerning the outcome of the evaluation.

If the CSE or CPSE determines that the child has a disability and is indeed eligible for special education and related services, the results of the committee's evaluation are then used to develop the IEP.

The SETT Framework

The information-gathering and decision-making activities of the CSE and CPSE are guided by the requirements of IDEA and other federal and state laws. In addition, these committees rely on systematic processes for gathering information and making decisions about students. For example, a widely used process for decision-making about assistive technology and other topics is the **SETT framework**. The acronym "SETT" stands for students, environment, tasks, and tools—four areas of inquiry that are used to identify supports and services for students with disabilities. The following are some of the questions a CSE or a CPSE might ask about each area:

- Regarding the student, what are his/her strengths and special needs? What are the student's goals and expectations? What does the student need to do that is currently difficult or impossible for him/her to do independently?

- Regarding the environment, how can the student's current physical and instructional arrangements be characterized? What types of materials and support are currently available? What are the attitudes and expectations of educational staff, family, and others? What are the specific concerns regarding the student's access to physical and instructional environments?

- Regarding the tasks, what activities normally occur in the student's instructional environment, what activities support the student's curricular goals, and what are the critical components of these activities? How could these activities be modified to accommodate the student's particular needs? What strategies could be used to facilitate the student's active engagement in these activities?

- Regarding the tools, what tools should be considered when developing instruction for the student and how might these tools be tried out in the environments in which they are ordinarily used? How could differentiated instruction enhance the student's performance? What other accommodations and services does the student need? Does the student have significant cognitive impairment that requires modifications to the curriculum?

Progress Monitoring

Progress monitoring is a commonly used approach for assessing individual student progress. This approach serves a number of purposes:

- Progress monitoring helps determine the extent to which instruction is generally effective, both overall and in specific areas.

- Progress monitoring helps determine the extent of each student's progress, both overall and in specific areas.

- Progress monitoring helps indicate how to modify instruction or provide other support for students whose progress is inadequate.

There are many different approaches to progress monitoring. Some of these approaches were discussed earlier in the chapter. This section focuses on a form of progress monitoring known as curriculum-based measurement.

Curriculum-Based Measurement

Curriculum-based assessment (CBA) provides information about student mastery of the general education curriculum. Such assessments are typically criterion-referenced. A prominent example of CBA developed for use in special education is **curriculum-based measurement (CBM)**, an approach to monitoring student progress that is relatively sensitive to changes in performance over time. CBM is based on the collection of samples of student performance on a specific task or test. Samples are obtained frequently (e.g., 1 to 3 times per week) and the tests are brief (e.g., 1 to 5 minutes).

As an approach to progress monitoring, CBM has a number of advantages:

- CBM can be carried out relatively quickly and easily with minimal disruption to daily routines.

- By means of CBM, student progress can be monitored with respect to a variety of basic academic skills (e.g., reading fluency, reading comprehension, spelling, mathematics and calculation).

- Because CBM is standardized (i.e., test administration, format, and scoring is the same from time to time) test performance can be readily compared across multiple instances of testing.

- The results of CBM are relatively easy to understand.

- The frequency of CBM testing allows teachers to quickly discern the impact of instruction and instructional changes on student performance.

To illustrate how CBM works, the following is a summary of how oral reading fluency might be monitored:

- The teacher or examiner works with the child on an individual basis.

- Once per week, the student is asked to read each of 3 passages out loud for 1 minute apiece.

- The student's score for each passage consists of the number of words read correctly and fluently minus the number of words read incorrectly.

- Clear rules are used to define correctly and incorrectly read words. For example, self-corrected words and repeated words are considered to have been correctly read. Substituted words and words that have not been read after 3 seconds are considered to have been incorrectly read.

- The median (i.e., middle) score across the three passages constitutes the student's fluency score for the week.

- Weekly fluency scores are plotted on a graph, which is then examined to determine the trajectory of student progress over time.

Studies have shown that CBM is a reliable and valid approach to progress monitoring. With respect to the assessment of students who have, or who are suspected to have disabilities, CBM offers a number of advantages, including the following:

- The quickness and ease of CBM administration and the nature of what is tested allows CBM to be readily used for the screening of all students as well as the progress monitoring of individual students with disabilities.

- The frequency of CBM administration allows lack of progress in particular areas to be quickly identified.

- The frequency of CBM administration and the nature of what is tested allows teachers to quickly determine the impact of instructional modifications.

- The standardization of CBM tests and the specificity of the results allow CBM to be a useful tool in IEP planning (see Chapter 2 for discussion of the IEP). That is, short- and long-term goals in the IEP can be expressed in terms of CBM scores.

PI (f): Strategies for communicating assessment results to all stakeholders and strategies and procedures for creating and maintaining records

This section describes strategies for communicating assessment results and for creating and maintaining records.

Communicating Assessment Results

When communicating assessment results, the teacher must keep in mind the audience. Whereas parents and students should not be expected to know anything about assessment, a special education professional, for example, can be assumed to have at least some knowledge and experience. The following are some questions that should be addressed when discussing assessment results:

- What kind of assessment was used? For example, norm-referenced, criterion-referenced, and individual-referenced assessments provide different kinds of information about students (see the discussion earlier in this chapter) and thus should not be confused.

- What kinds of knowledge or skills were assessed? The nature and scope of what was tested should be clearly stated. A test of oral reading fluency, for example, should not be described as "a reading test" since the results of such a test indicate nothing about other reading-related skills such as comprehension.

- How reliable and valid was the assessment? Although reliability and validity are technical concepts and not easily explained, the trustworthiness of the results should be considered when they are communicated. One may have greater confidence in the results of a standardized, widely used assessment, for example, than one that was created informally in order to measure the same skills. Both the strengths and the limitations of an assessment should be noted as appropriate.

- What are the main findings of the assessment? Rather than simply conveying statistical data, the meaning of the numbers should be clearly explained. Moreover, the practical implications should be discussed. Besides saying that a student scored in the 3rd percentile on some assessment and then explaining what a percentile is, the extent to which such a low score is problematic should be explained.

- How will the assessment results be used? The purpose and use of assessment results should be clearly indicated, particularly when communicating with families and students.

Confidentiality and Assessment Results

IDEA, FERPA, and other federal laws protect the confidentiality of assessment results and other educational records. Some of the legal requirements pertaining to confidentiality include:

- Parents may examine assessment results and other records, and if they request explanations of these materials, the school must comply. Parents may request that the records be amended if they feel the records are inaccurate, misleading, or violate the child's privacy.

- Generally, the school must obtain parental consent before disclosing assessment results and other records containing personally identifiable information about the child. (Personally identifiable information either names an individual directly or could be used by someone else to infer the individual's identity, location, and/or contact information.)

- Only parents and specific school personnel (e.g., teachers, educational specialists, and administrators) may have access to assessment results and other records. The school must document all instances in which records were examined; documentation must include information about when and why the records were examined, and who conducted the examination.

PI (g): Screening, prereferral (e.g., response to intervention), referral, and classification procedures

Assessment plays a central role in screening, prereferral (including response to intervention), referral, and classification. The role of assessment in these activities is discussed elsewhere in this book, including this chapter (section PI (e)) and Chapter 2 (section PI (e)).

This section discusses the continuum of services and placements available for students with disabilities, as required by IDEA and provided by New York State.

Continuum of Services

In order to meet the requirements of the least restrictive environment (see Chapter 2 for definition), schools must make available a continuum of services to meet the needs of individual students with disabilities. As per New York State law, these services include the following:

- Consultant teacher services are direct and/or indirect services provided to students with disabilities in the general education classroom and/or to their general education teachers.

- Resource room programs supplement the general or special education experience of students with disabilities by providing individual or small-group instruction (with other students who have similar needs) during part of the school day.

- Integrated co-teaching services consist of specially designed instruction as well as academic instruction provided to a combination of students with and without disabilities.

- Special classes consist of students with disabilities grouped on the basis of similar needs, who receive their primary instruction separate from the general education classroom.

- Related services consist of developmental, corrective, and other supportive services that help students with disabilities access the general education curriculum.

Teaching assistants and teacher aides can assist in the delivery of special education services, but they cannot be the only service that a student receives. Additional services that may be recommended for individual students with disabilities include the following:

- transition services (to help the student shift toward post-school activities)

- transitional support services (to help the student shift into a general education classroom or less restrictive environment)

- travel training (to help the student learn how to move effectively and safely through the environments of school, home, and community)

- adapted physical education (to provide the student with suitable activities when he/she cannot participate in regular physical education activities)

- 12-month special services and/or programs (to provide the student with year-round instructional services or programs to prevent substantial regression)

- special transportation (to help the student travel to, from, and within the school)

Continuum of Services and Programs for Preschoolers

A range of services and programs is available for preschoolers with disabilities, including the following:

- special education itinerant services

- half-day preschool programs

- full-day preschool programs

- 12-month special services/programs

- in-state residential special education programs

Continuum of Placement

In New York State, the continuum of placement choices includes the following:

- Public schools

- Boards of cooperative educational services

- Private approved day schools

- Private approved residential schools

- Home instruction

- Hospital instruction

In addition to these options, **interim alternative educational settings (IAES)** must be provided for students with disabilities who have been suspended or removed from their current placement for more than 10 school days. While in an IAES, the student must continue to receive educational services as well as behavioral intervention services and modifications intended to prevent reoccurrence of the problem behavior.

PI (i): The components of IEPs and the roles and responsibilities of special education teachers in developing, implementing, monitoring, and modifying IEPs, transition plans, and behavioral intervention plans.

In this section, you will find information about the requirements for IEPs and IFSPs that are specified by IDEA.

Within 30 days of determining that a child is eligible for special education services under IDEA, an **IEP team** must meet in order to create an IEP for the child. As you read this section, keep in mind that in New York State, the IEP team is the CSE or CPSE (see Chapter 2 for discussion of these committees).

Composition of IEP Team (CSE or CPSE)

The IEP team includes the following individuals:

- parents

- a special education professional from the local education agency (LEA) or school district who works with students with the same type of disability

- at least one of the child's general education teachers, if the child participates, or may participate, in activities with general education students

- a representative of the LEA who is knowledgeable about available resources and the provision of special education

- a professional who is qualified to interpret and explain the results of testing and other aspects of the evaluation (if such an individual is not already part of the team)

Parents may invite anyone whose presence they consider helpful, including outside experts, family members, or anyone else with pertinent knowledge about the child. The school may invite anyone who is providing disability-related services to the child, as well as guidance counselors and/or other experts. The child may be invited, as appropriate, and must be invited if one of the purposes of the meeting is transition services (see below for discussion of transition).

IEP Meeting

IDEA requires that school staff take responsibility for convening the first meeting to create a student's IEP, as well as for convening subsequent meetings. School staff must choose a meeting time and place that are convenient to the parents. They must inform the parents as to who will attend the meeting. They must also explain that the parents have the right to invite anyone else who has specific knowledge about the child.

Parents must be given a copy of the IEP. If parents disagree with the content of the IEP, they should attempt to negotiate an agreement with the IEP team. If an agreement cannot be reached, parents can request **mediation**. Briefly, mediation is a meeting between parents and school representatives conducted by a qualified, impartial mediator whose goal is to find a resolution that satisfies all parties. Mediation must be carried out at no cost to parents. Parents may also file a complaint with the state education agency and request a due process hearing concerning the IEP's contents.

The school is responsible for ensuring that the IEP is implemented. The IEP team must review the IEP at least once per year, as well as whenever the school and/or parents request a review.

IEP Content

IDEA requires that each IEP contain the following content:

- A summary of the child's current levels of functioning and educational performance. This summary is typically based on classroom performance (e.g., scores on tests and assignments), tests administered for the purpose of identifying a disability, and observations made by parents and school staff.

- A statement of annual goals. These are measurable goals that the child can reasonably accomplish in one school year, and they may pertain to the child's physical, behavioral, social, and/or academic functioning.

- A statement of short-term objectives. These are measurable goals that constitute steps toward achieving the annual goals.

- A list of services. This list consists of all services that the child needs in order to achieve the annual goals—both services directly provided to the child as well as support provided to school staff who work with the child.

- A description of timing for special education and related services. This description must indicate when the services will begin, as well as the frequency and duration of services. Location of services must also be indicated.

- An explanation concerning the extent of participation with non-disabled children. This explanation must account for situations in which the child is not present in the general education classroom and/or is not included in educational activities for children without disabilities.

- A statement concerning the child's participation in standardized testing. This statement indicates whether modifications are needed before administering any state- or district-wide achievement tests to the child. Also indicated is whether any of these achievement tests are not appropriate for the child to take (and whether alternative forms of testing will be provided).

- A description of how progress will be measured. This description indicates how the child's progress toward the annual goals will be measured and how parents will be kept informed of the child's progress.

IFSPs

The **Individualized Family Service Plan (IFSP)** is similar to an IEP, in the sense of being a written document that includes detailed information on the child's current level of functioning, a statement of goals, and a summary of how those goals will be met. Both the IEP and the IFSP are based on a careful assessment of the child's needs. However, the IFSP only pertains to the age range birth to 3 years. Once the child turns 3, the creation of an IEP must be discussed.

Another difference between the IFSP and the IEP is that the IFSP targets the family and those natural environments accessible to the young child, such as the home, child care programs, and parks. The IFSP often describes services that will be provided by representatives of one or more agencies to families in the home. In contrast, the IEP is typically restricted to the school setting.

Behavioral Intervention Plans

When a student with a disability has a behavioral problem that interferes with his/her learning or that of other students, IDEA requires that the IEP team explore the need for positive strategies, supports, and interventions to address the problematic behavior. In particular, the IEP team will need to conduct a functional behavioral assessment in order to identify the causes of problem behavior and to then develop an intervention.

Recurring and/or extreme misbehavior may result in a student being removed from his/her regular educational placement through suspension or through placement in an alternative educational setting. When such behaviors occur, the IEP team must involve school administrators and parents in a **manifestation determination review** in order to determine whether the misbehavior is a manifestation of the student's disability, or whether it resulted from the school's failure to appropriately implement the IEP.

If the conclusion of the manifestation determination review is that the misbehavior is indeed related to the student's disability, the IEP team must conduct a functional behavior assessment for the purpose of developing a behavioral intervention plan (a description of the problem behavior and the strategies by which it will be addressed). If a behavioral intervention plan already exists, the IEP team must meet in order to review and possibly revise the plan. Functional behavior assessment and behavior intervention plans are discussed in sections PI (b) and PI (c) of Chapter 8. (See also section PI (e) of Chapter 5.)

If the conclusion of the manifestation determination review is that the misbehavior is not related to the student's disability, the student may be disciplined in the same way that students without disabilities are disciplined in the particular school. A functional behavior assessment may still be conducted as appropriate.

Transition Planning

The free appropriate education (FAPE) requirement of IDEA was extended in the 2004 reauthorization to include not just current educational experiences, but also preparation for additional education or training, employment opportunities, and independent living. This new emphasis on **transition** is intended to help prepare students with disabilities for life after their K–12 education. The IEP team is required to take responsibility for planning transition services. Planning must begin when the student is 14, if not earlier, and the post-graduation plan must be included in students' IEPs by age 16. Transition services may include help with identifying and applying to college or vocational school, seeking employment, and finding a place to live in the community.

IEPs and Transition

By the time the student reaches the age of 16, the IEP must contain the following transition-related information:

- measurable goals for training, education, employment, and independent living post-school

- courses that should be provided to prepare the student for achieving post-school goals

- annual goals while in high school that will prepare the student to meet post-school goals

- transition services and activities that will facilitate the shift to life post-school

Transition planning and implementation are discussed in more detail in Chapters 7 and 8.

Practice Questions

1. According to IDEA, on what grounds can a student be considered eligible for special education and related services?

   A. Evidence that the student is failing or doing very poorly in two or more classes.

   B. Evidence that the student has a disability that impairs academic performance.

   C. Evidence that the student is not achieving his/her potential in school.

   D. Evidence that the student has limited English proficiency due to country of origin.

2. Brief, weekly tests of a student's oral reading fluency best represent which type of assessment?

   A. Diagnostic.

   B. Outcome.

   C. Screening.

   D. Progress monitoring.

3. Jimmy is an emotionally disturbed 2nd grade student who spends the entire school day in the general education classroom. Jimmy often shouts, cries, and engages in other distracting behaviors when he is frustrated. At the same time, Jimmy is receptive to cueing from the teacher and quickly settles down if he feels that his frustration has been noted. Which of the following is a setting accommodation that would be most suitable for Jimmy when he participates in the state assessment?

    A. A private room should be made available for Jimmy.

    B. Jimmy should be allowed to have extended time on the assessment.

    C. Jimmy should be seated as close as possible to the teacher.

    D. A scribe should help Jimmy record assessment responses.

4. A particular assessment reveals that Marisa has performed at the 37th percentile for her age group in reading comprehension. What type of assessment was used?

    A. Norm-referenced.

    B. Criterion-referenced.

    C. Individual-referenced.

    D. Performance-based.

5. During the second week of school, a teacher notices that the medication one of her students takes every day for a medical condition impairs the student's energy and concentration, and that as a result, the student needs frequent breaks during instruction and assessment. The teacher feels that the student's low performance on tests administered at the beginning of the year is not indicative of how well the student will function in class, because those tests were administered without breaks. What type of validity is the focus of the teacher's concerns?

    A. Content.

    B. Concurrent.

    C. Predictive.

    D. Construct.

NYSTCE STUDENTS WITH DISABILITIES

6. A CSE learns from anecdotal reports that a student with both hearing and speech impairments is performing well in some academic and social contexts while struggling in others. What type of assessment is most likely to help the team determine the extent of the student's difficulties and develop a plan of action for him?

   A. Standardized assessment.

   B. Ecological assessment.

   C. Authentic assessment.

   D. Portfolio assessment.

7. Disproportionality refers to which of the following?

   A. The relatively high rate at which students with disabilities are labeled as having a learning disability.

   B. The underrepresentation of privileged students among those who have been diagnosed with a disability.

   C. The overrepresentation of students from certain backgrounds among those in special education programs.

   D. The relatively high percentage of assessments that have been found to contain biased items.

8. Which of the following is true of curriculum-based measurement (CBM)?

   A. CBM is primarily a form of outcome assessment.

   B. CBM cannot be used for screening purposes under any circumstances.

   C. CBM works best as a tool for prereferral assessment.

   D. CBM is a reliable and valid approach to progress monitoring.

Answers to Practice Questions

1.   B.

Choice B is correct because according to IDEA, eligibility for special education and related services depends on evidence that the student has a disability and evidence that the disability impairs academic performance. Choice A is incorrect because academic failure does not necessarily indicate a disability. Choice C is incorrect for a similar reason—failure to achieve one's potential does not necessarily imply a disability. Choice D is incorrect because limited English proficiency due strictly to country of origin is not a disability.

2.   D.

Brief, weekly tests of a specific academic skill exemplify progress monitoring, and thus, choice D is the best answer. Although progress monitoring tests could be part of screening, diagnosis, or outcome assessment, such tests are not typical of these forms of assessment, and thus, choices A, B, and C are incorrect.

3.   C.

Choice C is correct because the extent of accommodation is minimal, and close proximity to the teacher will facilitate the use of cueing to manage Jimmy's distracting behavior, as it seems to during classroom instruction. Choice A is incorrect because the conditions of assessment should be as similar as possible to the conditions of instruction, and Jimmy always participates in the general education classroom. Choice B is incorrect because it does not represent a setting accommodation. Choice D is incorrect for the same reason that choice A is incorrect; in both cases, the conditions of assessment are very different from the conditions of instruction.

4.   A.

Choice A is correct because norm-referenced assessments yield scores that can be converted to percentile rankings within age groups. Choices B, C, and D are incorrect because scores on these assessments are not usually expressed as percentile rankings.

5.   C.

Choice C is correct because the teacher is concerned that for this particular student, low test performance does not predict impaired functioning in class. That is, the teacher is concerned that for this particular student, the tests have limited predictive validity. Choices A, B, and D are incorrect because the teacher is not directly concerned about these other forms of validity.

6.   B.

Choice B is correct because ecological assessment would allow the student to be observed in different settings and perhaps clarify which settings are problematic for the student and why he struggles in those settings. Choices A, C, and D are incorrect because they are unlikely to provide relevant information.

7.   C.

Choice C is correct because *disproportionality* refers to both overrepresentation and underrepresentation of certain groups in special education programs. Choices A, B, and D do not provide the correct definition.

8.   D.

Choice D is correct because CBM has been shown to be a reliable and valid form of progress monitoring. Although CBM scores can be used as outcome measures, this is not their primary purpose, and thus Choice A is incorrect. Choice B is incorrect because CBM can be used for screening purposes. Choice C is incorrect because although CBM can be used for prereferral assessment, it cannot be said to be "best" for that form of assessment.

CHAPTER 5

COMPETENCY 0004
Strategies for Planning and Managing the Learning Environment and for Providing Behavioral Interventions

This chapter introduces strategies for planning and maintaining safe, productive learning environments and for implementing effective behavioral interventions. The concepts discussed in this chapter apply to all students, including students with disabilities. In addition, the importance of differentiation with respect to individual students, including students with disabilities, is essential.

PI (a): How to create and maintain a safe, productive learning environment for all students, including establishing routines and appropriate physical arrangements

This section reviews the creation and maintenance of safe, productive learning environments for all students, including students with disabilities.

A safe, productive learning environment is the outcome of effective **classroom management** on the part of the teacher. Some examples of the dimensions that are critical to classroom management include:

- the physical layout of the classroom (e.g., the arrangement of students' desks)

- the types and distribution of materials (e.g., books and worksheets)

- the allocation of time (e.g., the amount of time spent on a particular hands-on activity)

- the establishment of class rules and routines (e.g., rules for use of the restroom)

- the monitoring of students' behavior (e.g., monitoring students during group work)

- the imposition of discipline (e.g., dealing with a student who has broken the rules)

Effective classroom management results when a teacher attends to dimensions such as those described above and makes modifications wherever appropriate. Most classroom management strategies pertain to the management of space, time, or behavior—that is, the physical environment of the classroom, the use of time during class, and the management of student behavior. These are not wholly independent dimensions. For example, student behavior is affected by the layout of the classroom and the teacher's use of time. Misbehavior is more likely when desks are located too close together, and there is a substantial amount of "down time" while the teacher prepares an instructional activity. Because dimensions such as this are interrelated, you will notice areas of overlap in the material presented in this section and across this chapter.

Safety

Safety is a fundamental concern in any learning environment. Teachers can promote a safe classroom through strategies such as:

- ensuring that the classroom is free of clutter, dangerous objects, and other potential hazards

- establishing routines that promote safety (e.g., when students transition in and out of the classroom)

- monitoring student behavior and addressing problems appropriately

- being aware of emergency procedures and reviewing these procedures carefully with students

- being prepared to provide extra support to students who need it (e.g., assisting students with sensory impairments and/or limited mobility in emergency situations)

Physical Environment

Effective classroom management depends on creating a physical environment that is clean, safe, minimally distracting, maximally engaging, and most conducive to instructional activities. To take just one example, to the greatest extent possible, desks and chairs should be arranged so that

- Students are not sitting so closely to each other that physical contact is inevitable.

- Both the teacher and the students can move throughout the room with minimal disruption.

- The teacher can maintain eye contact with students at all times.

- Areas used for group work are as separate as possible from individual desks.

Time Management

Effective classroom management depends on using time efficiently so that maximal time is devoted to the pursuit of instructional objectives, while minimal time is spent on discussing classroom procedures, transitioning between activities, clarifying behavioral expectations, and dealing with undesirable behaviors. (Discussing procedures and transitioning are essential to classroom management, but teachers should avoid spending more time on them than necessary.) For example, the following strategies promote effective time management in the classroom by minimizing the loss of instructional time:

- Teachers should come to class each day fully prepared for all lessons, activities, and transitions, so that minimal class time is spent getting ready for each.

- Teachers should provide students with clear explanations of the purpose, instructions, and expectations for each activity, in advance, so that minimal time is spent on merely reiterating this information during the activity.

- Teachers should keep track of time and modify activities accordingly so that instructional objectives can be achieved and time is not lost completing activities on a subsequent day that were intended to be completed the previous day.

- Teachers should delegate some work to aides and volunteers (if available) and to students (as appropriate to their age and capabilities) in order to reduce the amount of time needed to prepare for instructional activities.

- Teachers should describe and discuss classroom rules, routines, and expectations clearly, at the outset of the year, so that throughout the year minimal time will be needed to reiterate key points.

Student Behavior

Effective classroom management depends on keeping students engaged and attentive, confident about learning, clear about what is expected of them, and consistently on-task, while helping them avoid negative emotional states, tuning out, becoming distracted, or engaging in disruptive behaviors. The following are strategies that teachers use to promote positive classroom behaviors while discouraging negative ones:

- Setting reasonable expectations for classroom behavior, and making sure that students understand those expectations, helps promote positive student behavior. If students understand clearly what is expected of them, they will be less likely to engage in undesirable behaviors owing to confusion about the nature of the expectations or a sense that the expectations are unimportant. As noted earlier, teachers should take time at the beginning of the year to clarify rules, routines, and expectations, and then to reiterate key points as needed depending on student age and level of comprehension.

- Close attention to what is happening in the classroom helps teachers understand the basis of both positive and negative behaviors. By noticing the antecedents and consequences of a disruptive behavior, for example, the teacher will gain more insight into why the student is engaging in the behavior. Through such insights, the teacher will be better prepared to deal with the behavior.

- Creating a sense of community, by treating students positively, including students in decision-making processes, and enforcing the rules fairly and consistently, helps keep students engaged and in turn promotes positive behavior on their part.

- Differentiation helps teachers structure activities for individual students so that the students are appropriately challenged and neither feel bored by overly easy work nor frustrated by overly difficult work. Differentiation also helps promote good teacher-student relationships and allows teachers to interact with individual students in a way that encourages positive behaviors while discouraging negative ones.

- Modeling desirable behaviors and responding positively to desirable behaviors can promote further expression of those behaviors.

- Responding effectively to undesirable behaviors helps discourage those behaviors. Undesirable behaviors can be ignored if they constitute minor violations of the rules and are of short duration (e.g., a student who talks out of turn once, without receiving any response from his/her neighbor). When undesirable behaviors are more serious, longer in duration, or likely to spread or otherwise continue to be disruptive to other students, the teacher will need to intervene as soon as possible.

Section PI (e) below provides further information about student behavior.

PI (b): Ways in which teacher attitudes and behaviors affect all students, strategies for establishing and maintaining rapport with all students, and strategies for adjusting communication in response to student needs

This section discusses interactions between teachers and students, with emphasis on the development of rapport and communication between them.

Teacher Impact

Teachers' attitudes and behaviors have many kinds of effects on students:

- Through direct requests, explicit rules and expectations, and incentives, teachers impact student behavior. For example, the establishment of classroom routines provides a structure that guides student behavior in various situations.

- Through explicit instruction, both formal and informal, teachers influence student attitudes and behavior. For example, student attitudes toward certain groups of people (e.g., individuals with disabilities) can be modified through discussions led by the teacher.

- Through their interactions with individual students, student groups, and the entire class, teachers influence student attitudes and behavior. For example, students' self-esteem (i.e., how "good" they consider themselves as people) and academic self-efficacy (how "good" they think they are at learning) can be influenced by the way teachers respond to their questions and comments.

- Through their own speech and actions, teachers provide role models that students may emulate. For example, the teacher's response to a student who is behaving in an openly hostile way can provide students with guidance as to how to respond in a similar situation.

Building Rapport

Teachers can establish and maintain rapport through a number of strategies (which overlap with those that promote good behavior, as discussed in the previous section). The following are a few of the many strategies that build rapport:

- getting to know students individually

- treating students warmly while maintaining expectations for academic performance and classroom behavior

- being open with students while maintaining professionalism and appropriate boundaries

- conveying respect for each student and for the entire class

- engaging in active listening with students

- responding positively to students' ideas and opinions

- acknowledging students' feelings about classroom activities and about others

PI (c): Methods for ensuring individual academic success in one-to-one, small-group, and large-group settings

This section briefly discusses how academic success among individual students can be promoted through a mix of large-group, small-group, and one-to-one instruction.

Grouping Strategies

When teachers organize students into groups for instructional purposes, decisions must be made about the size and the composition of the groups.

- **Homogeneous groups** of students are similar to each other in some respect. Most commonly, homogeneous grouping is carried out in order to ensure that students with the same ability level work together. This practice enables differentiation, in the sense that students who have been placed in more skilled groups can receive more challenging tasks, and/or less teacher scaffolding, than students in less skilled groups.

- **Heterogeneous groups** of students are different from each other in some important respect. For example, the teacher can ensure that each group consists of at least one of the highest and lowest performing students in the class. In this way, low-performing students can benefit from modeling and other guidance provided by more advanced peers, while high-performing students can benefit from the challenge of taking on an instructional role.

Other approaches to grouping are sometimes used. For example, the composition of groups can be randomized through techniques such as counting off. In such cases, what is essential to the teacher is that students work in groups; the range of interests and ability levels represented in each group is not critical. Regardless of group composition, teachers need to be flexible, so that groups can be formed and reformed depending on instructional needs.

Group Roles

Effective grouping strategies depend not only on varying the composition of groups but also developing different types of grouping activities. The roles of students within each group may be the same or differentiated. In **reciprocal teaching**, for example, students take turns playing the role of teacher and providing instruction to each other and/or to the actual teacher. Reciprocal teaching can be used with a variety of topics and instructional levels. An example would be the use of reciprocal teaching to engage students in reading comprehension strategies.

Four such strategies would be:

- **Prediction**. Readers make predictions about what will occur next in a passage and the extent to which these predictions are confirmed is noted.

- **Questioning.** Readers generate questions about parts of a text that seem difficult or confusing or about how parts of the text are related to each other or to what the reader already knows.

- **Clarification.** Readers seek clarification about the aspects of different passages that are incomprehensible, confusing, or ambiguous.

- **Summarization.** Readers summarize part or all of the text in a way that captures the main theme or idea without including information of lesser importance.

Initially, teachers support the use of these four strategies through modeling, and through feedback to students when they ask questions, make statements, and so on. Students may then work together in groups of four, with one student in each group designated as the Predictor, the Questioner, the Clarifier, and the Summarizer, respectively. Over time, students increasingly take the lead in carrying out this activity.

Special Education and Grouping

When students with disabilities are grouped together for the purpose of special education (as opposed to participating in general education activities), they must be grouped according to similarities in individual needs. In such cases, New York State law requires limited variability within each group along the following dimensions:

- academic achievement, functional performance, and learning characteristics

- social development (including the student's social adjustment, relationships with others, and feelings about self)

- physical development (including health, vitality, motor and sensory functioning, and physical functioning of relevance to learning)

- management needs (i.e., the extent of environmental, material, and human support needed to benefit from instruction)

PI (d): Barriers to accessibility and acceptance of students with disabilities, adaptations that can be made to the learning environment to provide optimal learning opportunities for students with disabilities, and strategies for facilitating students' active participation and fostering their independence

Students with disabilities face physical barriers, which limit accessibility to general education experiences, as well as social barriers, which stem from the attitudes of others and can result in lack of acceptance. This section discusses some of the barriers to accessibility and acceptance that students with disabilities face, along with the adaptations that can be made to the learning environment in support of these students.

Classroom Management and Students with Disabilities

The principles of classroom management apply to general education students as well as to students with disabilities. For example, being aware of why a particular student is exhibiting a particular undesirable behavior will help the teacher respond appropriately to the behavior, regardless of whether or not the student is thought to have a disability. In the case of a student with a disability, the undesirable behavior may or may not be related to the disability. For example, a student with an intellectual disability may repeatedly talk out of turn because his disability makes it difficult for him to remember when he should avoid talking. Alternatively, this student may repeatedly talk out of turn because the work assigned to him is too easy and he is bored (a response that any student is prone to exhibit when insufficiently challenged).

The presence of students both with and without disabilities in the same classroom can pose unique challenges for classroom management, as described below.

Challenges and Strategies Related to Accessibility

Students with certain disabilities may be unable to access areas, facilities, materials, and other physical elements of the general education experience for a number of reasons, including:

- sensory limitations

- lack of sufficient mobility

- lack of coordination or bodily control

- inability to understand or follow complex procedures

- anxiety or fear regarding certain activities

The Individuals with Disabilities Education Act (IDEA) requires that schools make adaptations to increase the accessibility of materials, facilities, activities, and other resources to students with disabilities. Below are some examples of adaptations that teachers in particular can make which promote accessibility:

- The physical environment of the classroom can be modified to increase accessibility for individual students. For example, desks and other furniture can be arranged to allow sufficient space for students with wheelchairs or crutches to move around.

- Instructional activities and materials can be modified to increase accessibility for individual students. For example, papers and other materials can be taped or fastened to the desks of students with coordination problems or limited muscular strength.

- Technological devices can be used in the classroom to increase accessibility to instruction for individual students. (Assistive technologies are discussed in Chapter 6.)

Challenges and Strategies Related to Acceptance

Students with certain disabilities may be rejected to a greater or lesser extent by peers, owing to one or more reasons such as:

- Students without disabilities have stereotypes or other misconceptions about their disabled peers that are sometimes expressed by teasing and other forms of overt discrimination.

- Students without disabilities may view their disabled peers with anxiety or distrust, or with an extent of curiosity that is distracting.

- Students with certain disabilities may miss social cues or engage in behaviors that their non-disabled peers find distracting or offensive.

- Students with disabilities may feel anxious about the possibility of being rejected, or judged negatively, by their non-disabled peers.

Teachers should use a variety of strategies to promote the social acceptance of students with disabilities and to help students with and without disabilities develop more positive attitudes toward each other. For example:

- Teachers should reflect on their own attitudes toward each student with a disability, in order to determine whether they themselves are engaging in stereotyping or in treatment of students that is not called for in each particular case. For example, a teacher might tend to isolate an emotionally disturbed student more than necessary, in the interest of preventing the student from becoming frustrated. Since the decision of the individualized education program (IEP) team to allow the student to participate in the general education classroom indicates that the student should be treated like his classmates to the greatest extent possible, the teacher may need to reconsider how much the student needs to be sheltered from situations that create frustration.

- As appropriate, teachers can provide the class with information about a student's disability. The purpose of doing so is not to put the student "on display," but rather to provide the class with information that can dispel prejudices and other misconceptions, and to indicate what, if anything, the class might do to support the student. In some cases, this information can be provided before a student with disabilities joins the general education classroom. Such information is relevant not only to students but also to their parents.

- Students with disabilities can be provided with information that helps them adjust to the general education classroom. For example, if a student's social skills are much less advanced compared to peers, social skills training both before and after joining the general education classroom can be of benefit to the student.

PI (e) Strategies for developing, implementing, monitoring, and modifying behavioral interventions for students with disabilities, including strategies for providing positive behavioral interventions and supports

This section concerns behavioral interventions and supports for all students, including students with disabilities.

Traditional Approaches to Addressing Misbehavior

Traditional approaches to addressing misbehavior in school settings relied heavily on punitive measures ranging from verbal reprimands to the most extreme disciplinary measures of suspension and expulsion. Punishment was considered an essential deterrent for undesirable behavior, as well as an effective approach to dealing with misbehavior once it had occurred. Along with concerns about the actual effectiveness of such approaches, ethical concerns have been raised about the impact of punishment on students as well as the fairness with which punishments were traditionally administered. Concerns have also been raised about overreliance on suspension and expulsion as methods of addressing misbehavior among students with disabilities, as these practices create further isolation from the general education population.

Positive Behavior Support

In contrast to traditional approaches, **positive behavior support (PBS)** is an evidence-based approach to promoting desirable behaviors while discouraging undesirable ones. PBS is based on the assumption that problem behaviors cannot be effectively addressed unless their causes are understood. Knowledge about the causes of problem behaviors informs the development of interventions in which the goal is to replace these behaviors with more desirable ones. Successful intervention may require modifications to the student's educational environment rather than an exclusive focus on changing the problem behaviors directly. What constitute "desirable" behaviors, as well as the methods by which those behaviors are encouraged, must be acceptable to the community, to parents, and to the students themselves.

IDEA and PBS

IDEA recommends the use of PBS as a means of reducing problem behaviors in school settings, thereby minimizing the role of punishment, encouraging the respectful treatment of students, and reducing the need for suspension or expulsion as disciplinary strategies. The use of positive behavioral management strategies as a means of avoiding suspension or expulsion reflects IDEA's fundamental emphasis on inclusion.

Three-Tiered Approach to PBS

PBS systems are proactive. They attempt to prevent problem behaviors before they occur and to address problem behaviors before their severity intensifies. This proactive emphasis is illustrated by a three-tiered system of implementation:

- The first tier consists of school-wide preventative measures, such as making behavioral expectations clear to everyone present at the school, creating a system of positive reinforcements for desirable behavior, establishing consequences for undesirable behavior, and maintaining consistency in the handling of undesirable behavior. First-tier efforts are largely focused on prevention.

- The second tier consists of additional support available to students who have not responded to first-tier measures and currently exhibit problem behaviors. Supports such as mentoring, social skills training, friendship clubs, and simple behavior plans, are provided in the hopes of avoiding more serious consequences such as suspension or expulsion.

- The third tier consists of interventions created for individual students whose problem behaviors are most severe. In the case of a student with a disability, a behavior intervention plan will be created, monitored, and evaluated by the IEP team on the basis of a functional behavior assessment, as described in Chapter 8.

Preventative Strategies

At the classroom level, the teacher can use a variety of strategies that address problem behaviors in a proactive way, in the sense of attempting to prevent their occurrence or reducing the likelihood of their persistence. Examples of some simple preventative strategies include:

- The teacher should communicate behavioral expectations to students. Classroom rules should be explained clearly and concretely on the first day of class, for example, accompanied by demonstrations by the teacher and opportunities for student rehearsal as appropriate.

- The teacher should create a structured environment in which rules, routines, and procedures are consistent and clear. At any given time, students should know what they are supposed to be doing.

- The teacher should come to class fully prepared. Transitions between activities should be carefully planned, for example, so that transition time is minimized and expectations for students during the transition are clear.

- The teacher should continually monitor student behavior, making note of and responding appropriately to both desirable and undesirable behaviors.

- The teacher should create an atmosphere in which students focus on responding to positive behaviors rather than judging negative ones. Instead of "tattling," for example, students can be encouraged to recognize peers who engage in positive classroom behaviors.

- The teacher should implement specific strategies for promoting desirable behaviors—not only at particular moments, but throughout the school year. Positive reinforcement (discussed below) should be the typical incentive for desirable behaviors rather than threatening to punish students for failing to exhibit those behaviors. For example, if the teacher uses the opportunity for the class to receive a special privilege at the end of the year as an incentive for positive behavior, the teacher could create a system in which "points" are given for good behavior rather than deducted for bad behavior.

Reactive Strategies

Through positive behavior management, teachers engage in strategies for preventing problem behaviors rather than simply reacting to misbehavior punitively. However, preventative measures can only reduce the incidence of misbehavior to a greater or lesser extent rather than preventing it altogether. Thus, a proactive approach to behavior management includes strategies for implementing swift and appropriate responses to problem behaviors when they arise.

When responding to a problem behavior, the teacher should maintain a positive classroom atmosphere by selecting the minimal response that prevents the behavior from recurring. Below is a list of typical strategies ranging in order from the most minimal to the most intensive. (If one strategy is unsuccessful, the teacher usually will proceed to the next one.):

- The most minimal response to misbehavior is to ignore it. Minor misbehaviors such as talking out of turn or groaning during silent reading can be ignored if they are one-time occurrences and do not spread.

- The most minimal responses to a student who is misbehaving also include nonverbal cues such as looking at the student, frowning at the student, and/or moving closer to the student. Nonverbal cueing can be carried out while the teacher continues to address the class, or while the class continues to work independently. Other students may not even notice that cueing has taken place.

- If nonverbal cueing is ineffective, the teacher might resort to brief verbal cues that do not identify the student directly (e.g., "We're all paying attention now, right?"). Here too, regular class activities may not be disrupted if the student responds quickly to the verbal cue.

- The teacher might offer brief verbal cues directed specifically at the student, such as saying the student's name, or quietly asking the student to cease the problem behavior. Disruption to class activities is likely to be minimal if the student quickly responds to the cue.

- Interrupting regular classroom activities in order to explicitly address the problem behavior should be considered a last resort. Doing so may be necessary if the student is unwilling or unable to respond to brief verbal cues.

Processes of Learning and Behavioral Change

In this section, you will read about principles of learning and behavioral change that are widely applied when providing positive behavioral supports and interventions to all students, including those who have disabilities.

Ultimately, the goal of positive behavior management is to promote desirable classroom behaviors while discouraging undesirable ones using methods that respect individual students. This goal can be more readily achieved through an understanding of the general processes by which behaviors are learned and subsequently modified. Two such processes are modeling and reinforcement.

Modeling

Modeling, also known as observational learning, refers to learning that takes place by imitating someone else's behavior. The term "modeling" also refers to the demonstration of the behavior by the individual being modeled. Thus, a teacher might "model" a particular behavior that the students learn through "modeling."

Modeling reflects an explicit approach to instruction when explanations about how to perform the behavior are provided, or when prompts are given (as when a teacher says "Do what I do" and then performs some action while students watch). Modeling can also be implicit, as when a teacher expresses disagreement with a student's ideas in a positive and tactful way that is later reflected in students' interactions with each other. The teacher models a socially appropriate way of disagreeing with another person's ideas, but she does not describe or otherwise call attention to what she models.

Substantial learning takes place through explicit as well as implicit modeling. Teachers, however, cannot rely exclusively on modeling as a means of promoting desirable behavior in the classroom. Teachers must also explicitly discuss behavioral expectations with students, as well as responding to both desirable and undesirable behaviors that students exhibit.

Reinforcement

The likelihood of a particular behavior continuing to occur is influenced by the outcome of the behavior. This outcome is referred to as the **reinforcer**. A child who tries grapes for the first time and discovers that they taste pleasantly sweet is likely to eat grapes in the future in order to once again experience their sweet taste. In this example, eating grapes is the behavior, and sweet taste is the reinforcer. A child who touches a hot stove and experiences pain may not touch the stove again, because the child has discovered that touching the stove (behavior) leads to pain (reinforcer).

Positive Reinforcement

Positive reinforcement occurs when a behavior is followed by a desirable outcome that makes the behavior more likely to occur. For example, when a teacher praises a student for completing an assignment neatly, praise may serve as a positive reinforcer that increases the likelihood of the student completing future assignments neatly. Other examples of positive reinforcement in educational settings include the following:

- a special privilege granted for being helpful to classmates

- a positive note sent to parents regarding good classroom citizenship

- a special award given for effort

For positive reinforcement to be effective (i.e., cause a behavior to be exhibited more frequently), the following conditions must be met:

- The student must consider the reinforcer to be positive. Students vary widely in what they consider desirable; thus the teacher must consider each student's interests and abilities when selecting positive reinforcers. The opportunity to select and read an extra book would be viewed very positively by some students, for example, while others would consider it a form of punishment.

- The student must understand what behavior is being reinforced. Thus, telling a student that she did a "good job" on her writing assignment will not be as effective as a more specific statement such as "I like how neat your writing is this time."

Negative Reinforcement

Negative reinforcement occurs when a behavior is followed by the removal of an undesirable outcome, and the removal of that outcome makes the behavior more likely to occur. For example, when a teacher points out to a student that his handwriting on a homework assignment is sloppy, the teacher's comment is a negative reinforcer that makes it more likely the student will complete future assignments neatly. By doing his work neatly, the undesirable outcome (i.e., the teacher's negative comment) will be removed. Other examples of negative reinforcement include the following:

- frowning at a student who is slow to begin an activity

- warning a student to follow a particular instruction on homework assignments

- sending a note to parents commenting on inconsistency in following the classroom rules for polite interactions with peers

As with positive reinforcement, negative reinforcement will not be effective unless the student truly considers the reinforcer to be negative, as well as understanding what behavior is being reinforced. Frowning at a student who is slow to begin an activity will not constitute negative reinforcement if the student enjoys adult attention regardless of whether the attention is positive or negative. Moreover, even if the student does view the frown as a negative reinforcer, noticing the frown will not induce him to act more promptly in the future unless he understands that the frown was specifically elicited by his slowness. In such a case, the teacher may need to include a brief verbal explanation.

Punishment

Punishment occurs when a behavior is followed by an undesirable outcome that makes the behavior less likely to occur. For example, when a student loses recess privileges for throwing objects in the classroom, the loss of recess privileges is a punishment that makes it less likely the student will continue to throw things in class. Although negative reinforcement and punishment both consist of undesirable outcomes, negative reinforcement makes a behavior more likely to occur, while punishment makes a behavior less likely to occur. Thus, teachers can use negative (and positive) reinforcement to promote desirable classroom behaviors, while using punishment to discourage undesirable classroom behaviors. However, as noted earlier in this chapter, punishment is not intended to be a major element in positive behavior support systems.

A distinction can be made between positive and negative punishment. Positive punishment involves the introduction of an undesirable outcome, while negative punishment (also known as **response cost**) involves the loss of a desirable outcome. Requiring a student to redo an assignment or to complete an extra assignment would be examples of positive punishment, while loss of recess privileges would be an example of negative punishment.

Behavioral Instruction

Behavioral instruction, alone or as part of an intervention, often reflects the following sequence:

- Initially, the teacher engages in **task analysis**, or the division of what is to be learned into small components. Components are introduced separately. Once students have mastered one component, they proceed to the next one. **Chaining** refers to the teaching of complex behaviors whose components are linked sequentially.

- Instruction begins with the teacher describing to students what behavioral skills they will be learning.

- The teacher models the behaviors of interest for students. Explanations are provided as appropriate.

- Students are given opportunities to practice the desired behaviors, and the teacher provides feedback on student performance. Since students may not exhibit the desired behavior perfectly at first, the teacher may use **shaping**, or a process of reinforcing behaviors that are successively closer to the desired behavior until that behavior is finally achieved.

- As students practice the behaviors of interest, the teacher may provide **prompts**, which are cues or hints for appropriate action. Since the goal of instruction is for students to exhibit the behaviors independently, prompts are lessened and then completely withdrawn through a process of **fading**.

- To the greatest extent possible, the teacher will provide students with opportunities and support for **transfer**, or the generalization of the new behaviors to different people, places, and materials.

Environmental Modifications

Positive behavior management may focus on directly changing student behavior, as described above, on modifying the student's environment so that behavioral change is elicited, or on a combination of the two. The term "environment" is used in a broad sense here to include both the physical and the social environments in which learning takes place. Some of the ways the student's environment can be modified in order to reduce the incidence of a particular problem behavior include:

- A positive reinforcer for the problem behavior can be removed. For example, a student who deliberately breaks his pencil points because he enjoys using the pencil sharpener can be told that in the future he will not be allowed to use the pencil sharpener after engaging in this behavior. In this example, use of the pencil sharpener had been a positive reinforcer for the student's pencil-breaking behavior. (In the interest of avoiding a punitive atmosphere, the teacher might add that the student will be allowed to sharpen his pencils once per day, at a designated time.)

- A negative reinforcer for the problem behavior can be removed. For example, a student with an intellectual disability who is shouting in class because she fears that the teacher will think she is weak if she does not speak up for herself can be reassured that the teacher knows she is strong. In this example, the prospect of seeming weak had been a negative reinforcer for the student's shouting behavior.

- A positive reinforcer for a desirable alternative to the problem behavior can be introduced. For example, a student with an emotional disturbance who slouches, deliberately slips out of his chair, and makes noises during morning announcements can be told that if he sits up straight and quietly listens to the announcements, he can subsequently help the teacher pass out materials to the class. In this example, helping the teacher is a positive reinforcer intended to promote the desirable behavior of quiet attentiveness to morning announcements. (A key assumption here is that this particular student enjoys helping the teacher with class activities.)

- A token economy can be introduced that includes a positive reinforcer for a desirable alternative to the problem behavior, along with a response cost for that behavior. For example, a student with autism who sometimes mimics a statement from the teacher rather than responding meaningfully can be given a token each time he responds meaningfully, while losing a token each time he mimics the teacher. The tokens can be subsequently traded in for a privilege that the student desires.

- The teacher can modify his/her own behavior. For example, through conversations with a student who sometimes covers his ears when the teacher talks to him, the teacher may discover that the student feels threatened whenever the teacher speaks in unpleasant tones or stands too close to him when providing critical feedback. Upon reflection, the teacher may discover ways to modify her tone of voice and proximity to the student that make the student feel less threatened yet do not interfere with instructional and classroom management practices.

- The teacher can modify the behavioral expectations for the student. For example, a student with a traumatic brain injury who quickly becomes agitated by classwork she finds challenging can be allowed a short time to put her head down or to walk around the back of the classroom quietly, if such strategies prove effective at helping her to calm herself.

- The teacher can modify the physical characteristics of the classroom or the student's placement in it. For example, a student with autism who is easily provoked to disruptive behavior by innocuous movements and sounds originating from nearby students can be seated in the front row of the classroom, at one end of the row, in order to minimize the number of students seated in close proximity to him.

PI (f): Appropriate strategies for crisis prevention and intervention

This section describes strategies that teachers can use for crisis prevention and for intervention before crises occur.

Classroom Crises

Teachers must be prepared for rare but imminently dangerous situations such as the following:

- natural disasters, equipment malfunctions, and other situations that may pose immediate threats to the physical safety of individuals or the entire class

- medical emergencies, serious injuries, suicide threats, and other situations in which the well-being of individuals (and onlookers) is at risk

- hostile students, parents, staff, and/or outsiders who pose immediate threats to the class

Crisis Prevention

Strategies that can help teachers prevent crises include the following:

- Be aware of safety rules and emergency procedures used at your school, review these rules and procedures with students, and reinforce any rules or procedures that are not followed.

- Be aware of what is happening in the classroom at all times, and respond promptly to problematic situations.

- Make note of students and/or family members who appear to be troubled, reach out to these individuals as appropriate, and discuss your concerns promptly and in detail with relevant staff and administrators at your school.

- Learn how to recognize warning signs of extreme emotional states and the potential for violent behavior.

Crisis Intervention

In the rare event that a crisis has occurred, experts recommend a number of strategies for teachers to use, including the following

- Remain calm, so that you can respond effectively to the crisis.

- Prioritize, if possible, so that you can deal with the most imminent or serious threats first.

- Seek outside help, if possible.

- Isolate the source of the threat, if possible, by increasing the distance between the threat (whether a person or a thing) and the students.

- Choose the simplest approaches to dealing with the crisis that are likely to be effective.

- Monitor the situation and be aware of the consequences of your verbal and physical actions.

Practice Questions

1. Which of the following best illustrates heterogeneous grouping in a math class?

    A. The teacher ensures that each group of students consists of one student who scored an A on the previous test, along with one student who scored lower than a C.

    B. The teacher ensures that each group of students consists of individuals who scored the same letter grade on the previous test.

    C. The teacher ensures that each group of students consists of one student who scored a B on the previous test.

    D. The teacher ensures that each group of students is randomly chosen by means of a counting-off procedure.

2. An elementary school student asks her teacher in front of the class why one of her classmates, who has a speech impairment, "talks funny." How should the teacher respond?

    A. The teacher should explain that the student's question is rude and that in the future the class should avoid teasing the student with the impairment or otherwise discussing the topic.

    B. The teacher should reply that students must ask their classmate directly why he "talks funny," rather than spending class time discussing the topic and that they should feel free to ask the student any question about the impairment.

    C. The teacher should provide a brief explanation, ask the student with the impairment to pronounce certain phonemes in order to illustrate the disability, and then develop a thematic unit on speech impairments.

    D. The teacher should provide a brief, factual answer, comment favorably on some distinctive personal characteristic of the student with the impairment, and discuss how the class is more interesting owing to each student's distinguishing characteristics.

3. A student with a learning disability needs frequent reminders from her teacher with respect to preparation for tasks and staying on task. Each week her teacher has been deliberately reducing the number of reminders in order to promote the student's independence. Which of the following is illustrated by the teacher's actions?

    A. Transfer

    B. Fading

    C. Chaining

    D. Shaping

4. Which of the following most clearly illustrates the removal of a negative reinforcer for a problem behavior?

    A. A student who is whining about the difficulty of an assignment is told by his teacher that if he continues to whine, he will lose his chance to participate in the creation of a Christmas poster by the entire class.

    B. A student who is arguing about an assignment because he considers it unfair is told by his teacher that he should express his concerns in a more tactful way, so that the teacher will be more likely to take those concerns seriously.

    C. A student who is complaining about an assignment because he hopes to be disciplined and avoid completing the assignment is told by his teacher that if he continues to complain, he will be disciplined but still have to do the assignment.

    D. A student who is refusing to complete an assignment because he wants more attention from the teacher is told by the teacher that if he does not complete the assignment, he will receive a zero and have no chance to raise the grade.

5. Sally is a student with a traumatic brain injury who sometimes pushes, hits, or otherwise touches other classmates inappropriately. Sally's teacher reminds her at the beginning of a group activity that as long as Sally keeps her hands to herself during the activity, Sally will receive a gold star at the end of class. Assuming that Sally would like to have a gold star, which of the following does the teacher's comment represent?

    A. Positive reinforcement

    B. Negative reinforcement

    C. Positive punishment

    D. Negative punishment

Answers to Practice Questions

1. A.

   Choice A is correct because the groups will be relatively heterogeneous with respect to math achievement. Choice B is incorrect because the groups will be relatively homogeneous. Choices C and D are incorrect because it is not clear that the process of group assignment will result in heterogeneity.

2. D.

   Choice A is incorrect because the teacher's response would not help increase the students' understanding or appreciation of the student with the impairment, but rather may contribute to distance between this student and the rest of the class. Choice B is incorrect for similar reasons. Choice C is incorrect because the teacher's actions would place too much attention on the student with the impairment, when it is not clear that such attention is welcomed or would contribute to instructional objectives. Choice D is correct because the class would be provided a simple account for a characteristic that is already apparent to them, while promoting acceptance of the student with the impairment by helping the students view diversity (in the most general sense) in a positive way.

3. B.

   Choice B is correct because fading refers to a reduction in prompting in order to promote independent expression of a behavior. Choice A is incorrect because transfer refers to generalization of behavior. Choice C is incorrect because chaining refers to the teaching of a complex sequence of behaviors. Choice D is incorrect because shaping refers to the successive reinforcement of behaviors that are increasingly similar to a desired goal.

4. C.

   Choice C is correct, because in this scenario, the problem behavior is complaining and the negative reinforcer had been the prospect of completing the assignment. The student had been complaining in hopes of not having to complete the assignment. Choice A is incorrect because it illustrates negative punishment (i.e., response cost). Choice B is incorrect because it illustrates explicit instruction. Choice D is incorrect because it illustrates negative reinforcement (by completing the assignment, the student will avoid a grade of zero), but there is no removal of a negative reinforcer.

5.   A.

Choice A is correct because the gold star would serve as a positive reinforcer. Choice B is incorrect because the gold star is not a negative reinforcer. Choices C and D are incorrect because punishment is not indicated.

CHAPTER 6

COMPETENCY 0005

Instructional Planning and Delivery to Promote Students' Success in the General Curriculum

This chapter describes the planning and delivery of instruction that addresses the needs of individual students and enables students with disabilities to access and make progress in the general education curriculum.

> **PI (a): Applicable local, state, and national curriculum standards, including the NYS P-12 Common Core Learning Standards, and how to align instruction for students with disabilities to these standards**

In this section, you will read about the state and national curriculum standards that form education in the state of New York and about how instruction for students with disabilities can be aligned with these standards.

New York State Learning Standards

The **New York State Learning Standards** embody the curriculum standards for public schools in New York. These standards are organized into seven areas:

- arts

- career development and occupational studies

- English language arts

- health, physical education, and family and consumer sciences

- languages other than English

- mathematics, science, and technology

- social studies

Associated with each of these seven areas are specific standards linked to particular grades or grade ranges. These standards describe the knowledge, skills, and understanding that a student should be able to demonstrate after instruction and experience.

New York State P-12 Common Core Learning Standards

Recently, New York State joined other states in establishing a set of common standards for English Language Arts & Literacy, Mathematics, and the Prekindergarten Foundation for the Common Core. These **Common Core Learning Standards**, to which states voluntarily comply, replace the former standards used in New York for these areas.

Accessing the General Education Curriculum

Teaching students with disabilities so that instruction is aligned with state learning standards depends on ensuring these students access the general education curriculum. Many forms of support are available for these students.

Support for Children of Ages 3–21

As noted in earlier chapters, the Individualized Education Program (IEP) must contain a description of support that the student will receive in order to achieve the annual goals specified in the IEP, including access to the special education and general education curricula. Several types of support are available through schools for children ranging from 3 to 21 years of age:

- **Special education** is instruction designed to meet the particular needs of a child with a disability at no cost to parents.

- **Related services** are those services that students with disabilities need in order to benefit from special education. If the child uses a wheelchair, for example, the school must ensure that the child can ride the bus and enter the school building. Another example would be counseling or psychological services provided to a child who is classified as emotionally disturbed.

- **Supplementary aids and services** are those that students with disabilities need in order to participate in general education to the greatest extent possible. These aids and services help fulfill the least restrictive environment (LRE) requirement of Individuals with Disabilities Education Act (IDEA). An example would be audiotaped books for students with visual impairments. Arranging for a qualified individual to shadow a child with autism when that child is in the general education classroom would be another example.

- **Program modifications** consist of changes made to the general education experience that would benefit the educational progress of a particular student with disabilities. An example would be allowing a child with attention deficit hyperactivity disorder (ADHD) to walk around quietly in the back of class at specified times each day.

- **Supports for school personnel** consist of training, materials, and other resources made available to teachers and staff. An example would be professional development workshops designed for teachers to help them work with children who have particular types of disability.

Support for Infants and Toddlers

The services described above are provided through the school system. For infants and toddlers (birth through age 3), IDEA requires that **early intervention services** be provided in natural settings such as the home or a child care center. States have some latitude in determining eligibility for these services and in the nature of services provided. However, all states have a State Interagency Coordinating Council (SICC) that performs functions such as helping identify and coordinate the efforts of agencies that provide early intervention services. In addition, a service coordinator works with each family to ensure that the services described in the Individualized Family Service Plan (IFSP) are obtained.

PI (b): Co-planning and co-teaching methods to strengthen content acquisition of students with disabilities

This section describes the role of co-planning and co-teaching in promoting content acquisition among students with disabilities.

The LRE for students with disabilities is, of course, the general education classroom. In this context, **co-teaching** consists of a regular teacher and a special educator working together with a class composed of students with and without disabilities. The teacher and special educator co-plan instruction for their classroom. Then, the teacher leads instructional activities while the special educator provides additional support to individuals or small groups of students with disabilities. Other approaches to co-teaching include **parallel teaching** (each teacher works with a different group) and **station teaching** (heterogeneous groups of student work with each teacher for a period of time and then switch teachers).

PI (c): Research- or evidenced-based practices that have been validated for learners with specific characteristics and for specific settings and knowledge of how to differentiate instruction by selecting, adapting, and using instructional strategies and materials according to the characteristics of a given student with disabilities

This section describes how to differentiate and modify instructional methods, strategies, and materials in order to fit the characteristics of particular students with disabilities.

Differentiated Instruction

Differentiated instruction refers to the individualization of instruction within the general education setting. The purpose of differentiated instruction, or differentiation, is to meet the educational needs of each student. Not all students have the same needs in school settings or in particular classes. Rather, students have different needs because of their backgrounds, abilities, preferences, and interests.

Assessment is necessary to determine how particular aspects of instruction should be differentiated for individual students and to monitor the successfulness of specific differentiation strategies. In addition, as discussed in Chapter 4, assessment may need to be differentiated for some students.

Although differentiated instruction is a student-centered approach, it does not apply strictly to individuals but also to particular groups of students. Differentiation is carried out flexibly and with a degree of fluidity, as groups will be formed and reformed according to shifting instructional needs.

According to a prominent analysis, four aspects of instruction can be differentiated: content, process, products, and learning environment.

Differentiation of Content

The content of what is taught can be differentiated on the basis of what students know and what they are capable of learning. For example, when introducing concepts that are required learning according to state curriculum standards, the teacher may need to present material in greater depth to students who have already mastered the concepts, whereas background information will need to be provided to students who do not have knowledge that is prerequisite to learning these concepts. An English language learner may require simplification of the language through which new content is presented, although the student may be expected to engage in the same extent of critical thinking about the content as his/her classmates. In contrast, a student with an intellectual disability who also requires simplification of new content may be expected to engage the content in a very concrete way, as opposed to engaging in the higher-level thinking that is encouraged among other students. The teacher's specific approach to differentiating the content in this case would depend on the nature and severity of the student's disability.

Differentiation of Process

Teachers must differentiate the process or the activities by which individual students learn. For example, in light of differences in learning styles, the teacher may give students the option of visual as opposed to auditory presentation of certain materials. An English language learner might benefit from having visual and auditory materials, along with extra support from the teacher in understanding these materials and carrying out specific activities based on their content. In the case of a blind student, visual presentation of materials will not be an option, and differentiation of process will be reflected in the use of Braille texts, tactile materials, audio presentations, and other nonvisual formats to facilitate the instruction of this student.

Differentiation of Products

Differentiation may be needed for the products of learning—i.e., the tests, reports, projects, performances, and other means by which students demonstrate how well they have mastered the content of instruction. For example, the teacher may allow students in a math class to demonstrate their mastery of key geometric concepts through construction of a three-dimensional model, a two-dimensional drawing, or a narrative description of how such a model or drawing could be constructed. An English language learner might benefit from creating a model or drawing rather than providing a narrative description, or if evaluated in a way that narrative is required, given extra time and support to produce the narrative. In the case of an autistic student with a keen interest in visual patterns, differentiation of products would be reflected whenever a teacher modifies the regular classroom evaluations so that the student could express his/her learning through drawings and other two-dimensional representations.

Differentiation of Environment

Differentiation can be applied to various aspects of the learning environment, including the physical layout, the use of space, the distribution of materials, and the ambient lighting. For example, an English language learner might benefit from sitting close to the teacher or to a student who is verbally gifted, so that the teacher or student can easily provide language-related support on occasion. A student with a medical problem who needs to leave class periodically might benefit from being in a seat that allows easy access to the door. Students who are especially sensitive to distraction may create distractions for other students. The teacher should seat them away from windows and from other students who could be distracting. In some cases, they may be asked to complete individual work in a quiet area near the teacher. For these students, differentiation of environment is reflected in any way the teacher modifies the seating arrangements in the classroom.

Specific Strategies for Differentiation

Through differentiation, teachers modify various aspects of instruction to better meet the needs of individual students, groups of students, and/or entire classes. Instructional practices should be modified to meet student needs. Minimal changes should be attempted first, and only if they are not successful should teachers proceed to more substantial changes. In the most extreme case, new materials, activities, procedures, and/or tasks are substituted for existing ones. Before substitutions, teachers should attempt to modify existing elements of instruction. The following discussion illustrates some of the relatively minor changes that can be made.

Modification of Instructional Materials

One of the simplest approaches to the adaptation of instruction is to modify instructional materials through changes that make the material more suitable for particular students. Below are examples of relatively minor changes that can make task requirements more accessible:

- Task instructions can be restated, expanded, simplified, presented in more than one format, or otherwise changed in order to clarify the nature of the task and the expectations for performance. For example, a student with a hearing impairment might benefit from written instructions that are delivered to other students orally. A student with a visual impairment or with a learning disability such as dyslexia might benefit from the addition of oral instructions to an assignment in which the instructions are also presented in writing. A student with a specific intellectual disability might benefit from a brief, simplified summary of the instructions and expectations associated with a particular task.

- Prompts can be added to a task in order to highlight key information in the task, provide further details about expectations for performance, or otherwise provide students with guidance. For example, a student with a disability that results in attentional problems might benefit from the addition of arrows, underlining, or other graphics that demarcate key information in a text. A student with a specific intellectual disability might benefit from oral reminders to examine particular details in written materials or to follow a particular sequence of steps in solving a problem.

Modification of Instructional Procedures

Instructional procedures can be modified to meet the needs of individual students. For example, relatively minor changes that can be helpful when a student consistently makes the same kind of error include the following:

- Additional instructional time can be devoted specifically to the area in which errors are consistently observed. For example, a young student with a speech impairment might benefit from extended discussion of strategies for articulating phonemes that many students struggle with initially but he/she finds especially challenging. A student with an intellectual disability who consistently leaves out a step during long division might benefit from additional explanations of the importance of each step.

- Additional practice can be encouraged in the area in which errors are consistently observed. The additional practice can be guided, independent, or a combination of the two. Practice can be increased for familiar activities; in addition, the teacher may incorporate new activities to maintain student interest. For example, the students described in the previous bullet item might benefit from additional practice with articulation and mathematical problem solving activities.

Modification of Instructional Tasks

The requirements of instructional tasks can be modified in accordance with student needs. For example, below are a few of the relatively minor changes that can reduce the difficulty of a task:

- The number or complexity of task demands can be decreased, the amount of time required for the task can be lessened, or the task requirements can be modified in some other way to make it less difficult for the student. For example, during a group activity, a student with autism might benefit if required interactions with other students are scripted and minimized. A student with an intellectual disability might benefit from a simplified version of a task that all students complete.

- The criteria for successful performance on a task can be relaxed. That is, the teacher can indicate that in order to meet some benchmark, the amount of work required of a student, the accuracy of the work, and/or the speed with which the work must be completed will be reduced. Thus, a student with a speech or language impairment might be given more latitude in a task requiring an expressive reading of a poem. A student with a mild visual impairment might be allowed extra time to complete a task that involves visual processing.

Differentiation may involve just one type of modification to instruction, as in the case of a student with a mild hearing impairment who is given certain materials in visual form. In many cases, differentiation involves more than one type of modification. For example, a student with an articulation disorder might benefit from extra discussion of strategies for articulating difficult phonemes, extra guided practice with articulation of those phonemes, and reduced demands for tasks and assessments involving oral communication.

PI (d): Sources of specialized materials, curricula, and resources for students with disabilities; strategies for incorporating and implementing instructional and assistive technology into the educational program; and strategies for evaluating, modifying, and adapting instructional resources and curriculum materials for individual learners

In this section, you will read about materials, curricula, resources, and technologies used in the education of students with disabilities.

Instructional and Curricular Modifications

Modifications to instruction and/or curriculum for students with disabilities can be classified into four types.

- Modifications to presentation change the format of information presented in the classroom. An example would be the supplementary aids provided to students with visual impairments, such as audio-taped books, Braille texts, large print texts, and magnification tools. (Such modifications in turn fall under the heading of the modifications to instructional materials described in the previous section.)

- Modifications to response change the format in which students can respond to classroom tasks. An example would be allowing students with visual impairments to complete classwork using a Brailler (a

Braille keyboard), to dictate their work to a scribe, and to provide oral descriptions. (Such modifications fall under the heading of the modifications to instructional tasks described in the previous section.)

- Modifications to setting change the locations or conditions of the educational environment. An example would be allowing students with visual impairments to sit where they can best hear the teacher, to use specialized lighting or light filters, and to sit close to a natural light source. (Such modifications fall under the heading of modifications to instructional procedures described in the previous section.)

- Modifications to scheduling change the timing and scheduling of classroom activities. An example would be allowing students with visual impairments to have extended time on class assignments, to take breaks that prevent eyestrain, and to schedule assignments according to the availability of a scribe. (Such modifications fall under the heading of modifications to instructional procedures described in the previous section.)

The four types of modification are not exclusive. An individual student might receive one, some, or all of these modifications depending on need. For example, a child with a severe reading-related disability might be provided with classroom texts that have large fonts, wide margins, and extra space between the lines (presentation accommodations). This child might be allowed to provide oral responses to assignments that other students must complete in written format (response modification). The child might be permitted to sit close to the teacher, so that it is relatively easy for the teacher to assist with certain reading tasks (setting modification). Finally, the child may be allowed extra time on written tests (scheduling modification).

Specialized Materials

A variety of materials, curricula, and resources are available for the education of students with disabilities. For example, alternative and augmentative communication systems are discussed in Chapter 7. Other technologies, including assistive technology, are discussed in the present chapter, in section P (j). Here, for purposes of illustration, discussion focuses on the selection and evaluation of both print and nonprint media for instructional use. The following are some of the questions teachers should ask when considering a particular media item for use by the student or students who have disabilities:

- Is the level of difficulty suitable? This is a question about the content of the media item and, in the case of electronic media, about the technological expertise required to use the item.

- How well can the content promote instructional objectives? This is a question about alignment between the content and both curricular standards as well as specific lesson plans. It is also a question about the extent to which the student can benefit from the content.

- Is the content likely to be meaningful and engaging? This is a question about the extent to which the content matches student interests, the extent to which the content is culturally relevant, and—in the case of digital materials—the extent to which use of the materials is interactive.

- To what extent can the media item be used flexibly? This is a question about the extent to which use of the item can be modified to suit the needs of a particular student. It is also a question about the extent to which use of the item can be modified for use by other students.

PI (e): Evidence-based explicit and systematic instruction and intervention in reading for students with disabilities, including reading in the content areas

This section pertains to explicit, systematic instruction, and intervention in reading.

Phonological and Phonemic Awareness

Phonological awareness is the ability to consciously recognize, discriminate among, and manipulate language sounds, including syllables, onsets and rimes, vowels and consonants, and phonemes. **Phonemic awareness** can be defined as the ability to consciously recognize, discriminate among, and manipulate phonemes. Thus, phonemic awareness is a subset of phonological awareness—an important subset, as phonemes are the smallest units of sound that contribute to meaning in language. Preparation for reading instruction includes instructional activities that explicitly and systematically promote the development of phonological and phonemic awareness.

General Instructional Considerations

Phonological and phonemic awareness activities differ in their level of difficulty. Teachers should sequence activities so that the level of difficulty gradually increases and earlier activities provide the foundation for later ones. Generally speaking, the smaller the unit of sound on which an activity focuses, the more difficult the activity is likely to be. For example, it will be easier for young children to repeat a word than to repeat the word without the initial syllable, just as it will be easier for them to repeat a word without the initial syllable than to repeat the word without the initial phoneme.

Phonological and phonemic awareness activities also differ in the complexity of what teachers do with students. The complexity of the activity is largely independent of the difficulty. For example, asking children to repeat a word without the initial phoneme is a very simple activity, but it will be difficult at first for young children to perform successfully. By comparison, asking children to walk around the room in a circle while the teacher says words that rhyme, and to sit down whenever the teacher says a word that does not rhyme, is a more complex activity to organize yet one that would be easier for young children to perform successfully.

The goals of phonological and phonemic awareness instruction are to help develop the following:

- the ability to hear and produce rhymes and alliteration

- the ability to divide sentences into words

- the ability to segment words into syllables and to build words from syllables

- the ability to segment words into onsets and rimes and to blend these sounds into words

- the ability to segment words into individual phonemes and to blend phonemes into words

Simple Phonological and Phonemic Awareness Activities

The following are some examples of simple activities that consist of questions or requests that the teacher poses to students. (The first three promote syllable awareness, the next three promote rhyme awareness, and the final three promote phonemic awareness.)

- "Say the word *water*. Now say it without the *wa*."

- "How many syllables are in the word *potato*?"

- "I'm going to say the first part of the word *student* and you finish it. Ready? *Stu...*"

- "Do these words rhyme: *peek, week*?"

- "Which word does not rhyme: *cat, bell, pat*?"

- "Can you tell me some words that rhyme with *call*?"

- "What sound do you hear at the beginning of *panda*?"

- "What word do these sounds make: *rrr...ooo...mmm*?"

- "How many sounds can you hear in the word *six*?"

Complex Phonological and Phonemic Awareness Activities

The following are examples of more complex activities that involve more than a verbal exchange between students and teacher:

- After students learn the song "This old man," the teacher guides them in singing each pair of lines and identifying the rhyming words (e.g., "one" and "thumb" in the first pair, "This old man, he played one, he played knick-knack on my thumb"). Once students have become familiar with this activity, the teacher might sing the first line of each pair and ask students to recall the rhyming word in the second line. These are phonological awareness activities that help increase student awareness of rhyme.

- Students are given connector materials such as Legos or beads and told that they will be using them to break words into parts called syllables. The teacher begins by modeling the activity with a multisyllabic word, such as "barking." The teacher divides his/her own materials into two parts and indicates how each part stands for a different syllable ("bar" and "king"). At first, the students follow the teacher. Once they have become familiar with the activity, they can make their own guesses as to how to divide words into syllables, and the number of syllables in the words chosen by the teacher can increase. These are phonological awareness activities that help increase children's awareness of syllables. The teacher says "I'm going on a trip, and I'm bringing a bird." Children take turns saying the same phrase but substituting in another object whose name begins with the same sound (e.g., "book," "ball," etc.). When children run out of ideas, the teacher repeats the phrase with an object whose name begins with a different sound. Once children become familiar with this activity, they can try to incorporate what others have said before them. For example, if the teacher says "I'm going on a trip, and I'm bringing a bird," the child who goes first might say "I'm going on a trip, and I'm bringing a bird and a ball." The next child might say "I'm going on a trip, and I'm bringing a bird and a ball and a book." These are phonemic awareness activities that help increase children's ability to isolate phonemes.

Phonics

Phonics refers to a family of instructional methods designed to teach children letter-sound correspondences and to help them use these correspondences during the process of decoding text. Phonics is an important part of a broader approach to literacy instruction that is grounded in student engagement with meaningful texts. Information that falls under the heading of phonics instruction is briefly mentioned at various points in this chapter. The focus of this section is on describing some of the explicit, systematic instructional methods that develop children's phonics skills.

Explicit versus Implicit Phonics Instruction

Explicit phonics instruction, also known as synthetic phonics, can be contrasted with implict phonics instruction, or analytic phonics.

- **Explicit phonics instruction** proceeds from part to whole. The children are first instructed about letters and letter-sound correspondences and then taught how to blend sounds into syllables and words.

- **Implicit phonics instruction** proceeds from whole to part. The children are taught whole words and then learn how to analyze words into constituent parts, including syllables and letters.

There are other approaches to phonics instruction, varying in details and in the extent to which explicit and implicit methods are blended.

General Instructional Considerations

The following are a few of the characteristics associated with successful phonics instruction:

- direct, explicit instruction

- sequencing of vowels and consonants that allows students to read words as early as possible

- opportunities for students to practice and review what they learn

- opportunities for students to apply what they learn to meaningful texts

- progression from easier to more difficult activities

- age-appropriate pacing

Phonics and Phonological Awareness

Phonological awareness refers to the ability to consciously recognize, discriminate among, and manipulate language sounds. Phonics, in contrast, helps develop the ability to relate language sounds to written text. Phonics and phonological awareness thus support each other. In particular, phonological awareness activities are an indispensable component of early phonics instruction, because children cannot understand how speech is represented in text until they understand how spoken words are composed of various units of sound. The goals of such activities include helping students become aware of qualities of language sounds such as rhyme and alliteration; to learn how to divide sentences into words; to learn how to divide words into constituent sounds (e.g., syllables, onsets and rimes, and phonemes); and to blend constituent sounds into larger units such as words. Activities in a phonics program should contribute to these skills while also promoting skills related to correspondences between oral and written language.

Examples of Phonics Activities

The following are a few examples of simple phonics activities:

- The teacher puts a picture of a familiar object on the board along with the name of the object with the initial letter missing (e.g., a picture of a cat accompanied by the letters "at"). Children are asked to provide the missing sound.

- The teacher puts pictures of several familiar objects on the board. Underneath each object is its name with the final sound missing (e.g., "clo" for a picture of a clock). Children are asked to identify the pictures that would end with the same final sound (e.g., "ck" for pictures such as the clock).

- The teacher plays a variant of "I spy" with students by writing a letter group on the board and asking students to find an item in the classroom whose name contains the sound associated with the letter group.

Reading Fluency

This section introduces some of the explicit, systematic instructional methods that are used to promote **reading fluency**, which can be defined as the ability to read quickly, effortlessly, accurately, and expressively.

Practice with High-Frequency Words

Giving children practice with high-frequency words helps these words become part of their sight word vocabulary. The more sight words children can recognize, the more quickly and accurately they can read, and the more attention they can pay to reading with expression. Some materials and activities that teachers can use to promote the acquisition of high-frequency words are as follows:

- **Word walls** are organized lists of words placed on the wall of a classroom. The words may be arranged alphabetically or organized in some other fashion. The height of the word wall and the size of the words should allow for comfortable viewing from students' desks.

- **Word banks** consist of a collection of words stored in one place (e.g., index cards in a small box) that students can use for reading practice and for consultation when writing.

- **Word games** are structured activities that allow children to make use of words they are learning. For example, in word search games, children are instructed to find particular words in written materials. In illustration games, children draw pictures that illustrate particular words, or sentences in which those words appear.

Repeated and Timed Readings

Repeated readings promote fluency by allowing students to read the same passage more than once. The readings may be performed silently or out loud, alone or in groups. **Timed readings** are repeated readings in which the amount of time spent reading each passage is recorded, and targets are set for subsequent passages. The goal of a timed reading is for the student's reading rate to increase for each subsequent reading of the same passage. For example, after the student chooses a passage of interest, the teacher might read the passage out loud and then discuss with the student what aspects of the reading reflect good fluency. Next, the student reads the passage, and the teacher will help record how long the reading took. Following the student's first reading, the teacher might help the student identify words that were unfamiliar or difficult to read. The teacher and student might then choose a target reading rate for the passage, and in subsequent readings of the same passage, the student's progress toward that rate will be recorded.

Read-Alouds

As the name suggests, **read-alouds** involve reading texts out loud to children. Read-alouds benefit many aspects of children's literacy development, particularly when carried out interactively so that children have the opportunity to ask and answer questions, engage in analysis, and provide commentary. Read-alouds contribute to fluency by giving the teacher an opportunity to model fluent reading. Through interactive activities during a read-aloud, students can practice reading particular phrases, refrains, and short passages with expression.

Choral Reading

Choral reading occurs when an entire class or group of students reads together in unison, with or without the teacher. Choral reading contributes to fluency by giving students opportunities to practice reading out loud. Students who ordinarily feel uncomfortable about reading aloud can do so with less attention being drawn to themselves. Less fluent readers also have opportunities to hear and copy models of oral fluency in choral reading activities. The following are some of the different kinds of choral reading:

- The entire class, including the teacher, reads a passage together.

- The teacher reads a sentence from a passage, and the entire class repeats the sentence. The teacher then moves on to the next sentence.

- Students divide into groups, and each group reads a different part of a passage (following the order in which the passage was written).

- For texts such as poems, the teacher reads the main parts, and the students read the refrain.

Recorded Books

Recorded books allow students to listen to fluent reading being modeled. Students can listen, read along with the recording, or read the text after hearing part or all of it on the recording.

Vocabulary Acquisition

Children learn a great deal of vocabulary indirectly through reading and through conversations with parents, teachers, and others. At the same time, explicit vocabulary instruction is critical to literacy development. This section focuses on some of the explicit, systematic approaches to vocabulary instruction that teachers use.

Regardless of approach, explicit vocabulary instruction is facilitated when teachers choose new words appropriately. New words that are likely to be challenging to students but not too difficult should be the focus of vocabulary instruction. Teachers must also choose a grade-appropriate number of new words to introduce during each instructional activity.

Direct Instruction

In direct instruction, a teacher introduces new words and their definitions. Direct instruction will not be very successful, however, if students are simply expected to memorize definitions. Rather, teachers should engage in the following activities:

- offer students examples of how new words are used in different contexts

- give students opportunities to discuss new words

- give students opportunities to rephrase the definitions of new words, to create sentences with the words, and to provide synonyms and antonyms

- provide students with texts in which the words appear

Direct instruction is most beneficial when teachers identify a small number of new words in a text that students will be reading—particularly words that are important to the meaning of the text but not defined therein.

Multiple Exposures

Multiple exposures to a new word increase the likelihood that the word will become part of a student's receptive and expressive vocabulary. It is important that the word appears in different contexts because its meaning will become clearer from the different usages and because the meanings and usages of many words vary from context to context.

Word Analysis

A number of strategies can be used to facilitate vocabulary learning. For example, through **word analysis**, students use knowledge of the parts of new words to help determine word meanings. For example, understanding that the prefix "bi-" refers to two, as in familiar words such as "bicycle," can help students learn more advanced words such as "bipartisan" or "biennial."

Contextual Analysis

Another strategy that facilitates vocabulary acquisition is **contextual analysis**, in which students use information from the context in which a new word appears to help determine or make a reasonable guess about, the meaning. Some of the types of contextual clues may be available for the meaning of an unfamiliar word are as follows:

- The meaning of the word may be stated. For example, "Insects like crickets and grasshoppers make sounds by stridulation, or the rubbing together of body parts such as legs and wings." In this passage, the meaning of "stridulation" is stated.

- The meaning of the word may be indicated through comparison or contrast. For example, "Unlike most people, who are forgiving when others make a mistake, Rick was very intolerant." In this passage, "intolerant" can be understood as roughly the opposite in meaning of "forgiving."

- The meaning of the word may be indicated by means of a synonym or antonym. For example, "She plays the flute so mellifluously. It sounds so sweet!" In this passage, "mellifluously" appears to have approximately the same meaning as "sweet."

Dictionary Usage

The dictionary can be an effective tool for learning vocabulary if students are given guidance in its use. Dictionary entries may be too difficult for younger students, and multiple entries for the same word may be confusing. As with direct instruction, use of dictionaries is most helpful if students are actively engaged, by restating definitions in their own words, and using new words in sentences, rather than just passively copying out the definitions of new words.

Reading Comprehension

Even before students have entered the "reading to learn" stage, teachers should provide support for their reading comprehension and critical thinking skills. This section provides information about explicit, systematic instructional methods and strategies that can provide such support. Reading comprehension strategies refer to anything that promotes comprehension before, during, and/or after the reading of a text.

Graphic Organizers

Some of the strategies that support reading comprehension and critical thinking depend heavily on the use of materials. For example, **graphic organizers** are visual representations of concepts and facts as well as relationships between them. Examples of graphic organizers include Venn diagrams, flow charts, cause-and-effect diagrams, and story maps. A **semantic organizer** is a type of graphic organizer consisting of a central concept, to which related concepts are linked by means of branching lines. Graphic organizers can be used to illustrate a sequence of events, analyze cause-effect relationships, compare and contrast concepts, and summarize the connections among related concepts. Graphic organizers support reading comprehension and critical thinking skills by providing visual representations of abstract relationships. After reading a story, for example, students can create a graphic organizer that maps out the relationships among characters or the sequence of events in the story arranged in chronological order.

Structural Analysis

Reading skills progress as children become more aware of morphemes and their role in word meaning. As noted in Chapter 3, morphemes are the smallest units of meaning in a word. There are two types:

- **Free morphemes** can stand alone as words (e.g., the word "fire" serves as a morpheme in words such as "fireworks," "bonfire," and "firefly").

- **Bound morphemes** cannot stand alone as words. Examples of bound morphemes include prefixes such as "re-," "anti-," and "un-," as well as the letter "s," which can be added to the end of a word to indicate plural ("cats"), possessive tense ("John's"), or second person singular tense ("runs").

Structural analysis refers to the reader's use of knowledge about morphemes to help recognize familiar words, pronounce familiar as well as new words, and understand the meanings of new words. For example, a child who encounters the new word "untested" in a story can decode the word more quickly as a result of familiarity with the prefix "un-" and the suffix "-ed." The child's ability to infer the meaning of the word is also facilitated by knowledge of how this particular prefix and suffix contribute to word meaning. Through structural analysis of the word into a prefix, a root, and a suffix, the child's ability to decode and understand the word is enhanced.

Syntactic Cues

As discussed in Chapter 3, syntax pertains to rules governing the placement of words in phrases, clauses, and sentences. As children's reading skills progress, they rely increasingly on syntactic clues to recognize familiar words, anticipate upcoming words in a text, and infer the meanings of unfamiliar words. For example, consider the following passage:

The little tiger clambered into the boy's lap. The boy lifted the tiger. Lifting the tiger required all the boy's strength. Laughing, the boy said to himself, "This tiger is so....

Syntactic knowledge contributes in distinctive ways to the child's understanding of each sentence in this passage:

- In the first sentence of the passage, the word "clambered" may be unfamiliar to a young reader, but syntactic knowledge will allow the child to recognize that the word is a verb that describes an action by the tiger.

- The second sentence of the passage consists of five words. The syntax of this sentence will inform the child that it is the boy who lifted the tiger. A slight alteration in the order of these five words ("The tiger lifted the boy") would inform the child that it is the tiger that lifted the boy.

- Before the child has finished reading the final sentence of the passage, the child will know that the word or words following the word "so" will describe the tiger and that the word or words could only represent one of a few grammatical categories (e.g., an adjective or adjectival phrase).

Semantic Cues

As noted in Chapter 3, semantics refers to the meanings of parts of words, sentences, and larger units. As they read a text, children make use of background knowledge as well as semantic cues given in the text in order to recognize words, anticipate upcoming words, and infer the meanings of unfamiliar words. For example, in the excerpt about the boy and the tiger presented above, a young reader is likely to infer from knowledge about animals and from the context established by the first sentence that "clambered" is a word describing movement. Likewise, in the context of this passage, the child is likely to anticipate that the word following "so" in the final sentence will be "heavy" or something comparable in meaning.

Comprehension Monitoring

Unlike graphic organizers, strategies such as comprehension monitoring support reading comprehension and critical thinking without reliance on physical materials. **Comprehension monitoring** refers to the reader's ongoing awareness of whether the text makes sense or not. Through comprehension monitoring, the reader keeps track of how well he/she understands the text and makes notes of characteristics such as the following:

- elements of a text that are inconsistent with each other, or with the reader's prior knowledge

- elements of a text that are unclear, ambiguous, or lacking key information

- elements of a text that are too difficult for the reader to understand

- elements of a text that represent unwarranted conclusions or unexpected events

Comprehension monitoring is discussed further under section PI (i) on the next page.

Text Features

Text features are elements added to a text that facilitate the reader's comprehension. Examples of text features include the following:

- a table of contents
- a heading or subheading
- a figure or table
- a timeline
- an index
- a glossary

Instruction and Text Features

The following are some of the instructional strategies that help students recognize and make use of text features when they read, and to incorporate text features appropriately into their own writing:

- Students should be explicitly taught the names and purposes of each text feature and presented with examples of each.

- Students should be given opportunities to practice locating text features in meaningful texts, and deriving useful information from these features.

- Students should be given opportunities to add text features to enhance plain text that is provided to them.

- Students should be given opportunities to practice creating text features to accompany their own writing in useful ways.

Text Structures

Text structures consist of the ways that information is organized in a text. Examples of text structures include the following:

- A sequential structure presents information in chronological order.

- A compare-and-contrast structure presents a contrast among ideas, things, events, or people.

- A cause-and-effect structure presents one or more causes followed by one or more outcomes.

- A problem-and-solution structure introduces a problem and then presents one or more solutions.

Instruction and Text Structures

The following are instructional strategies that help students understand text structures in written texts, and to make use of these structures effectively in their own written work:

- Students should be explicitly taught the names and characteristics of each text structure and presented with examples of each. Instruction should focus on one text structure at a time.

- Students should be taught that certain words may signal particular structures. For example, words like "next" and "then" may indicate a sequential structure, and words like "because" and "as a result" may indicate a cause-and-effect structure. Although these signal words are not infallibly linked to particular text structures, students should be taught that such words are possible indicators of particular structures.

- Students should be given opportunities to discuss text structures in meaningful texts and to analyze the structures in these texts through discussion and representational means such as graphic organizers.

- Students should be given opportunities to practice writing texts that reflect each structure. Through writing, students will not only improve in their ability to express themselves using these structures but will also become more sensitive to the presence of these structures in the texts they read.

PI (f): Evidence-based explicit and systematic instruction and intervention in writing for students with disabilities

Writing

An effective approach to literacy instruction will always provide students with opportunities to read and write, as the development of reading and writing are intertwined and support each other. This section touches on explicit, systematic instruction in writing that focuses on four areas: mechanics, orthography, content, and process.

Mechanics

The mechanics of writing include the coordinated physical actions required to create text. During the early stages of writing instruction, students learn the following skills:

- good posture

- proper location of paper

- correct pencil grip

- letter formation

Orthography

As noted in Chapter 3, orthography is the representation of oral language by means of writing. Through instruction in writing, students learn orthographic rules in the following areas:

- orientation of text

- spelling

- capitalization

- punctuation

Content

The content of writing becomes important as students learn about the characteristics of difference genres and the importance of considering one's audience and purpose when creating a text. Elements of content that become increasingly important in writing instruction are the following:

- word choice

- sentence and paragraph construction

- organization

- clarity

Process

Writing instruction considers not only the form and content of a text but also the process by which it is written. Students learn about each of the following stages in the creation of a final written product:

- planning

- drafting

- editing

- revising

Writing Instruction

Effective writing instruction includes the following elements:

- explicit, systematic instruction in necessary skills

- opportunities to engage in meaningful writing

- instruction in the use of technology for writing

- integration of writing activities with content instruction

Attitudes and Literacy

It is important for teachers to not only promote reading and writing but to also foster a positive attitude toward literacy and an appreciation of written expression among their students. When a student seems reluctant to read and/or write, the teacher should consider the source of the student's reluctance. The following are some of the many possibilities:

- The student has poor literacy skills, or a disability specifically related to reading or writing, so that engaging in these activities is a perpetual struggle.

- The student has a visual impairment, or some other problem that is not specific to literacy, but which makes the experience of reading or writing difficult and unpleasant.

- The student has low self-confidence, or low self-efficacy with respect to reading or writing, so that the student believes he/she will not make progress in these areas.

- The student thinks of literacy activities as compulsory and class-specific, and is not aware yet that reading can be informative and rewarding, or that writing can be a satisfying and useful form of expression.

PI (g): Evidence-based explicit and systematic instruction and intervention in mathematics for students with disabilities

This section touches on some of the instructional methods that have been shown to be most effective for teaching mathematics and supporting the integration of math across the general education curriculum.

Systematic Instruction in Mathematics

Systematic instruction is essential to the introduction of new mathematical concepts and procedures, as well as to the process of making connections across different curricular areas. Although teacher modeling, student inquiry, and student observation contribute in important ways to learning, math concepts are most effectively taught by means of explicit, systematic instructional methods.

A fundamental step in systematic instruction is independent practice, through which students reinforce emerging skills and deepen their understanding. Teachers must ensure that students make use of metacognitive strategies during independent practice that foster successful learning. These strategies include the following:

- setting appropriate goals

- monitoring progress toward the goals

- checking one's work periodically

- seeking help when encountering difficulties

- taking steps to avoid distraction

Other instructional methods, such as peer tutoring, can benefit mathematics instruction. Authentic activities are especially helpful for integrating math concepts across the curricula. In addition, visual tools are critical components across the different instructional methods. Some useful visual tools in math instruction include the following:

- pictures

- number lines

- graphs

- computer-generated animations

- manipulatives

PI (h): Research- or evidence-based strategies for identifying and teaching essential concepts, vocabulary, and content across the general curriculum

This section briefly discusses instructional strategies that can be used to teach concepts, vocabulary, and content across the general education curriculum.

Instructional Goals

Apart from specific curricular areas, three of the most important goals of instruction are acquisition, maintenance, and generalization:

- **Acquisition** refers to the initial learning of new content or skills. Instruction begins with a focus on acquisition, and the purpose of many instructional strategies is to help students with the initial learning process.

- **Maintenance** refers to the recall of what has been learned. Successful acquisition does not guarantee that new information will be maintained, because it is relatively easy to forget what one learns as time passes and newer content and skills are learned. Thus, instructional strategies are needed that will help promote maintenance.

- **Generalization** refers to the application of what has been learned to new situations. Just as acquisition does not guarantee maintenance, so maintenance does not guarantee generalization. In other words, students may be able to learn and remember new content and skills yet fail to generalize what they have learned to new situations. Thus, instructional strategies are also needed to help students transfer what they learn beyond the original context in which it was learned.

As is evident from these definitions, students cannot benefit much from instruction unless acquisition, maintenance, and generalization take place. An effective approach that supports these processes, particularly when learning specific skills, is systematic instruction.

Systematic Instruction

The phrases "systematic instruction," "explicit, systematic instruction," and "direct instruction" are used in many different senses and are sometimes treated interchangeably. **Systematic instruction** involves breaking new knowledge or skills into small elements and then presenting them to students in a sequence from simple to complex. Systematic instruction is grounded in five types of activities: planning, review, presentation, guided practice, and independent practice.

Planning

Prior to engaging in instructional activities, the teacher selects the knowledge or skills that will be presented, divides the new content into manageable elements, and decides on the appropriate sequence with which the new material will be introduced. For example, a math teacher who is developing a unit on long division will plan a sequence in which simple division problems are discussed first, and then long division problems with no remainders are studied before turning to problems in which the solutions contain remainders.

Review

The teacher begins each instructional unit by reviewing what was previously learned and by discussing connections between prior learning and the current unit. The purpose of what will be learned in the new unit is also explicitly discussed with students. For example, a math teacher who is introducing long division to students will review simple division problems and then provide explanations and examples illustrating the need for long division.

Presentation

In the presentation phase, the teacher explains and models the new knowledge or skills that students are to learn. The knowledge or skills are broken down into small components and presented in a sequence from simple to complex. Examples of presentation include the following:

- A math teacher introduces the elements of long division to students, first through graphic means and then using numerical examples.

- A language arts teacher who wants her students to memorize a particular poem recites the poem and encourages students to notice her phrasing and expression as they follow along in the text.

- A social studies teacher interacts with a student while others listen. The teacher structures the conversation so that a key idea is articulated and discussed. The teacher then describes the key idea in a subsequent discussion.

- A chemistry teacher introduces a new formula and, using this formula, solves two problems on the board as students watch. While solving the problems, the teacher explicitly notes how each part of the formula is being applied.

- A music teacher briefly analyzes a particular passage and then plays the passage for students as they listen.

Guided Practice

In the **guided practice** phase, students are given the opportunity to practice, under the supervision of the teacher, what was presented to them in the demonstration phase. During this time, the teacher will provide feedback to students, indicating when they are expressing their new knowledge or skills correctly, and correcting them when mistakes occur. The goal of guided practice is to facilitate the acquisition of new knowledge and skills. Guided practice contributes to maintenance as well and can also provide opportunities for generalization under the guidance of the teacher. The following are examples of guided practice:

- After a mathematics teacher has explained long division, students are asked to summarize the correct procedures for solving simple long division problems and are given opportunities to solve problems. Corrective feedback is provided if the procedures are summarized or applied incorrectly.

- After a language arts teacher has recited a poem, students are given the opportunity to recite the poem while looking at the written text as little as possible. The teacher provides corrective feedback with respect to students' accuracy as well as their phrasing and expression.

- After a social studies teacher has interacted with a student in front of the class, indicated which elements of the interaction correctly reflect an important idea, and then reiterated the idea, students are asked to respond to similar questions and given the opportunity to restate the idea. The teacher provides corrective feedback.

- After a chemistry teacher has used the same formula to solve two problems on the board, students are asked to solve similar problems that also require the application of this formula. Errors are corrected by the teacher.

- After a music teacher has performed a particular passage for students and discussed some of the key elements, students are asked to perform the passage. The teacher provides corrective feedback on students' performances.

Independent Practice

Following guided practice, students are given further opportunities to practice what they are learning. During the **independent practice** phase, students practice without supervision from the teacher. Teachers may still continue to provide students with feedback on their performance, but practice takes place independently. The goal of independent practice is to facilitate acquisition and maintenance of new knowledge and skills, and in some cases to provide opportunities for generalization. Examples of independent practice include the following:

- After students have solved long division problems under their math teacher's guidance, they receive a homework assignment that contains long division problems.

- After students have practiced reciting a poem for their language arts teacher, they work together in groups on reciting the poem with good phrasing and expression, and with minimal reliance on the written text.

- After students in a social studies class have learned a new concept by observing and then participating in interactions with the teacher, they are asked to write a short essay paraphrasing and critically evaluating the idea.

- After students have received support from their chemistry teacher in solving problems that require the use of a particular formula, they take a short, informal quiz that tests their ability to apply the formula to a variety of problems.

- After students have performed a particular passage for their music teacher, they are asked to continue working on the passage at home prior to the next class.

Assessment in Systematic Instruction

Although not a separate phase, systematic instruction includes an assessment component, as teachers regularly monitor their students' acquisition, maintenance, and generalization of new knowledge and skills, particularly during the guided and independent practice phases.

Explicit and Systematic Instruction

The phrase "explicit and systematic" instruction can be used to indicate systematic instruction in which new information is presented explicitly by the teacher (as opposed to presented by modeling, discovered through student inquiry, and acquired by passive observation).

Scaffolding

Scaffolding refers to direct support given to students during the learning process by a teacher or some other experienced individual. Scaffolding can consist of verbal support (e.g., giving a hint) or physical support (e.g., guiding a student's hand as the student writes a particular letter). The extent of scaffolding varies widely depending on student need. The following are examples in which the extent of scaffolding is relatively minimal:

- A teacher periodically looks over the shoulder of a student who is working independently on a project and offers a brief comment or suggestion.

- A teacher briefly summarizes the main theme of a passage before asking students to read the passage independently.

- A teacher briefly models the correct approach to solving a particular type of mathematics problem before students complete a worksheet containing this and other types of problems.

In the following examples, the extent of scaffolding is much greater:

- A teacher sits with a student who is working on a project and reiterates instructions and expectations, offers specific directives about what to do next, and provides corrective feedback.

- Before asking students to read a passage independently, a teacher summarizes the main theme of the passage and then reads the passage aloud, pausing to emphasize how particular details contribute to the theme.

- A teacher models and thoroughly explains the correct approach to solving a particular type of math problem, and then supervises guided practice before asking students to complete a worksheet that only contains the same type of problem.

As these examples imply, scaffolding can be provided to groups of students or tailored to an individual student. The extent of scaffolding provided to a student with a disability depends on the nature and severity of the disability.

Modeling

Modeling refers to the process by which the teacher demonstrates whatever students are intended to learn, and students then attempt to mimic what they have observed. Modeling can take place with or without explanation, and either prior to or following students' first attempts to demonstrate their learning. Modeling can contribute to a variety of instructional goals, including the following:

- mastery of specific behaviors (e.g., the formation of a particular letter during a handwriting lesson)

- application of problem-solving strategies (e.g., using the Internet to conduct research on a particular question)

- development of reasoning skills (e.g., making inferences from story events about the motives of key characters)

Integrating Across the General Curriculum

In order to integrate concepts, vocabulary, and content across the general education curriculum, the individual elements must be connected in a meaningful way. One way to achieve meaningful connections is to ensure that instructional activities require different concepts and to be integrated for some common purpose. For example, consider a simple activity in which the teacher reads students a short story and then asks the students to write down their favorite part, share what they wrote with a partner, and engage in discussion. In this activity, listening, writing, reading, and speaking are integrated in a purposeful way.

> **PI (i): Research- or evidence-based methods for explicitly teaching learning strategies, listening skills, study skills, and test-taking skills to help students with disabilities acquire academic content; strategies for explicitly teaching students to use self-assessment, problem-solving, and other cognitive strategies to meet their own needs; and explicit teaching methods to help students strengthen and compensate for deficits in perception, comprehension, memory, and retrieval**

In this section, you will read about methods for explicitly teaching strategies and skills that help all students, including students with disabilities, acquire academic content, apply cognitive strategies, and compensate for cognitive deficits. The focus of this section is on the role of metacognition in promoting these strategies and skills.

Metacognition

One of the most important contributors to effective listening, studying, and test-taking is **metacognition**, or the process of thinking about one's own knowledge, mental capacities, and thought processes. Examples of metacognition include reflecting on what you have learned from a text and how well you understand it, recognizing the steps by which you drew conclusions from the text, and making note of gaps in your knowledge about the text. Thus, when you read a mystery novel, merely stating that Patricia is the thief or that Patricia behaved suspiciously on Thursday would not be examples of metacognition. Rather, metacognition would involve when you state that Patricia is the thief but acknowledge that this conclusion reflects a bias on your part rather than incontrovertible evidence, and that if you just had one more piece of information about Patricia's whereabouts on a certain day, your conclusion might be stronger. In this example, you are not just stating knowledge about Patricia but also commenting on your thought process—on the certainty of what you know and the origins of that knowledge. Another example of metacognition would be your statement that it was easy for you to figure out that Patricia is the thief, because you are a very logical person. Likewise, it would reflect metacognition if you commented that identifying the thief was difficult for you, because logical reasoning is not one of your strengths.

Metacognition and Reading

Some metacognitive strategies focus specifically on the acquisition of academic content through reading. For example, the **SQ3R** is a reading comprehension strategy consisting of the following steps:

- Survey. The student briefly glances through the material that will be read in order to obtain information about headings, length, and other important features.

- Question. The student formulates general questions (e.g., what is the main point of this material?) as well as more specific ones (e.g., what information will be provided under such-and-such heading?).

- Read. The student begins reading, keeping in mind the results of the previous two steps.

- Recite. The student speaks, writes, or thinks about the answers to his/her questions indicated by the reading.

- Review. The student reviews what he/she learned.

Whether engaged in reading, problem-solving, or some other academic activity, the metacognitive strategies most suitable for students depends on their age and ability levels. For example, the SQ3R method is a relatively advanced strategy that requires facility with basic reading skills (e.g., decoding). An example of a simpler strategy would be the **KWL chart**, a graphic organizer in which the student makes note of what he/she knows, what he/she wants to know, and then what he/she learned.

Metacognition and Self-assessment

The examples of metacognition described above require the student to consider what he/she already knows. Metacognition is also illustrated when a student reflects on his/her own abilities and preferences, and uses that information to make decisions about how to proceed with studying and other academic activities. Examples of this kind of metacognition are as follows:

- During a short lecture, a student decides that taking notes will be necessary, because the amount of information the teacher is providing seems to be greater than what he can remember without notes.

- While studying, a student creates a flow chart, because she knows that she is a visual learner and would benefit from a visual representation of the material.

- While brainstorming solutions to a problem during a group setting, a student is careful about what he says, because he senses that he does not understand the material well.

- While taking a timed exam consisting of 50 questions, each worth 2 points, a student decides to answer one of the questions at the end because she can tell that it is especially difficult and might take too much time away from other questions.

Metacognition as a General Strategy

Comprehension monitoring was defined under section PI (e) above as a reading comprehension strategy. It is a form of metacognition in the sense that the reader asks questions such as: How well do I understand? What do I know? What do I not know? How can I find out what I need to know? Questions like this are not restricted to reading; they can also be asked while listening or viewing. Moreover, these questions can be asked when studying as well as taking tests, and either with or without support from graphic organizers. Thus, comprehension monitoring illustrates that metacognition can be used as a general, multipurpose strategy in academic settings.

PI (j): The use of technology for promoting academic success for students with disabilities

This section describes the use of technology in the instruction of students with disabilities.

A variety of technologies are available for classroom use, many but not all of which are computer-based. The term **assistive technology** refers to any device that maintains or improves the functioning of individuals with disabilities. Examples of assistive technologies used in the classroom include the following:

- wheelchairs, walkers, and other devices that support students with limited mobility

- large pencils, pencil grips, and paper fasteners for students with limited fine motor control

- sentence windows, graphic organizer software, and editing devices for students with limitations in attentional or cognitive processing

- alternative and augmentative communication devices for students with communication-related impairments (see Chapter 7 for details)

Assistive Technologies and Visual Impairments

To illustrate the role of assistive technology in instruction, consider the challenges faced by students with visual impairments. These students can be supported by means of tactile symbols, objects, and systems of representation, the most famous of which is the **Braille** system.

Braille consists of raised dots that represent letters, numbers, and punctuation marks. Blind and visually impaired children can read Braille by touch, and they can create Braille texts by means of special devices, including Braille typewriters and computers. However, Braille does not consist of a simple one-to-one representation of orthographic marks (e.g., letters) as raised dots. For example, Braille is based on complex rules governing the use of contractions (e.g., the word "but" is represented with the letter "b," but the note *b* in the musical scale is represented differently). For this and other reasons, mastery of Braille is a gradual process.

In recent years, students with visual impairments are being increasingly supported by special computer programs. The following are some examples:

- **Screen readers** read aloud text that is presented on a computer screen, including the main text as well as "extras" such as drop-down menus and dialog boxes.

- **Digital book readers** read books aloud and provide numerous interactive features.

- **Scan/read systems** allow printed materials to be scanned and then read aloud.

- **Screen magnification software** allows the user to magnify all or part of what is presented on a computer screen.

Practice Questions

1. A teacher who sometimes repeats instructions more slowly for a student with a learning disability is engaging in differentiation of what?

    A. Content.

    B. Process.

    C. Product.

    D. Environment.

2. Which of the following is the correct sequence of activities in systematic instruction?

    A. Review, presentation, guided practice, planning, independent practice.

    B. Planning, presentation, review, independent practice, guided practice.

    C. Review, presentation, guided practice, planning, independent practice.

    D. Planning, review, presentation, guided practice, independent practice.

3. Jason is a hearing-impaired 10th grader whose biology teacher provides him with written versions of the lectures she delivers in class. This scenario represents a modification of what aspect of instruction?

    A. Presentation.

    B. Response.

    C. Setting.

    D. Scheduling.

4. Which of the following concepts is illustrated by the math teacher who allows a mildly autistic student to quietly draw and fold paper while the teacher is lecturing as long as the student appears to learn from the lectures?

    A. Differentiation.

    B. Independent practice.

    C. Scaffolding.

    D. Modeling.

5.   A teacher engages students in an activity in which they compare the written words "sight, "light," "tight," and "fight," in order to call attention to the fact that "ight" makes the same sound in each case. What phase of decoding is the teacher attempting to promote?

   A.   Pre-alphabetic.

   B.   Partial-alphabetic.

   C.   Full-alphabetic.

   D.   Consolidated-alphabetic.

6.   A kindergarten teacher reads a familiar passage out loud and asks a student with a learning disability to clap his hands once every time he hears the "b" sound. What skill is this activity intended to promote?

   A.   Awareness of syllables.

   B.   Phonics.

   C.   Phonemic awareness.

   D.   Structural analysis.

7.   Which of the following most directly illustrates a limitation in metacognition?

   A.   A student consistently fails to remember instructions when completing in-class activities and consequently performs poorly on these activities.

   B.   A student vastly overestimates his ability to remember information from a lecture and consequently sees no purpose in taking notes.

   C.   A student often misremembers information gleaned from written text and consequently fails to engage with the main themes of the texts.

   D.   A student frequently remembers task-irrelevant information while forgetting task-relevant information and consequently performs slowly on tasks.

Answers to Practice Questions

1. **B.**

   Choice B is correct because differentiation of process involves tailoring learning activities for individual students. Choice A is incorrect because there are no changes to the content of the instructions. Choice C is incorrect because there are no changes to what is required of the student. Choice D is incorrect because there are no changes to the learning environment.

2. **D.**

   Choice D presents the correct order of activities in systematic instruction. Choices A, B, and C present incorrect orderings.

3. **A.**

   Choice A is correct because modifications of presentation change the format of information presented in the classroom, and the teacher in the scenario has changed the format of her lectures for Jason from oral to written. Choice B is incorrect because modifications of response change the format in which students can respond to classroom tasks, but nothing is mentioned in the scenario about Jason's response. Choice C is incorrect because modifications of setting change the location of the educational environment, but nothing about such changes is noted in the scenario. Choice D is incorrect because modifications of scheduling change the timing of classroom tasks, but no mention is made in the scenario of timing-related changes.

4. **A.**

   Choice A is correct because the teacher is engaging in a differentiation of the teaching process in order to accommodate the student's particular needs. Although the student may be "practicing" representational skills, choice B is incorrect because the student is not engaging in independent practice of what is being taught, as would take place during systematic instruction. Choice C is incorrect because the teacher is not directly supporting the student's learning but rather simply relaxing one of the class rules pertaining to attentiveness. Choice D is incorrect because the student is not copying the teacher's actions.

5.   D.

Choice D is correct because the consolidated-alphabetic phase involves the under-standing of how groups of letters function as units. Choice A is incorrect because children have not begun the process of decoding in the pre-alphabetic phase. Choices B and C are incorrect because in either phase, any decoding that takes place is carried out letter by letter.

6.   C.

Choice C is correct because the activity helps the student develop the ability to iso-late specific phonemes in the flow of speech. Choice A is incorrect because the "b" sound does not consistently correspond to a syllable. Choice B is incorrect because phonics pertains to letter-sound correspondences. Choice D is incorrect because structural analysis pertains to the identification of morphemes.

7.   B.

Choice B is correct because the capacity to estimate how well one can remember information is a reflection of metacognition. Choices A, C, and D are incorrect be-cause they illustrate cognition and do not directly reflect metacognition.

CHAPTER 7

COMPETENCY 0006

Strategies for Teaching Communication Skills, Social Skills, and Functional Living Skills

This chapter introduces strategies for teaching communication skills, social skills, and functional living skills, with emphasis on strategies that benefit children with disabilities who have impairments in one or more of these areas.

PI (a): Instructional strategies for fostering communication skills of students with disabilities, including students from various cultural and linguistic backgrounds

In this section, you will read about different types of communication deficits as well as interventions and strategies to help children overcome these deficits and develop communication skills.

Types of Communication Deficits

Children with communication deficits exhibit a variety of receptive and/or expressive language symptoms, depending on the nature of the deficit. What these deficits have in common is that the child's communication is significantly poorer in some respect than would be expected for age and that the deficit interferes with academic performance and/ or social communication. The severity of these deficits typically varies from child to child. For some children, the deficit is temporary while for others it will be lifelong.

Communication deficits can be subdivided into speech impairments and language impairments.

Speech Impairments

Speech impairments can be divided into four types: motor speech disorders, articulation disorders, fluency disorders, and voice disorders. These impairments tend to reflect limitations in expressive rather than receptive language skills.

Motor Speech Disorders

Motor speech disorders reflect anatomical or physiological limitations in the physical mechanisms used to produce speech. The two general categories of motor speech disorders are dysarthria and apraxia.

- **Dysarthria** is a weakness or paralysis of the musculature that controls speech, typically resulting from illness or injury. The symptoms of dysarthria vary widely and may include excessively rapid or slow rate of speech, slurred speech, distorted vowels, unmodulated pitch and/or word flow, and overly nasal speech.

- **Apraxia** is an impairment in the ability to translate speech plans into actual speech. Children with apraxia know what they wish to say, but their brains do no readily translate planned speech into the necessary movements of lips, tongue, and other parts of the speech apparatus. As a result, these children experience difficulties initiating speech and producing language sounds. They may appear to be groping as they attempt to form sounds. Their utterances may exhibit abnormal rhythm, stress and intonation, and errors of articulation that are not consistent each time a word is produced. Children with the disorder are aware of their speech errors and may attempt to correct themselves. If the apraxia is not the result of illness or injury, the problem is referred to as **childhood apraxia of speech (CAS)**. Children with CAS will show language delays and other abnormalities beginning in infancy.

Articulation Disorders

Articulation disorders are reflected in difficulties producing certain speech sounds. The mispronunciations that occur reflect one or more of several types:

- Omissions occur when the child leaves out sounds, as in the sentence "I ha a boo" ("I have a book").

- Substitutions occur when the child uses an incorrect sound in place of the correct one. In such cases, the incorrect sound is usually easier to imitate. An example would be the child who says "wight" when attempting to say "right."

- Distortions occur when the child produces the correct sound but does not articulate it clearly, as in the case of a slight lisp.

Articulation disorders should be distinguished from the errors of articulation that young children make and usually grow out of (and from alternative pronunciations reflecting accents or dialects). Teachers should recognize that articulation errors are common among young children and do not necessarily imply the presence of a disorder.

Fluency Disorders

Fluency disorders are reflected in difficulties with the rhythm and timing of speech. Two prominent examples are stuttering and cluttering:

- **Stuttering** is a problem in which speech is disrupted by involuntary pauses, also known as blocks, as well as repetitions and/or prolongations of sounds, syllables, words, or phrases. Although all people exhibit pauses, repetitions, and prolongations from time to time, these dysfluencies are especially severe in the case of stutterers. The extent of severity varies not only across individuals but also within individuals, in the sense that stuttering is more likely in some situations than in others. Stuttering is typically developmental but may be acquired.

- **Cluttering** is a problem in which speaking rate is unusually fast and/or irregular. Fluency is affected owing to a lack of phrasing, to omissions and/or slurring of syllables, and to other dysfluencies resulting from the high rate of speed. Stuttering and cluttering may occur together, although they are distinct disorders. For example, stutterers tend to struggle, while clutterers produce streams of speech relatively effortlessly. Whereas stutterers typically know what they wish to say but have difficulty expressing themselves fluently, clutterers experience some disorganization or uncertainty in what they intend to say.

Voice Disorders

Voice disorders are manifested as difficulties in producing language sounds of appropriate quality, pitch, and/or loudness. These disorders can be subdivided into phonation disorders and resonance disorders.

- **Phonation disorders** result in excessive hoarseness, raspiness, sudden changes in volume, and/or sudden changes in pitch while speaking.

- **Resonance disorders** result in either too much or too little nasal emission of air while speaking.

Language Impairments

Language impairments can be discerned when children have difficulties in expressing their thoughts, needs or feelings, and/or in understanding what others say. Three of the main types of language impairments are phonological disorders, expressive language disorders, and mixed receptive-expressive language disorders.

Phonological Disorders

Phonological disorders refers to impairments in the ability to distinguish specific phonemes. The extent of impairment is greater than would be expected given the child's age and dialect.

Phonological disorders can be classified as impairments of language rather than speech. Although phonological and articulation disorders may both result in specific mispronunciations, articulation disorders reflect limitations in the ability to produce specific language sounds, while phonological disorders reflect limitations in the ability to distinguish phoneme contrasts. A child with a phonological disorder does not recognize differences between certain phonemes and, as a result, may pronounce different phonemes the same. Unlike children with expressive language disorder or mixed receptive-receptive language disorder, the difficulties that children with phonological disorder experience are limited to specific sounds. These children may omit certain sounds, distort the sounds, or substitute one sound for another. Children with a phonological disorder do not have impairments in other aspects of oral fluency such as rate, stress, pitch, and loudness.

Expressive Language Disorders

Expressive language disorder, also known as **specific language impairment (SLI)**, refers to expressive language abilities that are much lower than expected for age, although mental functioning and receptive language skills fall within the normal range. Expressive language disorders may be developmental, and thus noticeable when the child first begins to talk, or they may be acquired as the result of disease or injury to the brain. A child with an expressive language disorder is likely to have difficulty expressing himself/herself with anything more than a few words or simple sentences. Symptoms vary from child to child and may include grammatical errors, difficulty constructing coherent sentences, and limited vocabulary.

Mixed Receptive-Expressive Language Disorders

Mixed receptive-expressive language disorder refers to a disorder in which both receptive and expressive language abilities are affected. As with expressive language disorder, mental functioning falls within the normal range, and the disorder may be developmental or acquired.

Prevention and Intervention

A number of steps can be taken to help prevent speech and language disorders, including attention to signs such as delay or regression, and consideration of risk factors such as hearing impairment, a family history of communication disorders, and a medical disorder such as cleft palate. A child who is suspected of having a speech or language disorder can be screened and, depending on the results of the screening, evaluated in depth.

If the results of in-depth assessment suggest that intervention is necessary, the intervention can be direct (i.e., focused on the child) or indirect (i.e., focused on parents, teachers, or anyone else who will intervene with the child). Direct interventions can be carried out with the individual child or with small groups of children.

A further distinction can be made between directive and naturalistic interventions, although most interventions reflect a mix of both approaches.

- **Directive interventions** are structured learning activities in which the professional responsible for the intervention models speech, prompts the child for specific responses, and offers incentives for desired responses. Through these techniques, the professional attempts to develop targeted aspects of the child's communication.

- **Naturalistic interventions** are activities carried out in day-to-day settings in which the professional responsible for the intervention makes use of opportunities for the child to learn. The professional may engage in modeling, prompting, and the use of incentives, but he/she will also allow the child's interests to influence the content of communication with the child.

Segregated vs. Integrated Instruction

In segregated models of instruction, emphasis is placed on the development of discrete skills. In such models, content areas such as math, science, and social studies are treated separately from each other and from instruction in language. With respect to language, skills such as reading, writing, and speaking are treated largely independently, and language instruction is separated to some extent from the development of communication skills.

Integrated instructional approaches are based on the assumption that content areas overlap with each other and with language and that language skills such as reading, writing, and speaking are interdependent. According to this view, language skills are interdependent in the sense that development in one skill fosters development in the others, and all of these skills are supported by underlying cognitive abilities such as memory and attention. Integrated instructional approaches also assume that sharp distinctions between language and communication are unnatural, since language is ordinarily used for the purpose of communication.

Content-Based vs. Task-Based Instruction

Two versions of integrated instruction are content-based and task-based instruction, both of which are considered desirable in the classroom.

- **Content-based instruction** involves teaching language and content simultaneously. For example, language skills may be taught in the context of an age-appropriate theme. Themes can be relatively specific (e.g., current threats to the ecology of South American rain forests) or relatively broad (e.g., outer space). Content-based instruction is considered desirable because it promotes student interest, because it breaks down artificial barriers between content areas (and between language and content), and because it reinforces learning by making connections between content areas.

- **Task-based instruction** involves the teaching of language by means of age-appropriate tasks that require meaningful communication. For example, language skills may be taught in the context of group activities such as the creation of a class newspaper or website. Task-based instruction is considered desirable because it promotes student interest and engagement, because it breaks down artificial barriers between language and communication, and because it fosters authentic use of language in meaningful communicative contexts.

PI (b): Communication and social interaction alternatives for students with disabilities, including strategies for planning and implementing instruction in the use of alternative and augmentative communication (AAC) systems

This section describes the use of communication alternatives for students with disabilities, particularly among children with communication-related disabilities. (Social alternatives are discussed under section PI (d) below.)

Alternative and Augmentative Communication Systems

As noted in the previous chapter, an assistive technology is any device that maintains or improves the functioning of individuals with disabilities. Discussed in this section are assistive technologies of direct relevance to communication (as opposed to assistive technologies such as wheelchairs and walkers that are not primarily intended to support individuals with communication-related impairments). The term **alternative communication system** refers to any system of communication other than the conventional natural language systems of reading, writing, hearing, and speech. Finally, the term **alternative and augmentative communication (AAC)** is often used to describe a broader category of methods that includes both assistive technologies and alternative communication systems.

AACs can be classified in terms of the types of students they primarily support. In this section, children with hearing, speech, and language impairments will be discussed.

Children with Hearing Impairments

Students who are deaf or hearing-impaired can receive support from hearing technologies, alerting devices, and/or communication supports.

Hearing technologies enhance the volume and quality of spoken language and other sounds. The following are the two primary examples:

- **Assistive listening devices** increase volume as well as minimize the effects of background noise and the acoustics of the surrounding room. These devices can be used by individuals or groups.

- **Personal amplification devices** such as hearing aids increase the quality of sound for individuals.

Alerting devices are designed to gain the attention of an individual by means of an amplified sound, flashing light, or vibration. These devices can be used to alert the deaf or hearing-impaired student of an emergency as well as for more routine situations such as the need to move to another part of the classroom.

Communication supports consist of technologies that facilitate communication among students who are deaf or hearing-impaired. The following are some examples:

- Conventional word-processing programs
- Conventional cell phones (with texting capacity)
- Text telephones

- Videoconferencing devices and programs

- Closed captioning

- Speech-to-text translators

Finally, **sign language** is an alternative communication system that is used by many children who are deaf or who have significant hearing impairments. In American Sign Language (ASL), meaning is conveyed through hand movements, bodily gestures, and facial expressions. However, just as Braille is not a simple one-to-one representation of letters and other orthographic elements, so ASL is not a simple manual representation of English. Rather, ASL represents a distinct natural language, with rules of semantics, grammar, and pragmatics that are largely independent of spoken English.

Children with Speech or Language Impairments

Along with sign language, a number of technologies are available to support children with speech or language impairments. Some of these technologies are "low-tech," meaning that their use is relatively simple and does not require batteries or electricity, while others are "high-tech" and consist of sophisticated devices. Two of the most prominent examples of technologies designed specifically for speech or language impairments are as follows:

- **Communication boards** allow students to choose among photos, pictures, or symbols arranged on a board. A communication board could be as simple as a piece of paper containing pictures, in which case the student communicates by pointing to individual pictures. This "low-tech" communication board would be appropriate for a student with impaired speech who has no other disability. An example of a "high-tech" communication board would be one in which images, symbols, and/or text are presented on a computer screen, and the student makes choices by means of shifting his/her gaze. This board would be appropriate for a student who has impaired speech as well as limited mobility and is unable to point.

- **Voice output communication aids** (also known as "speech-generating devices") are devices that produce speech. What they say may be pre-recorded, produced by synthesizers, or both. Students with impaired speech but no limitations in mobility may use a keyboard or touch screen to operate such a device. Students with limited mobility may use movements of head and/or eyes to operate the device.

Adaptive Life Skills

PI (c): Strategies for integrating affective, social, career, and life skills with academic curricula

This section pertains to the integration of adaptive life skills with instruction.

Adaptive life skills consist of a broad variety of skills that allow people to care for themselves, interact with others, and cope with the demands of everyday living. When considering how much support a student with a disability needs for the development of his/her adaptive life skills, the following areas will be considered:

- self-care (e.g., eating, using the toilet, personal hygiene)

- health and safety (e.g., avoiding danger, preventing illness, making food choices)

- domestic living (e.g., cooking, cleaning, maintaining clothes)

- communication (e.g., asking questions, expressing needs, using the phone)

- social (e.g., forming relationships, negotiating conflicts, understanding customs)

- community use (e.g., using public transportation, shopping, obtaining services)

- functional academics (e.g., telling time, writing notes, keeping a budget)

- self-direction (e.g., managing time, seeking assistance, solving problems)

- work (e.g., accepting supervision, completing tasks, cooperating with others)

- leisure (e.g., making use of free time, choosing activities, participating with others)

Students with disabilities exhibit much variability in the extent to which they need support for these skills. At one end of the spectrum, a student with dyslexia might need very little support for adaptive life skills other than knowledge about how to compensate for the problem in particular situations. At the other end of the spectrum, a student with a severe intellectual disability may need lifelong support for every aspect of daily life, including personal care routines such as eating. All students, including those with disabilities, need instruction in adaptive life skills, particularly as they get older and the prospect of an independent life beyond graduation grows nearer, but the type of instruction that each student needs will vary from student to student.

Integration through Instruction

Multiple approaches to assessment are needed to determine the adaptive life skills for which a particular student needs the most support. Based in part on assessment results, instructional methods for teaching adaptive skills will need to be chosen. A variety of methods are available, and the choice of particular methods will depend on the types of needs revealed by prior assessment. Regardless of which instructional methods are used, hands-on activities and modeling will be essential to the learning process, given that adaptive life skills tend to require independent action. Group work and role play will be important too, given the social nature of some adaptive life skills. Finally, authentic activities and community learning will be critical given that adaptive life skills reflect applied knowledge that contributes to functioning in natural settings. These strategies are not fully independent of each other, nor do they reflect the same level of analysis in the classification of instructional strategies, but together they illustrate some of the most effective instructional procedures for teaching adaptive life skills.

Hands-on Instruction

Hands-on instruction refers to a broad category of instructional strategies in which students learn by actively applying the knowledge or skills being taught rather than passively listening to the teacher. Hands-on instruction is essential for learning skilled behaviors, since mastery of these behaviors requires performing them rather than merely understanding how they are performed. Thus, hands-on activities will be central to instruction in adaptive life skills involving skilled behaviors, such as cooking and grooming.

Modeling

As noted in Chapter 6, **modeling** refers to the process of learning through observation. Modeling contributes to the learning of both physical and verbal behaviors. Thus, modeling can be a useful strategy for teaching a variety of adaptive life skills ranging from self-care routines to verbal strategies for effective communication with others. In practice, modeling and hands-on instruction will be closely connected, as the teacher will often demonstrate a behavioral skill for students (and provide commentary) before giving students the opportunity to practice what they have been observing.

Group Work

A variety of instructional activities can be implemented within the context of **group work**, in which groups of two or more students work together in their efforts to achieve a common goal. Because group work requires individual initiative, collaborative interactions among group members, and progress toward a shared goal, any group work activity will provide students with the opportunity to practice social and occupational skills. Thus, group work activities will help students develop adaptive life skills such as conflict resolution and cooperation.

Role Play

In **role play** activities, students each assume the identity of a character other than themselves in order to act out a narrative, or they pretend to be themselves as they respond to others in a fictional setting. Role play benefits adaptive life skills involving communication and social functioning, because cooperation is required in order to carry out the role play, perspective-taking and empathy are fostered by assuming the identity of another individual, and imagining oneself responding to others in a fictional setting promotes thinking about social interactions and social relationships.

Authentic Activities

Authentic activities are tasks that are identical or highly similar to meaningful real-life tasks. A distinctive characteristic of authentic activities is that they reflect the ultimate purpose of instruction. The purpose of learning how to add and subtract, for example, is not merely to solve addition and subtraction problems on a test but to use these mathematical operations to solve real-world problems such as balancing a budget. Instructional approaches that incorporate authentic activities are inevitable when teaching of adaptive life skills, as practice with these skills constitute authentic activities.

Community-Based Instruction

As the name suggests, **community-based instruction** consists of instructional activities that take place in community settings. Instructional activities are grounded in meaningful, everyday tasks—in effect, they are authentic activities carried out in the community. However, community-based instruction is not the same as a field trip. A field trip consists of a visit to a particular community setting for the purpose of extending instruction. Community-based instruction consists of repeated visits to a community setting in which instruction takes place and is cumulative over time. Community-based instruction is an especially effective means of teaching adaptive life skills, as students can be given the opportunity to practice the skills in these actual settings in which they will someday be applied.

The Role of Explicit, Systematic Instruction

Although some adaptive life skills consist of learned physical behaviors, others depend in part on the application of basic academic skills such as literacy and numeracy. For this reason, explicit, systematic instruction in these skills contributes to the development of adaptive life skills. To take just one example, the ability to read the following types of information will contribute to an individual's functioning in a variety of settings:

- signs
- instructions
- labels
- application forms
- contracts
- policies
- informational resources

The Role of Differentiation

Teachers differentiate instructional methods and strategies for individual students depending on each student's strengths and needs, as well as on the types of skills being supported. For example, with respect to adaptive life skills that require complex physical behaviors, the teacher will need to consider whether the student has any physical limitations that would prevent him/her from performing the behavior. Limitations in the student's attention, memory, understanding, or impulse control may need to be considered when selecting the instructional approach. The teacher will need to decide on the amount of scaffolding initially needed, and student progress will help determine the tempo of instruction and the rate at which fading occurs.

PI (d): Social skills needed for educational and other environments and strategies for designing, implementing, and evaluating instructional programs that enhance the social participation of students with disabilities across environments

In this section, you will read about strategies for enhancing the social skills and social participation of all students, including students with disabilities.

Social Skills

The acquisition of social skills is a critical part of development. The following are a few of the many types of social skills that are particularly important when interacting with teachers and peers in educational environments:

- holding a conversation

- making a request using clear, tactful, and appropriate language

- responding appropriately to others' distress

- accepting and responding appropriately to criticism

- negotiating conflict with others

Instructional Strategies

The AACs described earlier in section PI (b) are appropriate for use by students with sensory impairments, or with impairments in the ability to comprehend or produce language. However, some students with disabilities have difficulty communicating for cognitive and/or emotional reasons. Students with autism, and some students with emotional disturbances and/or intellectual disabilities, will have limitations in social competence that result in impaired communication with others. These students may benefit from the following activities:

- explicit instruction in specific social behaviors and in the nature of social relationships

- modeling of social behaviors by teachers and/or others

- creation of role-play activities that include the student

- use of social narratives (self-created stories in which the student depicts himself/herself in a social situation requiring a particular social skill)

- creating activities in which the student is paired with a socially skilled peer

Training

One or several of the activities described above may be incorporated into training programs that enhance social skills and social participation among students with disabilities.

For example, **social skills training** focuses on providing students with a variety of skills that benefit their interpersonal relationships and communication with others. Examples of social skills that can be enhanced through behavioral training include the following:

- how to establish and maintain friendships

- how to effectively communicate one's needs

- how to listen to and cooperate with others

- how to recognize and respond to conflict with others

- how to deal with frustration, loss, and other negative outcomes

- how to deal with being bullied or neglected

PI (e): Strategies for teaching self-advocacy and self-determination skills and for encouraging increased independence

This section introduces the characteristics and promotion of self-determination and self-advocacy, which are extremely important to independent functioning in and beyond the classroom.

Self-Determination

Self-determination refers to the ability to make choices for oneself. Through self-determination, an individual becomes able to function independently. Adaptive life skills depend on general self-determination abilities such as the following:

- the ability to set goals

- the ability to choose actions that will help achieve goals

- the ability to monitor progress toward goals and make adjustments as necessary

Examples of specific self-determination behaviors include:

- choosing what foods to eat

- choosing what clothing to wear

- choosing which service provider to use

- choosing how to budget money

- choosing how to spend free time

- choosing who to establish friendships with

- choosing where to seek employment

- choosing when to seek assistance

- choosing when to reject advice

Promoting Self-determination

Teachers can use a number of strategies to promote self-determination among students with disabilities, including the following:

- maintain positive expectations for students

- facilitate students' self-esteem

- help students identify their own strengths and interests

- teach students about their own disabilities

- teach students planning skills

- provide students with information about choices

- teach students strategies for obtaining information about choices

- provide students with opportunities to make meaningful personal choices

- provide guidance for students' personal choices

- allow students to make independent choices

- positively reinforce students' planning and choice-making behaviors

- allow for mistakes and negative outcomes for students' choices

Each of the strategies in this list can be supported in multiple ways by the teacher. For example, to foster a student's self-esteem, the teacher should engage in a variety of activities such as the following:

- model positive self-esteem

- create opportunities for student success

- encourage increasing student independence

- help the student recognize his/her strengths and achievements

- use praise and other positive reinforcers judiciously

Self-Advocacy

Self-advocacy includes the ability to assert one's own needs and to obtain assistance in meeting those needs. Students with disabilities will use self-advocacy skills in order to meet the kinds of needs that anyone might have (e.g., obtaining a particular product in a store) as well as to meet needs related specifically to their disabilities (e.g., obtaining accommodations for which they are eligible).

Need for Self-advocacy Skills

Students with disabilities who are weak in one or more adaptive life skill may face significant challenges in school and in their lives beyond school. The support that these students can obtain from people around them may be lacking in some key respect such as the following:

- Parents or school staff may have low expectations for a student's future independence and productivity.

- A student may have little or no awareness of successful role models who share the same disability.

- The student may have limited informational support from parents or school staff whose knowledge of disability rights laws is lacking.

- Parents or school staff may be unable to provide adequate support for the student in some specific respect.

Students with disabilities need self-advocacy skills not only as a means of self-expression, but also to help ensure that they can achieve their potential when environmental support is lacking.

Promoting Self-Advocacy

Students' self-advocacy is fostered by the promotion of self-determination and by the enhancement of other skills related to the ability to independently assert and gain assistance with one's needs. The following are some examples of how teachers can promote self-advocacy:

- encourage students to communicate their needs

- encourage students express their ideas, attitudes, and interests

- provide guidance to students, as appropriate, for effective communication of needs and ideas.

- positively reinforce students for assertiveness and appropriate self-expression

- provide students with opportunities for self-advocacy and leadership activities

- teach students about the social and occupational experiences of individuals with disabilities

- teach students about legal rights and responsibilities pertaining to disabilities

- encourage student communication of disability-related needs

- teach students how to obtain informational and service-related resources for individuals with disabilities

Integration of Approaches

As this chapter suggests, teachers can use a variety of specific strategies to promote self-determination and self-advocacy among students with disabilities. In practice, teachers and other educational professionals often use approaches that integrate specific strategies. For example, **person-centered planning approaches** support the transition to life beyond graduation by helping students achieve their goals for the future. A person-centered planning team, including the student, will help the student articulate goals, pursue his/her goals with increasing independence, identify community members and resources that can be of support, find ways of increasing the student's participation in the community, and empower the student to achieve his/her goals and dreams.

> **PI (f): How to plan and implement instruction in personal management skills, career development and occupational skills, and independent living skills, including instruction in community-based settings**

This section pertains to activities that support career development, personal management, and independent living, which are among the critical areas of focus in a student's transition to life beyond high school.

Stages of Career Development

Student knowledge about careers and career-related activities change over time. Four stages of career development that are often discussed include career awareness, career exploration, career preparation, and career placement. These stages overlap, and the types of activities that support one stage tend to support the other stages (assuming age-appropriate modifications to each activity).

Career Awareness

During the career awareness stage, students become aware of the purpose of work and of the existence of an increasing number of different types of jobs. During this time, they also become increasingly aware of personal interests, strengths, and goals that may be relevant to later work experiences. Activities that support career awareness include the following:

- lessons, instructional materials, and other resources that provide information about different professions

- field trips and classroom visits that provide opportunities to interact with people from different professions

- discussions and activities that promote work-related values such as cooperation and a collaborative attitude

- encouragement to reflect on personal strengths and interests and how they might relate to the performance of certain kinds of jobs

Career Exploration

During the career exploration stage, students become increasingly knowledgeable about the characteristics, social importance, and interconnectedness of different types of jobs. Activities that support career exploration include those described above in connection with career awareness, as well as the following:

- critical reading of autobiographies, biographies, and work-related narratives

- authentic activities with work-related themes

- informal and formal assessments of vocational skills and interests

Career Preparation

During the career preparation stage, students acquire more detailed information about job opportunities and how various educational and vocational training experiences might prepare them for these jobs. As they are now on the verge of graduation, students will need to decide soon whether to work after graduation or to pursue further education or training. Activities that support the career preparation stage include those mentioned in connection with the previous two stages, as well as the following:

- opportunities for interviewing professionals

- opportunities for shadowing professionals in the workplace

- assistance with job search

- assistance with the evaluation of different job opportunities

- instruction in appropriate interview behavior

Career Placement

During the career placement stage, students acquire jobs through their own efforts and with support from the Individualized Education Program (IEP) team, school staff, and possibly also community agencies such as the vocational rehabilitation agency. Follow-up efforts will be needed, given that individuals may need additional education or training, and given that their career-related interests and priorities may evolve.

Further Education

Following high school, some students will pursue further education in the community on a part-time or full-time basis. Support for these endeavors begins in high school with transition-related activities specified in the IEP. For example, if the postsecondary goal is for the student to "enroll in business-related courses at the local community college within one year of graduation," the specific IEP goals might be for the student to have done the following by a certain time:

- accurately summarize the published admissions criteria for the college

- accurately state the admissions deadlines for the college

- identify three business-related courses in the college that the student would be eligible to take and that would serve the student's stated interests

Personal Management and Independent Living

Transition planning in the IEP must also include personal management and independent living skills in areas such as the following:

- transportation

- medical

- financial

- time management

- leisure

- relationships

- parenting

- self-advocacy

> **PI (g): Strategies for promoting successful transitions between various environments during the school years (e.g., home to school, classroom to classroom, school to school)**

This section discusses transitions during the school years for all students, including students with disabilities.

Transitions

During the school years, all students experience the following transitions:

- transitions from home to school

- transitions from grade to grade

- transitions from one area of the school (e.g., classroom) to another

In addition, some students experience transitions that many of their peers do not experience, such as a change in schools or a transition within school to a special area.

Coping with Transitions

All students benefit from strategies that make transitions understandable, predictable, and minimally disruptive. For example, when going to school for the first time or when changing schools, a number of strategies can be helpful, such as

- Explain the need for the transition and answer any questions in a straightforward but positive manner.

- Discuss the potential benefits of the transition as well as any particular challenges.

- Allow the child to visit the school and meet the teacher(s), if possible.

Transitions During the School Years

During the school years, transitions may pose physical, cognitive, and/or emotional challenges for students with disabilities.

Physical Challenges

Students may struggle with the physical movements necessary for within-school transitions if they have a medical condition, a sensory impairment, or a physical condition resulting in limited mobility, or if they rely on an assistive technology such as a wheelchair. Teachers can help these students through the following strategies:

- arrange the classroom and the student's desk in a way that facilitates transition

- establish a routine in which the student begins the transition early, with minimal disruption

- establish a routine in which the student may complete the transition late, with minimal disruption

- establish routines for peer support when possible (e.g., the last general education student in line for recess holds the classroom door open for a student in a wheelchair)

Cognitive Challenges

Students with a disability that impairs their cognitive functioning may forget transition routines and/or become confused during the process of transitions. These students may benefit from one or more of the following strategies:

- additional explanations and discussion of transition

- verbal or written reminders of routines

- graphic depictions of routines

- teacher- or peer-modeling of routines

- teacher support during routines

- peer support during routines

Emotional Challenges

Students with autism or emotional disturbances may become frustrated by changes to their routines that result from transitions within and beyond school. Students with cognitive challenges may also become frustrated when they are enjoying their current situation and do not understand the need for the transition. Parents, teachers, and other professionals will need to be resourceful to minimize the negative emotional impact of the transitions. For example, in school settings, autistic students may benefit from the following strategies that help increase the predictability of transition:

- verbal reminders of when an activity will end and a transition will begin

- verbal reminders of how transition will proceed

- use of visual cues related to transition

- use of timers that mark the beginning and end of activities

PI (h): Strategies for promoting successful post-secondary transitions

This section concerns **transition planning**—the supports and services that are designed to help students with disabilities shift from life in a secondary school environment to adult life in the community.

■ IDEA and Transition

The Individuals with Disabilities Education Act (IDEA) requires that transition planning be coordinated by the IEP team, which includes the student and the parents, and that the student must be invited to any IEP meeting in which transition-related issues are considered. Specifically, IDEA requires that when a student with a disability turns 16, if not earlier, the student's IEP must include a description of goals for employment, education, and other significant dimensions of postsecondary life. These postsecondary goals must reflect two characteristics:

- They must be measureable, meaning that whether or not they are achieved will be directly observable. For example, "enrolling in business-related courses at the local community college within one year of graduation" would be an example of a measurable goal.

- They must be based on age-appropriate transition assessments that reflect the student's particular strengths, interests, preferences, and needs.

The IEP must also contain a description of transition services (including courses of study) that will be needed to help the student achieve his or her postsecondary goals. **Transition services** consist of a set of activities that facilitate transition. These services must reflect several characteristics:

- Transition services must be coordinated, in the sense of converging on common goals (e.g., independent living) rather than being separate activities.

- Transition services must be tailored to the individual student (i.e., based on the transition assessments noted above).

- Transition services must be results-oriented and foster the development of academic and adaptive life skills that will help students become engaged in a variety of personal, social, educational, and occupational activities following school. "Result-oriented" means that the transition services must focus on creating improvements in the student's ability to function during postsecondary life.

- The transition services themselves may consist of instruction, community experiences, employment assistance, and postsecondary adult living support.

Postsecondary Goals and IEP Goals

During transition planning, the IEP team will develop specific IEP goals that support the student's progress toward his/her postsecondary goals. Essential domains of transition planning by the IEP team include the following:

- postsecondary education

- vocational training

- employment

- continuing and adult education

- adult services

- independent living

- community participation

As can be seen from this list, transition planning involves virtually every aspect of life beyond school. An individual student may need support in all or just some of the domains listed here, depending on the student's postsecondary goals and particular strengths and needs. For example, some students will need postsecondary education or training in order to achieve employment goals, while other students will need no further education or training. Some students will need substantial support for independent living, while others will need little or no support in this domain.

Transition and Characteristics of Students and Families

Although postsecondary outcomes such as duration and quality of employment tend to be less favorable on the whole for students with disabilities than for the general population, the relative success of these outcomes varies widely among students with disabilities. Student and family characteristics are among the key variables that influence the quality of postsecondary outcomes.

Student Characteristics

The IEP team must take into account the nature and severity of the student's disability during transition planning. The greater the number of areas of functioning affected by a disability, the greater the obstacles to successful transition. A student with a hearing impairment, for example, may need a small number of specific, readily identifiable kinds of support in order to achieve postsecondary goals, while a student with an intellectual disability may need a broad range of supports and services in a variety of domains.

Transition planning should also attempt to anticipate any changes in the severity of a disability. For example, the severity of medical conditions such as multiple sclerosis may wax and wane over time, leading to significant variability in the individual's ability to function. Other medical conditions such as amyotropic lateral sclerosis are associated with progressive degeneration, while still others, such as severe injuries, may create significant impairments for the student at the present time yet can be expected to gradually improve.

Apart from the characteristics of each student's particular disability, the IEP team should also take into account the student's personal, family, and cultural background during transition planning. The following are a few examples:

- Each student is likely to have personal strengths as well as areas of need that are unrelated to his/her disability. For example, a student with an emotional disturbance may be relatively good (or relatively poor) at using computers and other electronic devices, and this consideration might influence the types of jobs and vocational training the student would be encouraged to consider following graduation.

- Some students are more likely than others to experience prejudice and/or discrimination in the form of lower expectations, negative stereotyping, and diminished job opportunities. In some cases, visible evidence of a disability, such as a wheelchair, is the trigger for prejudicial or discriminatory treatment. In other cases, the student may have characteristics unrelated to the disability that foster negative treatment, as in the example of students who are subject to racist attitudes and behaviors owing to their skin color.

- Students whose family environment is unstable (e.g., owing to change in the marital or employment status of parents) may experience additional challenges following graduation that are unrelated to their disabilities. For example, a student whose father becomes extremely ill or passes away around the time of graduation will find it challenging to focus on postsecondary goals while simultaneously dealing with personal grief and additional responsibilities at home.

- Students whose native language is not English may face additional challenges in postsecondary life over and above those posed by their disabilities. In such cases, the postsecondary goals may need to include continuing education or other activities intended to promote English language skills and to provide assistance with the adjustment to a more or less unfamiliar culture.

Family Characteristics

Characteristics of the student's family have a significant influence on the success of transition. Students whose families are more affluent and more highly educated, for example, tend to have more successful transition outcomes owing to the greater extent of material support their parents can provide. (The term "parents" is used here as shorthand for "parent, parents, or guardians"—in other words, the adult or adults who are legally responsible for the student prior to age of majority.)

A particularly important family-related characteristic is parental involvement. The greater the parents' involvement in transition planning and in providing support for the student following graduation, the more readily the student's postsecondary goals will be achieved. However, there are many obstacles that can prevent parents from being as involved as they might wish to be, as illustrated by the following examples.

- The parents may have disabilities themselves which limit their ability to provide support.

- The parents may lack confidence in their ability to provide support.

- The parents may experience unusual demands on their time owing to multiple jobs and special family obligations.

- The parents may be recent immigrants to the United States and lack knowledge about local customs, opportunities, and resources.

- The parents may be poor and consequently struggle to provide necessary medical or psychological support, transportation, a stable residence, or highly specific resources such as clothing of the quality necessary for certain kinds of jobs.

Parents who have little or no English language skills are at a particular disadvantage, in that even with sufficient material resources and a strong desire to help their children, the language barriers they face may limit the extent to which they can be supportive.

Finally, regardless of cultural and linguistic background, the parents may wish to be involved, provide support, and engage in advocacy. but simply lack knowledge as to how to best proceed. These examples illustrate the importance of the IEP team not only involving parents in the transition process but also attempting to understand the unique situations of each family, including potential obstacles to involvement. The IEP team has an obligation to provide resources to parents who experience certain kinds of obstacles, such as limited English proficiency or lack of knowledge about local employment opportunities, if these obstacles interfere with the parents' ability to participate in IEP meetings to the extent they would like.

Following are some of the questions that the IEP will need to ask in considering how to gauge the extent to which parents can support the transition process as well as their children's postsecondary goals:

- Are parents fully informed about opportunities to participate in transition planning, and do they experience logistical challenges to participation (e.g., difficulties attending IEP meetings)?

- Are parents' ideas, interests, and needs understood and respected during transition planning by the IEP team?

- What information do parents need about their rights, the rights of their children, and the availability of local resources? What information do they need about their children's disability?

- Can parental involvement be increased in constructive ways that are consistent with parental attitudes and interests?

Practice Questions

1. Which of the following is not an adaptive life skill?

   A. Use of number knowledge to tell time.

   B. Use of multiplication to calculate a tip.

   C. Use of division to adjust a recipe.

   D. Use of addition to solve a formula.

2. According to the requirements of IDEA, which of the following would be an acceptable postsecondary goal?

   A. With support from his parents, John will develop a considerably more positive outlook on life.

   B. John will be able to get around town successfully, with very little assistance from friends and family.

   C. John will join one organization that promotes cycling, one of his favorite leisure activities.

   D. Before graduation, John will identify a community college to which he may be eligible to apply.

3. Which of the following activities would be most suitable for helping to develop students' perspective-taking skills?

   A. A role play activity in which students take different positions in a debate.

   B. A hands-on activity in which students interpret the meaning of challenging instructions.

   C. An authentic activity in which students follow recipes to create healthy snacks.

   D. A group activity in which each student summarizes a different reading for the group.

4. During the first week of kindergarten, Mary's teacher observes that although Mary has no difficulty understanding requests and other verbal information, she has a definite lisp and pronounces the "s" sound as "th." What can Mary's teacher infer from this observation?

    A. Mary should be observed more closely, because she may have a receptive language impairment.

    B. Mary's lisp indicates that she has an articulation disorder and is in need of speech therapy.

    C. Mary's expressive language limitation is likely to create significant challenges to her learning.

    D. Mary may have a speech disorder, or she may just need more time to learn how to pronounce "s" correctly.

5. Following a head injury, a student experiences some paralysis in his tongue and other areas, resulting in slurred speech and distortions of certain phonemes. Which of the following is the most likely description of his impairment?

    A. Dysarthria.

    B. Phonological disorder.

    C. Cluttering.

    D. Resonance disorder.

6. Which of the following students seems to need the most support for self-determination skills?

    A. A student who prefers to be alone and devises strategies for working in isolation from peers and otherwise avoiding social interaction.

    B. A student who is experiencing anxiety because she has no preferences as to what career she might pursue following graduation.

    C. A student who is unsure which peer to ask for help with a math problem because he cannot tell which one has stronger math skills.

    D. A student who is rigid in her decision-making process and rarely revisits her decisions once they have been made.

7. Which of the following students seems to need the most support for self-advocacy skills?

   A. A student who is confident and assertive but is sometime tactless about asserting his interests.

   B. A student who has difficulty processing complex texts and prefers to read simple texts for pleasure.

   C. A student who is very hesitant about raising his hand in class or expressing himself to peers.

   D. A student who has impulse control limitations that result in her interrupting others at times.

8. Which of the following agencies would provide the most career-related counseling to an individual with a disability?

   A. Independent living center.

   B. Disability rights organization.

   C. Assistive career service.

   D. Vocational rehabilitation agency.

Answers to Practice Questions

1. D.

   Choice D is correct because it is not clear that solving the formula has any relevance to functioning in everyday settings. Choices A, B, and C are incorrect because each option describes a meaningful everyday action.

2. C.

   Choice C is correct because it identifies one clear, measurable, postsecondary goal. Choices A and B are incorrect because they are too vague to be readily measurable—it is unclear what exactly it means to have a "more positive outlook" or to be able to "get around town" successfully.

3. A.

Choice A is correct because by taking different positions on a debate topic, students may gain insight into perspectives other than their own. Choice B is incorrect because the focus will be on interpreting instructions, and if there are inconsistencies or ambiguities, the students will probably focus on the possible meanings of inconsistent or ambiguous items rather than analyzing the perspective of the individual who created the instructions. Choice C is incorrect because perspective-taking skills are not likely to be involved when following a recipe (except perhaps in the limited sense of trying to interpret inconsistent or ambiguous statements in the recipe). Choice D is also incorrect because the activity does not appear to directly involve perspective-taking skills.

4. D.

Choice D is correct because lisping could indicate a problem such as articulation disorder, but given Mary's age, it might instead simply reflect a temporary difficulty with the pronunciation of one particular sound. Choice A is incorrect because Mary's difficulty falls under the heading of expressive rather than receptive language. Choice B is incorrect because, as noted, it is not certain that Mary has an articulation disorder. Choice C is incorrect because it is implausible that difficulty producing one sound would impair a child's learning experience.

5. A.

Choice A is correct because dysarthria is illustrated by speech impairments such as slurring and distortions as a result of paralysis to the musculature that controls speech. Choice B is incorrect because phonological disorder is an impairment in the ability to distinguish specific speech sounds. Choice C is incorrect because cluttering is indicated by speech that is too fast and/or irregular. Choice D is incorrect because resonance disorder is indicated by too much or too little nasal flow during speech.

6. B.

Although anxiety about future careers is commonplace among students, choice B is correct because the student is not even able to articulate her preferences for her future career. Choice A is incorrect, even though the student's behavior is problematic, because the student seems to have no difficulty formulating a goal (being alone) and implementing strategies for achieving that goal. Choice C is incorrect, because even though the student is experiencing difficulty making a choice, there is a good reason for his uncertainty. Choice D is incorrect because the student appears to have no difficulty making decisions.

7.   C.

Choice C is correct, because the student is experiencing difficulties expressing himself in more than one setting. Choice A is incorrect, because the student seems to have no trouble advocating for himself; he simply needs some guidance about conventions of polite interaction. Choice B is incorrect because there is no information about self-advocacy skills but simply about the student's preferences. Choice D is incorrect for the same reason as choice B.

8.   D.

Choice D is correct, because career-related counseling is among the many services provided by a vocational rehabilitation agency. Although an independent living center might assist with career counseling, such centers provide non-vocational services as well, and thus choice A is incorrect. Although a disability rights organization might direct an individual to a career counseling service, choice B is incorrect because such services are not part of the mission of such organizations. Choice C is incorrect because there are no agencies that are routinely identified as "assistive career services."

CHAPTER 8

COMPETENCY 0007
Analysis, Synthesis, and Application

This chapter discusses how teachers develop and implement instruction and interventions for students with disabilities on the basis of numerous sources, including background knowledge, student profiles, and the results of formal and informal assessments.

The competencies discussed in earlier chapters are tested on the NYSTCE Students with Disabilities exam by means of selected-response questions. The competency discussed in the current chapter is tested by means of one constructed-response question in which you are presented with a scenario and asked to analyze artifacts such as samples of student work or excerpts from an Individualized Education Program (IEP). Thus, a number of scenarios involving individual students are presented in this chapter.

PI (a): Analysis of profiles of students with mild, moderate, severe, or multiple disabilities

This section touches on the analysis of the profiles of students with different levels of disability. A **profile** is a summary of a student's strengths and areas of need, created on the basis of formal assessment, informal observation, and/or other sources of information.

A disability is not an all-or-nothing entity. There is variability in level of severity for each of the 13 categories of disability outlined in the Individuals with Disabilities Education Act (IDEA). When planning instruction or interventions for a student, the teacher will need to attend to the level of severity of the student's disability. For example, compared with students who have mild or moderate disabilities, students with severe disabilities

- tend to spend more time outside of the regular classroom.

- tend to need support in a broader range of areas, including adaptive life skills.

- tend to need more intensive support in each area.

- may not respond as readily to intervention.

- may not progress as much in independence.

Profile Analysis

In this chapter, and throughout the book, emphasis has been placed on the uniqueness of each student. For example, when modifying instruction and developing interventions for a student with a disability, the teacher or Committee on Special Education (CSE) will need to be aware of those characteristics and patterns of change that distinguish the student. In addition, some aspects of the student's profile, such as the student's age, gender, and primary language, as well as the nature of the student's disability, will provide general guidance as to the best way to support the student. This point can be illustrated by a consideration of the areas in which the student struggles, and by a contrast between skill deficits and performance deficits.

Areas of Need

When examining information about a student with a disability, the teacher or CSE will need to consider the area or areas in which the student is likely to need support. The following are some of the key areas that should be considered:

- cognitive functioning

- linguistic functioning

- communication

- social interaction

- self-control and self-regulation

- self-esteem and self-efficacy

- mobility and physical access

- adaptive life skills

For example, a blind student whose cognitive and linguistic functioning are normal will need support with written communication, with physical access to facilities, and with adaptive life skills that require vision. This student may need support in other areas, such as social interaction and self-esteem, depending on the particulars of his situation.

Skill Deficits vs. Performance Deficits

A **skill deficit** is implicated when a student does not know how to perform a particular behavior. Examples of skill deficits with respect to participation in social interactions, for example, include the following:

- A student responds to a verbal challenge with silence, because she does not know any verbal strategies for responding to challenges.

- A student responds inappropriately to the tears of another student, because he does not know what constitutes a supportive or polite response.

- A student does not join peers in the use of a particular piece of playground equipment, because he does not understand how the equipment works.

- A student does not join in group activities during recess, because she does not know how to initiate contact with peers.

A student who knows how to perform a behavior but chooses not to, or is incapable of doing so owing to some mental or physical barrier, has a **performance deficit**. Examples of performance deficits with respect to participation in social interactions include the following:

- A student responds to a verbal challenge aggressively, although she understands what a more appropriate response would be, because she experiences difficulty controlling her anger.

- A student responds to the tears of another student by laughing, even though he knows this is an inappropriate response, because he becomes very upset in the presence of suffering and laughs in order to hide his distress.

- A student does not join peers in the use of a particular piece of playground equipment, although he understands how to use the equipment, because his disability has temporarily reduced his physical dexterity.

- A student does not join in group activities during recess, although she is aware of how to initiate contact with peers, because she is extremely anxious about being teased for her disability.

The Case of Sheila

From the preceding examples, it should be clear that concerns about an individual student's behavior must be addressed differently depending on whether the underlying issue is a skill deficit or a performance deficit. For example, consider the following teacher note about a 3rd grade student with an emotional disturbance:

"Yesterday Sheila completed her in-class essay for the first time all year. It was a vivid description of her younger brother, with fewer grammatical errors and more varied word choice than usual. She also commented insightfully that when he gets older he will probably want to spend more time with male friends than with her. Today Sheila turned in a fragment more typical of prior work, an uninspired, poorly written description of a local park."

Apparently, Sheila has a performance deficit rather than a skill deficit with respect to essay writing. She is capable of writing well but does not usually demonstrate that skill. The teacher should consider the possibility that Sheila only writes well when the topic inspires her. If this is the case, the teacher could support Sheila through strategies such as the following:

- Learn more about what topics do versus do not interest Sheila. Topics that interest her may include anything of personal relevance, people in general, her family in particular, or specifically her brother.

- Ensure that Sheila understands that she is capable of writing well.

- Help Sheila understand that variability in her writing performance is related to her interest level. Discuss with her the idea that not all writing tasks will be equally interesting.

- Explore ways of helping Sheila make connections between writing assignments and topics that interest her.

> **PI (b): Interpreting and synthesizing information from formal and informal assessments (e.g., individual achievement tests, curriculum-based assessments, adaptive behavior scales, functional behavioral assessments, teacher observations) of academic and/or functional performance to determine a student's strengths and needs**

The role of assessment in determining a student's strengths and needs in various areas is discussed in Chapter 4. This section focuses on the interpretation and synthesis of information from behavioral assessments in particular.

Data Collection by Teachers

Teachers encourage desirable classroom behaviors in order to maintain a positive classroom environment and to help students develop good habits and social skills. For example, teaching students how to disagree with each other's ideas in a respectful way serves the dual purpose of helping maintain a positive classroom environment and helping students develop a social skill of great importance both within and beyond the classroom.

In order to encourage desirable classroom behaviors while discouraging undesirable ones, teachers need information about students' current behavior, particularly if a student is struggling in some respect or has a disability that seems to manifest in problem behaviors. A variety of strategies, both indirect and direct, are available to teachers for obtaining information about student behavior:

- Indirect assessment can be used to obtain information about behavior without directly observing the student. For example, a teacher who is concerned about a particular student's social awkwardness may interview the student, as well as parents, other teachers, educational specialists familiar with the child, and school administrators. If the student has a disability, data previously gathered by the Committee on Special Education (CSE) is likely to be considered as well. Although these strategies can yield essential information, direct observation of the student in social settings such as the classroom would be needed in order for the teacher to be fully informed about the extent and possible causes of the student's awkwardness.

- Direct assessment is used to obtain information about student behavior through first-hand observations of the student. For example, teachers can use observational assessments to obtain descriptions of student behavior in natural settings such as the classroom. Assessments such as checklists, rating scales, duration records, and time-sampling records all rely on direct observation, as does simply observing a student in an informal way.

Regardless of the specific approaches to gathering data that are used, it is critical for the teacher to develop a system for recording the data, so that student behavior can be monitored over time and changes more readily understood.

Data Collection by the CSE and Others

The CSE, as well as educational professionals who are not part of the team, will typically use a combination of direct and indirect assessments as a basis of learning more about the behavior of a student with a disability. As discussed in Chapter 4, the CSE may also need to conduct a functional behavior assessment.

Functional Behavior Assessment

IDEA requires that a functional behavior assessment be conducted if the CSE has concerns about the behavior of a student with a disability or if the student has engaged in extreme misbehavior that would result in suspension or removal from the current educational setting for more than 10 days. Functional behavior assessments can also be conducted with students who exhibit problem behaviors but have not have been identified as having a disability.

A functional behavior assessment (FBA) consists of strategies for determining what causes and sustains problem behaviors, and for developing interventions that might best address those behaviors. FBA is based on the assumption that behavior serves specific purposes in specific situations. When a student misbehaves, the misbehavior serves some particular purpose, and intervention is not likely to be effective unless this purpose is understood.

The need for understanding the purpose of a problem behavior is illustrated by the fact that the same behavior may serve different purposes for different students. For example, one student who repeatedly talks back to the teacher may do so because he resents the way the teacher treats him, while another student may exhibit the same behavior because she is seeking peer approval. Clearly, a different remedy is needed for each student. The first student needs to develop a more effective and appropriate way of expressing concerns about the teacher, while the second student needs to learn more appropriate ways of seeking approval from peers. In short, the intervention that will be most suitable for each student is different because the causes of their misbehavior are different, even though the same sort of misbehavior is expressed in each case.

For students such as those described above, FBA would address questions about how to describe the problem behavior, where and when the problem behavior is observed, what the underlying cause of the behavior seems to be, and what intervention(s) are most likely to be effective.

Description

Descriptions of problem behavior in FBA should consist of concrete, specific statements rather than vague summations. For example, rather than stating that a student is "rude," a description of the problem behavior might be "the student talks back to the teacher during one-on-one interactions initiated by the teacher." Judgments about the student's character, hypotheses about the causes of the problem behavior, and predictions about future behavior should be avoided in these descriptions.

Context

FBA requires the gathering of information about contextual influences on the problem behavior. That is, information is needed about when, where, and under what conditions the problem behavior is exhibited and about what contextual factors seem to increase or diminish the frequency and intensity of the behavior. In order to obtain such information, the student will need to be observed in different contexts. Conversations with the student, and perhaps also parents and other adults, will be helpful as well.

Although IDEA specifies when FBA must be conducted, the law does not indicate which methods of assessment should be used. Generally, information is needed about the antecedents as well as the consequences of the targeted behavior in order to understand its causes. For example, regarding a student who repeatedly talks back to his teacher, it might be noted whether the student talks back to just one particular teacher, to all teachers, or to all adults generally. It might also be noted whether the student is more likely to talk back when peers are present, and if so, how these other students respond. If the student's tendency to talk back seems relatively independent of context, an interview might be needed with the student to determine whether he is aware that talking back is considered inappropriate and whether he is capable of more appropriate exchanges if motivated to do so and not distracted by anger or some other strong emotional state.

Cause

FBA yields hypotheses about the underlying cause of a problem behavior—i.e., informed guesses about what purpose or purposes the behavior serves for the student. Talking back to the teacher, for example, might reflect one or more of the following causes:

- resentment toward authority figures

- concerns about one particular teacher

- insecurity about the ability to succeed academically

- lack of knowledge about appropriate interaction with others

- poor impulse control

- a need for more attention from adults

- a need for approval from peers

The list presented above is not exhaustive. The fact that there are many possible causes for the same behavior highlights the importance of multiple approaches to gathering data, including observation of the student and conversation with the student about his/her thoughts and feelings.

Although there are many possible specific causes for a problem behavior, the CSE will need to be particularly cognizant of the distinction between skill deficits and performance deficits discussed earlier in the chapter, as the distinction has important implications for intervention.

Further information about FBA is provided in the next section. The following is an example.

Example of FBA: John Doe

Following is a brief example of an FBA for a mildly retarded 1st grader who has some difficulties with impulse control.

Name: John Doe   **Date:** 9/14/15

Description of Behavior	
Behavior:	Talks out of turn; interrupts teacher & peers.
Setting(s):	Classroom and wherever else students congregate (e.g., cafeteria and playground).
Antecedents:	Seems more common when anxious.
Frequency:	At least once per set of remarks by teacher or conversation with peers.
Duration:	Interjected comments are usually brief.
Impact:	No apparent academic or emotional effects. Some peers seem to get angry.
Prior interventions:	None
Hypothesized Function of Behavior	
Emotional:	Seems anxious; speaking freely seems to reduce anxiety.
Cognitive:	States that he likes talking to people; considers his interruptions "talking."
Behavioral:	Some peers laugh when he interrupts the teacher; laughter may be reinforcing.
Social:	Seems to want to engage with peers and fit in.
Other:	He is the second youngest of five siblings.

PI (c): Strategies for developing and implementing behavioral interventions for students with disabilities, including strategies for providing positive behavioral interventions and supports

This section focuses on strategies for developing and implementing behavioral interventions for all students, including students with disabilities.

FBA and Intervention

As noted earlier, FBA yields hypotheses about which interventions might reduce the incidence or intensity of the problem behavior. These interventions will be closely related to hypotheses about the underlying cause of the behavior and will include suggestions for "replacement behaviors" or behaviors that are likely to serve the same purpose as the problem behavior. In short, emphasis is placed on changing the behavior rather than the purpose that it serves. A student who talks back to the teacher because he seeks approval from peers must learn effective strategies for gaining approval rather than being expected to give up the desire for approval. In this example, the strategies for gaining peer approval that might be taught to the student during an intervention are the replacement behaviors for the undesirable behavior of talking back to the teacher.

Behavior Intervention Plan

The CSE uses information from the FBA to develop a **behavior intervention plan (BIP)**, which describes the behaviors that are to be changed as well as the intervention strategy or strategies for effecting change. The focus of these interventions is not on controlling the problem behaviors but rather on fostering positive replacement behaviors.

Content of BIP

IDEA requires that the following elements be described in the BIP:

- the targeted problem behavior
- the types and effectiveness of interventions that have been tried already
- the interventions that will be used

- the specific goals of the interventions

- the approach to evaluating the effectiveness of the interventions

- the plan for reviewing the success of the interventions

- the plan for disseminating intervention results and other information to parents

- the plan for how to support the student if his/her behavior reaches crisis proportions

Other information is recommended for inclusion in the BIP but not required. This information includes, for example, the following:

- a summary of student strengths

- a statement regarding the purpose of the problem behavior

- a description of the positive replacement behavior

Success of BIP

An intervention proposed in the BIP is most likely to achieve long-term success if the following conditions are met:

- close alignment between intervention and cause of problem behavior

- close alignment between intervention and student's strengths and needs

- choice of replacement behaviors most likely to receive environmental support

- choice of least intrusive and least complex intervention

- choice of intervention most acceptable to those responsible for implementing the plan

- choice of intervention most acceptable to the student

- choice of intervention with greatest systemic support

Example of a BIP: John Doe

The following is an excerpt from a BIP for the mildly retarded first grader described earlier.

Name: John Doe

Behavior:	Talks out of turn; interrupts teacher and peers.
Causes:	Belief that interruptions are appropriate; desire for acceptance from peers; mild anxiety may contribute.
Goals:	Reduce interruptions of teacher and peers; increase appropriate conversational input.
Strategies implemented by:	Teacher, counselor, parents.
Preventive strategy:	Use social narratives, modeling, and informal discussion to teach that interruptions are not desirable conversational input, and to enhance conversational skills.
Preventive strategy:	Use reminders when appropriate prior to interactions with others.
Preventive strategy:	Teach simple self-control strategy for use in conversational settings.
Reactive strategy:	Use cueing following interruptions.
Other:	Discuss possible anxiety issues with CSE.

PI (d): Applying research- or evidence-based practices that have been validated for learners with specific characteristics and for specific settings by recommending appropriate interventions for a given student

The importance of research- and/or evidence-based practices, and the importance of tailoring interventions to given students, is stressed throughout this book. An intervention may work well with some types of students, or in some settings, but not with other students or in other settings. For example, a student with a traumatic brain injury and a low-performing student with attention deficit hyperactivity disorder may struggle to an approximately equal extent with academic material, but the support that each student needs will differ somewhat, as the former struggles to comprehend the material while the latter struggles to pay attention to it. Moreover, the interventions most appropriate for a given student will need to be tailored to that particular student's combination of strengths and needs, so what works best with one student may need to be modified for another student, even if both students experience the same disability to approximately the same degree of severity, and have similarity in age and other characteristics. For example, two sixth graders with mild mental retardation will require somewhat different kinds of support if one student gets along well with peers and enjoys learning while the other one dislikes learning and feels insecure in social settings. Both students will need specific kinds of academic support, but the second student will also need emotional and social support in order to promote more positive attitudes toward school and greater self-confidence in interactions with peers.

> **PI (e): Applying research- or evidence-based explicit and systematic instruction and intervention in reading, including reading in the content areas, by recommending appropriate interventions for a given student**

This section provides information on both prevention and intervention as methods of addressing reading difficulties.

Reading Programs

Programs designed to teach reading can be distinguished in terms of their content and their specific role in the classroom. For example, a distinction can be made among the characteristics and purposes of core reading programs, supplemental reading programs, and intensive intervention programs.

Core Reading Programs

A **core reading program** is the basic program for teaching reading in the general education classroom. Although teachers may use supplementary materials and methods as well, the core reading program is the one that all teachers will rely on to support instruction in all aspects of reading.

A strong core reading program will provide teachers with clear descriptions of the following:

- Program objectives

- Scope and sequence of program

- How program materials are organized

- How to implement instructional approaches used in program

- How to manage specific details of program activities

- How to assess student progress in reading

In addition, if implemented appropriately, a strong core reading program will reflect characteristics such as the following:

- Explicit, systematic, balanced instruction in all reading-related skills

- Coherent instructional design

- A variety of texts, instructional approaches, and student activities

- Opportunities for student practice, participation, discussion, and feedback

- Progression from easier to more challenging activities

Supplemental Reading Programs

As the name suggests, **supplemental reading programs** are used to supplement a core reading program. The supplemental program does not replace the core program but rather supports and extends the core.

Typically, a supplemental program focuses on one or two components of reading (e.g., word identification and fluency). The supplemental program will be needed in a particular school for one of two reasons:

- If evidence suggests that the core reading program is not sufficiently effective or is not providing sufficient support for one component of reading, such as fluency, a supplemental reading program can fill in the gap.

- Individual students who are not performing well with respect to one component of reading, including students with reading-related disabilities, may benefit from a supplemental reading program.

Intensive Intervention Programs

Intensive intervention programs are intended to support students with reading difficulties. These programs may focus on one, several, or all components of reading. The goal of these programs is for students to be functioning at grade level. The students who are served by intensive intervention programs may be poor readers, or they may have a reading-related disability.

Response to Intervention

Implementation of supplemental and intensive intervention programs for reading are often carried out within a Response to Intervention (RTI) framework. As noted in Chapter 2, RTI is a school-wide, multilevel approach to identifying students at risk for reading difficulties and other problems, monitoring student progress, and providing increasingly tailored interventions to students who need them.

Prevention

The first step in preventing reading difficulties is making sure that good instructional practices are being implemented in the general education classroom. In addition, it is critical that supplemental reading programs are available for struggling readers. Teachers and reading specialists should provide extra support for struggling readers as soon as possible, including explicit, systematic, and intensive support in areas for which weaknesses are discernible.

Intervention

Reading interventions focus on developing one or more of the reading skills discussed in Chapter 6, including phonological and phonemic awareness, decoding, fluency, and comprehension. Regardless of skill, the components of an effective intervention include the following:

- clear instructional objectives

- activities appropriate to the child's level and interests

- guided practice

- independent practice

- regular reviews

- formative evaluations

> **PI (f): Applying research- or evidence-based explicit and systematic instruction and intervention in writing by recommending appropriate interventions for a given student**

Writing instruction is discussed in Chapter 6, section PI (f). This section presents a case study to illustrate the process by which a teacher might develop an appropriate intervention for a given student who struggles with writing.

The Case of Jay

Jay is a fourth grade student with mild dyslexia who also experiences difficulties with some but not all aspects of writing. Jay's posture, pencil grip, and handwriting are roughly normal for his age. The content of his writing is average; although when he addresses a topic that inspires him, the teacher feels that his writing is quite strong. He seems to write more slowly than average, but not to the extent that he runs short of time on tests and in-class activities. On the whole, Jay's teacher has two main concerns. First, Jay performs very poorly on assignments in which he must self-correct, incorporate feedback, or otherwise edit work that he has already completed. He tends to make few or no changes to what he has already written. Second, the teacher's concern is that Jay dislikes writing, particularly when he knows that he may need to revise his work. Apart from these concerns, the teacher gathers from Jay's Individualized Education Program (IEP), from observation, and from conversations with parents as well as Jay himself, that Jay is a happy, socially well-adjusted student who struggles with reading owing to his dyslexia and with the elements of writing described above. Jay receives all of his instruction in the general education classroom, with some modifications to instructional methods and assessment as necessitated by his dyslexia. Jay has an open, friendly relationship with the teacher.

Developing an Intervention for Jay

The writing process is often divided into the stages of planning, writing, and revision.

Although Jay has negative feelings toward writing in general, it appears that his main issues are with the revision stage, as his ability to plan and write are at least average for his age.

Because Jay has a good relationship with the teacher, the teacher might begin by talking openly with him about why he dislikes writing and, in particular, the revision process. The teacher needs to determine whether the problem is a skill deficit or a performance deficit (see section PI (a) above for definitions).

If the problem is a skill deficit, the teacher will need to seek information about the cause. For example, it is possible that Jay dislikes revisions because, owing to his dyslexia, he finds it difficult to read his own writing. If this is the case, the intervention might focus on providing Jay with support during the revision process similar to what he ordinarily uses when reading. For example, Jay could be encouraged to write using large font and to use rereading strategies when reviewing what he has written.

If the problem is a performance deficit, the nature of Jay's reluctance will need to be explored. For example, it may be that Jay is simply impatient and does not enjoy revisiting prior work. Another possibility is that the revision process sparks insecurity about his ability to write. Jay's openness with the teacher may allow the teacher to explore these and other possibilities in conversation with him.

> **PI (g): Applying research- or evidence-based explicit and systematic instruction and intervention in mathematics by recommending appropriate interventions for a given student**

Mathematics instruction is discussed in Chapter 6, section PI (g). This section presents a case study illustrating how appropriate interventions can be developed for an individual student.

◼ The Case of Rhonda

A high school math teacher joins the CSE of a student who she will have in her ninth grade class. The following is some of the information the teacher obtains from discussions with the team and examination of the IEP:

- Rhonda is a 14-year-old student who has been diagnosed with dyscalculia and who has received special education services since fourth grade.

- Rhonda is diabetic and manages the disease independently through dietary choices and self-administered medication.

- Rhonda's grades in classes other than math are mostly As and Bs. Her scores on standardized tests in subjects other than math have ranged from the 47th percentile to the 73rd percentile.

- Rhonda's physical, emotional, social, and behavioral functioning appears to be normal. Her study skills are appropriate for her age. Apart from mathematics, her cognitive functioning appears to be normal.

- Rhonda generally enjoys school and hopes to attend college upon graduation.

- Rhonda's dyscalculia manifests in all aspects of mathematics. She has difficulty understanding, recalling and applying mathematical knowledge. Her mathematical working memory is limited, resulting in difficulties with calculation and problem solving.

- Rhonda works very hard at mathematics, but she dislikes the subject because she frequently experiences confusion and disorientation during mathematical activities. She also states that in recent years the anxiety she experiences during mathematics is minimal, because she knows what to expect but that she continues to be easily frustrated when she fails to understand or remember key information and when her performance is poor.

- Rhonda has received instructional modifications such as supplementary materials, instructional support such as tutoring, assistive technology such as calculators, and accommodations such as extended time on tests. She has never been removed from the general education setting or received anything other than the general education curriculum in mathematics.

- Evidence suggests that the special education supports and services provided to Rhonda are effective. Prior to receiving these supports and services, Rhonda was unable to pass her math classes, and she scored in the 1st percentile on standardized tests of mathematics. Since receiving these supports and services, she has passed all of her math classes, and she has scored between the 14th and 19th percentiles on standardized tests of mathematics.

Developing an Instructional Plan for Rhonda

The teacher will need to consult with the rest of CSE when developing an instructional plan for Rhonda. Although special education supports and services appear to have been effective, the teacher should keep the following points in mind when developing an instructional plan:

- Not all of the supports and services formerly available to Rhonda may continue to be available in high school.

- High school mathematics differs in content and difficulty from what Rhonda has previously experienced. Thus, some of the supports and services she receives may need to be modified or replaced. The teacher should try to anticipate such changes in advance, based on her knowledge of content and her pedagogical content knowledge.

- Rhonda's math achievement still has room for improvement. Moreover, the frustration she continues to experience over mathematics is an important area to address.

In summary, a suitable instructional plan for Rhonda is likely to include the following elements:

- a continuation of the supports and services formerly provided, to the greatest extent possible, with modifications as appropriate

- strategies for helping reduce the frustration that Rhonda experiences when working on mathematics

PI (h): Applying research- or evidence-based strategies for identifying and teaching essential concepts, vocabulary, and content across the general curriculum by recommending appropriate interventions for a given student

Section PI (h) in Chapter 6 describes instructional practices for teaching concepts, vocabulary, and content across the general curriculum; sections PI (b) through PI (d) also include information about tailoring instruction to individual students.

PI (i): Applying research- or evidence-based practices for teaching learning strategies and study skills by recommending appropriate interventions for a given student

Sections PI (h) and, especially, PI (i) in Chapter 6 describe instructional practices for teaching learning strategies and study skills. The current section illustrates how a study skills intervention can be designed and implemented with a particular student.

The Case of Pete

Pete is a third grader with multiple, mild learning disabilities. One of the short-term goals developed by the CSE is to foster Pete's homework skills, as it has been discovered that Pete's work on homework assignments is sporadic and unfocused. The team believes that better homework habits will reinforce in-class activities designed to promote Pete's success with the general education curriculum and will provide Pete with skills that can contribute to future academic success. The team has noticed that Pete's parents do not provide him with much guidance about homework.

Developing an Intervention for Pete

Both Pete and his parents would benefit from direct instruction in strategies that support a beneficial homework experience. Pete could be taught the following strategies:

- use an assignment book to keep track of homework assignments

- find a comfortable, distraction-free place to work on homework

- estimate the time needed for each assignment

- set goals for the completion of each assignment

- plan a strategy for the completion of each assignment

- use metacognitive strategies (see Chapter 6 for examples) to monitor progress on each assignment

- proofread assignments before turning them in

Pete's parents could be taught strategies for supporting his homework activities, including the following:

- help establish homework routines

- help provide a minimally distracting place for doing homework

- provide necessary supplies for homework activities

- allow sufficient time for doing homework

- through words and actions, show that homework is important

- offer praise for completion of homework assignments

- discuss instances in which homework benefitted comprehension and/ or achievement

PI (j): Applying research- or evidence-based strategies for teaching communication and social skills by recommending appropriate interventions for a given student

Chapter 7 describes the teaching of communication and social skills to all students, including students with disabilities. This section uses a case study to illustrate how interventions can be developed for a particular student.

The Case of Jill

Jill is a 6th grade student with a traumatic brain injury that results in difficulties with impulse control and emotional self-regulation. Although Jill's academic functioning and social skills are generally normal, she struggles with anger management, particularly when interacting with others. The CSE is concerned that Jill is increasingly alienating her peers, including friends, through outbursts and hostile remarks she often makes during social interactions. Jill shares these concerns. She feels that she can control herself sometimes but that she needs to be able to do so more consistently.

Developing an Intervention for Jill

Jill might benefit from anger management training that is tailored to her particular age and cognitive abilities. Generally, **anger management training** focuses on providing students with skills that help them to avoid situations that create anger, to deal with their anger when it is experienced, and to manage conflict with others. The following are some of the strategies that may be provided in anger management training:

- Relaxation techniques can help students reduce the likelihood of becoming angry as well as the severity of anger when it is experienced.

- "Self-talk" strategies can help students monitor their responses in different situations, so that they can manage their own anger in its early stages, as well as reframing social situations in more positive ways so that the severity of their anger (or the likelihood of their becoming angry in the first place) is diminished.

- Social skills training in areas such as conflict resolution can help students avoid conflict and develop positive verbal strategies for dealing with conflict when it is inevitable.

Because of Jill's brain damage, danger may continue to be a regular presence in her life, but relaxation techniques may reduce its severity to manageable levels. Self-talk strategies may also help with anger management. Although Jill may not need training in all types of social skills, since her social functioning is generally normal and she maintains friendships, she may benefit from training in specific areas, such as how to apologize for and provide explanations for her outbursts.

Chapter 7 describes the teaching of functional and independent living skills to students with disabilities. This section provides additional information, with an emphasis on transition.

Academic vs. Functional Skills

Academic skills are critical to functioning in daily life, but mastery of these skills does not guarantee that a person will be able to function independently. For example, knowledge about the nutritional content of different foods, although critical to survival, does not guarantee that a person can independently prepare a healthy meal. In contrast, **functional skills** allow a person to function independently in real-life domestic, occupational, and social settings. Functional skills include the ability to select, purchase, and cook nutritionally beneficial foods. (See discussion of adaptive life skills in section PI (c) of Chapter 7 for further discussion.)

Functional Skills

Functional skills are an integral part of the general education curriculum. In addition, for a student with a disability, the CSE must make decisions about the kinds of functional skills that should be supported and the extent of support, particularly if the nature of the disability prevents full mastery of general education curricula.

Once they have graduated from school, students with disabilities may find it challenging to function independently in domestic, occupational, and/or social settings. For this reason, the CSE may need to develop and oversee means of supporting the functional skills of these students. In order to do so, the CSE will need to address a number of critical questions.

The first question for the CSE is whether a functional curriculum needs to be developed for the student, particularly as the time of graduation nears. Such a curriculum may be needed if the following conditions are observed:

- The student has significant difficulties with learning and transfer.

- The student seems well below peers in skill development.

- The student spends relatively little time participating in the general education curriculum.

Other questions for the CSE pertain to the details of the student's life after graduation. For example:

- Where might the student live?

- What kind of work does the student hope to do?

- Who might the student associate with?

- What kinds of support might others provide to the student?

When considering these questions, the CSE will need to monitor the extent to which the student's planned educational experience is aligned with post-graduation goals and whether progress toward those goals has been adequate or will require some adjustment to the support currently being provided to the student.

Systematic Instruction and Functional Skills

Systematic instruction has been shown to be an effective method of teaching functional skills to students with disabilities. Characteristics of systematic instruction that contribute to its effectiveness in this regard include the focus on specific skills or components of skills, the sequencing of skills in order of increasing complexity, the creation of opportunities for student practice, and the provision of teacher guidance throughout the learning process.

This section touches on some of the resources and strategies available to assist students as they transition into postsecondary environments, particularly those involving employment and independent living. Some of these resources and strategies are school-based, in the sense of being provided by the CSE and others in the secondary school setting, while others are provided by individuals and agencies in the community.

School-Based Support for Transition

School-based resources and strategies that provide transition support to students include the following:

- training in self-determination and self-advocacy

- social skills training

- psychological services

- community experiences

- opportunities for work experience

- vocational guidance

- higher education-related guidance

Individual Support for Transition

Transition can be facilitated by the addition of key community members to the CSE or by involving these individuals in the collaborative task of providing support to the student. The following are some of the important roles that can be played by these individual community members:

- role model

- mentor

- informational resource

- service provider

- advocate

- liaison between agencies

As this list suggests, individual community members can play a variety of different roles during the transition process and in supporting postsecondary living.

Agency Support for Transition

Successful transition can also be facilitated by the involvement of community agencies. For example, **independent living centers** are local, nonresidential agencies that help individuals with disabilities lead self-sufficient lives. A specifically work-related example is the **vocational rehabilitation agency**, a federal- and state-funded agency that provides employment-related services to students who qualify. This agency provides services such as the following:

- career counseling and guidance

- resume development

- postsecondary training and education

- job placement

- job coaching and training

- assistive technology

- supported employment

Supported Employment

Supported employment is a community-based approach to promoting the employment of individuals with disabilities in integrated settings (i.e., those in which a substantial number of employees do not have disabilities) through various kinds of support. For example, in the **Individual Placement and Support (IPS)** approach, supported employment teams housed within community agencies provide coordinated services to individuals with disabilities, beginning with the development of a plan for seeking employment, and continuing with job search assistance, interview training, and on-the-job support.

Coordination of Support

The school- and community-based resources and strategies used to facilitate postsecondary goals should be coordinated, in part because each individual's goals will tend to be related. An individual with limited mobility, for example, will have transportation needs that include access to stores (in order to achieve domestic living goals) and access to the workplace (in order to achieve employment goals). For this individual, the achievement of transportation goals may be related to decisions about place of residence, place of employment, and allocation of personal finances. Thus, transportation needs should not be considered an isolated problem during transition planning.

Practice Questions

1.   Under which of the following conditions would a functional behavior assessment be legally required for a student with a disability?

   A.   The student exhibits rude and intolerant behavior toward classmates throughout the school year.

   B.   The student commits an act of aggression that would ordinarily result in a two-week suspension.

   C.   The student leaves school early one afternoon without informing anyone of his destination.

   D.   The student complains of diminishing intellectual functioning that impairs his ability to learn.

2.   Which of the following would be the most appropriate description of problem behavior in a functional behavior assessment?

   A.   Juan is an angry young man.

   B.   Juan frequently exhibits verbal hostility toward classmates, and he sometimes gets into physical fights with them.

   C.   Juan feels threatened by his peers, so he often interacts with them in a hostile manner, picking fights with them on occasion.

   D.   Juan responds to criticism from peers with verbal and physical aggression because he has learned these patterns of response from his father.

3.   Which of the following is not a required part of a behavioral intervention plan?

   A.   A list of all possible interventions for the student.

   B.   A summary of the goals of the proposed intervention.

   C.   A description of how intervention results will be evaluated.

   D.   A discussion of how intervention results will be communicated to parents.

4. Devon, a student with an intellectual disability, is having difficulty operating a new software program that his classmates have been successfully using for several days. Devon's teacher believes that he has the ability to use the program successfully and independently but that he becomes confused when attempting the sequence of steps necessary to run the program's basic functions. Although the teacher is likely to use more than one approach to help Devon, which of the following approaches should be the focus of the teacher's efforts?

A. The teacher should provide Devon with explicit instruction in which the steps for using the program's basic functions are defined and explained.

B. The teacher should create a group activity in which students in each group take turns using the program while the others record data from the screen.

C. The teacher should model for Devon the sequence of steps by which the programs' basic functions are run.

D. The teacher should develop an alternative activity for Devon that would achieve the instructional objectives for him.

5. Which of the following students appears to have a skill deficit?

A. A student ignores his teacher when she questions him because he has a hearing impairment and did not realize that she had been talking to him.

B. A student ignores his teacher when she questions him because he is unaware of the social convention of responding to people when questioned.

C. A student ignores his teacher when she questions him because he is angry with the teacher and wishes to convey his anger indirectly.

D. A student ignores his teacher when she questions him because he is distracted by an emotional conflict he is currently experiencing.

6. Lina is a high school senior with a mild emotional disturbance. The CSE determines that one of Lina's postsecondary goals should be to establish a relationship with an experienced individual in order to obtain regular, on-the-job support concerning non-technical matters (e.g., getting along with co-workers). In particular, Lina needs to find someone she can call for guidance when she becomes frustrated or angry. The CSE decides that the most suitable individual for this role would be Lina's guidance counselor at school, as all agree that Lina has an excellent relationship with the counselor. What is likely to be the main limitation of the CSE's choice?

    A. The guidance counselor is unlikely to know much about issues that Lina will face in the workplace.

    B. The guidance counselor will probably be unwilling to help Lina further once she graduates.

    C. The guidance counselor may not have time to help Lina at the times when she needs immediate support.

    D. The guidance counselor may provide the wrong kinds of advice to Lina in critical situations.

7. Which of the following resources would most benefit a high school junior who has entered the career preparation stage and who has been learning about the postsecondary training needed to become an auto mechanic?

    A. The autobiography of an automobile executive who began his career as a mechanic.

    B. A field trip to a local garage in order to observe mechanics at work.

    C. A documentary about careers in auto mechanics and related fields.

    D. The opportunity to shadow an actual mechanic in his place of work.

8. Laura is a blind elementary school student who has begun thinking about the kinds of careers that would suit her. Which of the following actions would best promote Laura's growing self-determination?

    A. Encouraging Laura's teacher to use authentic activities when teaching Laura.

    B. Asking Laura's parents to discuss careers and career choices with her.

    C. Helping Laura develop academic skills that will support her choice of careers.

    D. Inviting Laura to join the CSE and participate in planning discussions.

Answers to Practice Questions

1. B.

   Choice B is correct because IDEA requires that a functional behavior assessment be conducted when a student with a disability engages in behavior serious enough to merit suspension. Choices A and C are incorrect because neither of the particular behaviors in itself would be sufficient to require a functional behavior assessment unless the IEP team were concerned about the behavior. Choice D is incorrect for similar reasons, and because the student's complaint pertains to cognitive functioning rather than behavior.

2. B.

   Choice B is correct because it presents a clear, concrete description of the problem behaviors. Choice A is incorrect because the description is vague. Choices C and D are incorrect because they include interpretations of the causes of Juan's behavior rather than focusing exclusively on the behavior.

3. A.

   Choice A is correct because there is no requirement that all possible interventions be listed in the behavioral intervention plan. Choices B, C, and D are incorrect because the inclusion of each is required by IDEA.

4. C.

   Choice C is correct because the teacher believes that Devon is capable of learning the program but is simply confused by the necessary sequence of steps. By observing the teacher run the program, Devon might be able to learn through observation of the correct sequence. Although explicit instruction might be useful, Choice A is incorrect because Devon seems to need the most support for applying his knowledge of the necessary steps. Choice B is incorrect, even though Devon might benefit from observing peers, because when he is not using the program he will be recording data from the screen rather than focusing on a group member's use of the program. Choice D is incorrect because the teacher should not exclude Devon from the use of instructional technology if he is capable of using the technology but simply struggling with its use.

5.   B.

Choice B is correct, because the student seems to lack the necessary skill rather than simply having difficulty expressing it. Choices A, C, and D are incorrect because they reflect performance deficits—in each case, the student has the necessary ability to respond to the teacher but cannot express that ability owing to some temporary condition.

6.   C.

Choice C is correct, because Lina needs someone she can call upon during regular business hours without prior notice, and the guidance counselor is likely to be busy on many of the occasions that Lina calls. Choice A is incorrect because Lina needs non-technical support, particularly concerning issues that upset her, and the guidance counselor most probably understands the workplace well enough to appreciate the context for those issues. Choice B is incorrect because there is no reason to suppose that the guidance counselor, with whom Lina has an excellent relationship, is completely unwilling to provide extra support. Choice D is incorrect because anyone regardless of background could conceivably provide less-than-ideal advice in a critical situation. There is no reason to suppose that the guidance counselor is more likely than any other experienced individual to provide such advice.

7.   D.

Choice D is correct, because it would allow the student to have significant experience observing and interacting with a mechanic during an ordinary work day. Choices A, B, and C each consist of resources that would be useful to the student, but none of them would be likely to provide as much specific, career-related information as the shadowing opportunity provided by choice D. Moreover, choices A, B, and C would not allow the same extent of interaction as the opportunity to shadow a working mechanic.

8.   D

Choice D is correct, because participation in IEP planning with the CSE would allow Laura to exercise choices about issues of direct personal relevance. Although authentic activities can promote self-determination, they do not automatically do so, and thus choice A is incorrect. Likewise, discussions with parents may, but do not necessarily, promote self-determination, and thus option B is incorrect. Option C is incorrect because the teacher will promote academic skills anyway, and doing so will not automatically foster self-determination.

PRACTICE TEST 1

NYSTCE
Students with Disabilities

Also available at the REA Study Center (*www.rea.com/studycenter*)

This practice test is also available online at the REA Study Center. The NYSTCE Students with Disabilities test is only offered as a computer-based exam; therefore, we recommend that you take the online version of the practice test to receive these added benefits:

- **Timed testing conditions**—Gauge how much time you can spend on each question.

- **Automatic scoring**—Find out how you did on the test, instantly.

- **On-screen detailed explanations of answers**—Learn not just the correct answer, but also why the other answer choices are wrong.

- **Diagnostic score reports**—Pinpoint where you're strongest and where you need to focus your study.

TOTAL TIME: 195 minutes
90 selected-response questions
1 constructed-response question

Each question in the first section is a multiple-choice question with four answer choices. Read each question CAREFULLY and choose the ONE best answer.

---

1. Mr. Graham is a specialist who works with students who have special needs. You observe Mr. Graham and he is working with a group of students on the tasks of cutting with scissors, holding a pencil, and writing sentences using the same hand without switching to another hand. Mr. Graham is the

   A. special education teacher
   B. physical therapist
   C. occupational therapist
   D. motor planning specialist

2. Which is an example of an unmet need that can be addressed prior to the referral process?

   A. conducting a formal assessment to pinpoint the student's reading capabilities
   B. creating an IEP with goals for the student
   C. selecting related services that the student will receive
   D. providing assistance to help the student increase his/her attendance rate

3. Which of the following is the best example of a chronic behavioral pattern that is problematic?   X situation

   A. Taylor throws chairs to express her anger concerning her parent's divorce
   B. Sal gets into fights when he is attacked
   C. Kelly cannot verbally sound out digraphs when reading aloud
   D. Shawn is sometimes late to school because he misses the buses

4. The first step in addressing an identified unmet need is to

   A. refer the student for special education
   B. set up counseling
   C. contact the family or guardian
   D. meet with the principal

5. The multidisciplinary team is creating Jenna's IEP. In regards to placement in general education, the team must

    A. place Jenna in a general education class
    B. justify her placement if she is not participating in general education
    C. explain her placement to the Board of Education
    D. report her placement in special education to the Board of Cooperative Educational Service

6. Lisa is a new student in your class. She has an IEP. You are planning instruction but need to know what Lisa is expected to achieve by the end of the year. Which section of the IEP best articulates this information?

    A. The Present Levels of Performance
    B. The Annual Goals
    C. The Short-Term Objectives
    D. The Evaluation Scores

7. On Sheldon's IEP, it states that Sheldon will attend a two-year college with the purpose of taking courses in child day care. Where on the IEP should this information be documented?

    A. Present Levels of Performance
    B. Management Need
    C. Post-Secondary Goal
    D. Evaluation Statement

8. Which is the best example of an IEP Annual Goal?

    A. Scott will solve math problems that involve addition and subtraction of three- and four-digit numbers with 90% accuracy on 7 out of 10 tests, in which he will be assessed weekly through the use of classroom assessment and classwork worksheets.
    B. Scott will solve math problems that involve addition and subtraction of three- and four-digit numbers with 80% accuracy on 9 out of 10 tests, in which he will be assessed weekly.
    C. Scott will solve math problems that involve addition and subtraction of three- and four digit numbers with 70% accuracy on 8 out of 10 tests.
    D. Scott will solve math problems with 90% accuracy on 7 out of 10 tests, in which he will be assessed weekly through the use of worksheets.

9. Which is the best example of the information concerning a related service found on an IEP?

    A. speech language, Individual delivery, 30 minutes, in the classroom
    B. physical therapy, small group delivery, twice a week, 40 minutes, in the therapy room, beginning 10/2015
    C. occupational therapy, twice a week, 30 minutes
    D. adaptive physical education, 45 minutes, in the gym, beginning 3/2015

10. Maya has difficulty with speech and language tasks. She uses text-to-speech on her iPad to express thoughts, needs, and wants. Implementing the use of this in your classroom *best* demonstrates

    A. specialized curriculum
    B. assistive technology
    C. annual goals
    D. speech as a related service

11. A classroom setting in which a General Education Teacher and Special Education Teacher work together with students who are typical and have disabilities is *best* described in Part 200 of the Regulations of the New York State Commissioner of Education as a(n)

    A. integrated co-teaching class
    B. resource room class
    C. special education class
    D. inclusion class

12. In reference to testing accommodations for the IEP, which statement covers (1) the type, (2) the conditions, and (3) the implementation recommendation criteria needed (in order to report a testing accommodation completely)?

    A. The student will have extended time that will be administered in the resource room.
    B. The student will have time and a half on essay exams concerning writing five paragraphs or more.
    C. The student will have time and a half on math tests that will be administered in the resource room.
    D. The student will have accommodations for reading tests that will be administered in a separate location.

13. Activities that facilitate a student's <u>movement</u> from school to post-school activities and also constitute a section on the IEP are titled

    A. Present Level of Performance Activities
    B. Evaluation Activities
    C. Post-School Activities
    D. Transition Activities

14. On Keisha's IEP there is a statement of Placement Recommendations stating where her IEP will be implemented. Which one of the following choices is *not* a probable location?

    A. self-contained class (service)
    B. approved private pre-school
    C. public school   locations
    D. residential care facility

15. Long-term goals that are Post-Secondary Goals include all of the following *except*

    A. education/training
    B. employment
    C. independent living skills
    D. counseling

16. Measurable Annual Goals must include all of the following *except*

    A. testing modification
    B. criteria
    C. evaluation method
    D. evaluation schedule

17. Gloria is beginning her special education program services next week. To prepare Gloria for the program, what three essential parts about her services does she need to know which are also required on the IEP?

    A. the program's location, frequency, and duration
    B. the program's student roster, duration, and teacher's name
    C. the program's location, student roster, and school name
    D. the program's duration, location, and teacher's name

18. The nature and degree to which environmental modifications, human resources, and material resources are required to enable the student to benefit from instruction defines

    A. Present Levels of Performance
    B. Social Needs
    C. Management Needs
    D. Academic Needs

19. In Present Levels of Performance, Social Development includes all of the following *except*

    A. relationships with peers and adults
    B. feelings about self
    C. adjustment to school and community
    D. perspectives on health and well-being

20. Physical Development in Present Levels of Performance is partly defined by each choice *except*

    A. the degree and quality of motor and sensory development
    B. health and vitality
    C. physical skills or limitations related to learning
    D. audio and visual stimulation

21. Present Levels of Performance on the IEP include all of the following *except*

    A. academic achievement and functional performance
    B. social development and physical development
    C. learning characteristics and management needs
    D. related services and transition plans

22. Mr. Johnson is a specialist who works with students who have special needs. You observe Mr. Johnson work with students on verbally labeling objects, sentence combining, and auditory tasks. Mr. Johnson is

    A. a sign language interpreter
    B. an occupational therapist
    C. a speech and language therapist
    D. a physical therapist

23. Kelly has difficulty communicating verbally. She has developmentally hit most expected benchmarks, but her communication skills are delayed. Which classification would most likely appear on Kelly's IEP?

   A. autism
   B. speech and language impairment
   C. intellectual disability
   D. emotional behavioral disability

24. Joseph has some communication deficits. He also lacks appropriate social responsiveness, which was identified when he was very young. Joseph has difficulty with eye contact at times and is able to go into his own world. Joseph's characteristics may indicate which of the classifications?

   A. a learning disability
   B. a speech and language disability
   C. autism
   D. an emotional behavioral disability

25. Sheena is a student who is persistently withdrawn in school and at home. Her teacher reports that Sheena is capable of completing the classwork and seems academically intact. Sheena doesn't speak to the other students in class and at recess rarely socializes. Sheena reports that she has obsessive thoughts and fears. Sheena's characteristics may indicate which classification?

   A. learning disability
   B. traumatic brain injury
   C. autism
   D. emotional behavioral disorder

26. According to IDEA, how many federally defined disability classifications are there?

   A. 12
   B. 14
   C. 13
   D. 10

27. Jenna is a student in an inclusion class. Which of the following educational environments would be less restrictive?

   A. day treatment
   B. self-contained class
   C. general education class with speech therapy twice a week, 30 minutes
   D. general education class with resource room five times a week, 60 minutes

28. The Americans with Disabilities Act introduced the idea of universal design. The goal of universal design is to

    A. place students in the least restrictive environment
    B. provide students with a free and appropriate education
    C. ensure all students have due process rights
    D. remove barriers in the environment to allow better access

29. All of the following are components of the IEP *except*

    A. behavioral plan
    B. modifications needed
    C. instructional methods
    D. transition plan

30. Mrs. Alverez and Mrs. Chen are co-teachers. While Mrs. Alverez teaches, Mrs. Chen gathers data. This collaboration approach is called

    A. one teach, one observe
    B. one teach, one drift
    C. cooperative learning
    D. station teaching

31. Mrs. Smith and Mrs. Kendall are co-teachers. Their classroom students are divided into three groups. One group works with Mrs. Smith and one group works with Mrs. Kendall. The third group works on a group project based on pre-planned activities designed by the teachers. This collaboration approach is called

    A. cooperative learning
    B. station teaching
    C. parallel teaching
    D. alternative teaching

32. Mr. Poole and Miss Granger are co-teachers. They are teaching the same topic, but have divided their class into two groups. One group consists of auditory learners and the other kinesthetic learners. Mr. Poole and Miss Granger are able to give the students more opportunities to participate in the lesson and design the instruction based on learning style. This collaborative approach to teaching is called

    A. station teaching
    B. cooperative learning
    C. parallel teaching
    D. one teach, one observe

33. Mrs. Raymond and Mr. Devon are co-teachers. Mr. Devon takes the lead and teaches students how to use the order-of-operation strategy known as PEMDAS. While Mr. Devon teaches, Mrs. Raymond walks around the room helping students and making sure they are following the correct order. This collaboration approach is called

    A. one teach, one drift
    B. one teach, one assist
    C. one teach, one score
    D. one teach, one alternate

34. Which of the following is a method of collaboration that strengthens the home–school relationship and provides the teachers and parents opportunity for direct communication?

    A. parent education
    B. parent conferences
    C. parent involvement
    D. parent associations

35. At school, Linda's mother has been invited to read a book to the class. Mrs. Daley, Linda's teacher, invites parents to come to the school and collaborate with her. Mrs. Daley attempts to encourage

    A. parent associations
    B. parent complexity
    C. parent involvement
    D. parent position

36. Collaboration with teachers requires all of the follow *except*

    A. parity
    B. a shared goal
    C. shared accountability
    D. power

37. All of the students in Mrs. Perrone's class are being assessed for academic problems early to identify those who are having difficulties despite an evidenced-based Tier 1 program. This assessment is part of the RTI process and is called

    A. universal design
    B. universal screening
    C. criterion-based assessments
    D. norm-based assessments

X 38. For purposes of progress monitoring as part of the RTI process, which type of assessment would be the *least* useful?

→ A. norm-referenced test (him x school pop)
    B. curriculum-based assessment
    (C.) universal screening measures
    D. class tests

39. Which of the following is *not* a testing accommodation?

    A. providing adaptive or special furniture
    B. allowing a flexible schedule
    C. securing papers to work area with tape or magnets
    (D) collaborating with peers

40. Tests such as the New York State English Language Arts Assessments and the Regents exams

    A. show growth between student populations
    (B.) are criterion-reference tests
    C. are norm-reference tests
    D. are screening measures

41. Mrs. Hays is using an assessment tool to evaluate Sherman. One of the tasks measures how quickly Sherman can perform a skill or recall academic tasks. Mrs. Hays can use this information to determine Sherman's

    A. potential
    B. grade average
    C. fluency – the rate @ which
    D. latency

X 42. Mr. Wise is an inclusion teacher planning for the upcoming school year. To begin, he thinks about the four major areas that make up instructional environments and ponders how he will accommodate all of his students. What are the four areas Mr. Wise has in mind?

    (A.) physical organization, cooperative learning, materials, and assistive technology
→ B. organization, grouping, technology, and methods
    C. routines, organization, physical plant, and technology
    D. cooperative learning, station teaching, parallel teaching, and technology

43. Maria is a student who tends to be off task only when the teacher moves on to a new topic or activity. Mrs. Little, her teacher, could provide Maria with a behavior chart or checklist to help Maria with

    A. attention
    B. conduct
    C. transitions
    D. visual perception

44. In determining eligibility for special education services, tests of adaptive behavior are important for assessing

    A. hearing impairments
    B. speech and language disorders
    C. blindness
    D. intellectual disabilities

45. Mr. Tsu is planning a reading unit for his 7th grade science class. Assessment from the last unit shows that the majority of the students scored above 75%. Mr. Tsu begins to analyze the other 25%. Before he begins his planning, he uses this information to make a(n)

    A. data-based decision
    B. individualized assessment plan
    C. individualized education plan
    D. unit plan

46. At the beginning of a lesson, Ms. Canty uses a discussion to introduce the new material. During the discussion, Ms. Canty guides students to connect their life experiences to the new topic. She probes to see what they may know about the topic and how their associations can serve as a base for the new information they will learn. This is an example of

    A. guided discussion
    B. motivation
    C. activating prior knowledge
    D. associations

47. Jonathan has been diagnosed with autism. He often does not understand social expectations. To teach Jonathan how to respond in social situations, Mrs. Mohammad, Jonathan's teacher, uses examples and situations known as

    A. social stories
    B. social studies
    C. social dynamics
    D. social relationships

48. A strategy used to teach individuals with low-incidence disabilities to communicate with another person through the structured use of pictures is known as

    A. PECS (picture exchange communication system)
    B. PMS (picture memory system)
    C. PMDS (picture memory decoding system)
    D. PRTS (picture recall to tell system)

49. Mary has been diagnosed with autism and needs a clear, consistent schedule explained to her ahead of time. Mary needs which of the following aids displayed in the classroom?

    A. behavior chart
    B. rules chart
    C. visual schedule
    D. picture chart

50. Matthew has been diagnosed with a seizure disorder. Peter has been diagnosed with sickle-cell disease. Tanisha has severe asthma. Jennifer has a cochlear implant. Which student is most likely *not* classified under OHI?

    A. Matthew
    B. Peter
    C. Tanisha
    D. Jennifer

51. Mrs. Tau is teaching her students how to give positive feedback during student presentations. Part of her lesson includes listening behaviors. Mrs. Tau then teaches the students how to take turns when speaking and giving compliments. This is an example of

    A. manners training
    B. social skills training
    C. social advocacy training
    D. self-determination training

52. Emanuel has a 12-month IEP and in the summer months the focus is on an expansion of the core curriculum. Of the following, which would be a part of an expanded core curriculum?

   A. the writing process
   B. reading informational text
   C. using manipulatives for math
   D. orientation and mobility

Questions 53–55 refer to the following:

Mr. Tower is conducting a Functional Behavioral Assessment with Tyrone. Tyrone's target behavior is that he puts his head down on the desk during his 5th period science class for about half of the class period. Mr. Tower notes that Tyrone has lunch during 4th period. Mr. Tower usually ignores Tyrone's behavior, but now realizes it must be addressed.

before the beh

53. What is a possible antecedent for Tyrone's behavior?

   A. Tyrone is bored in science class
   B. Tyrone does not sleep at home
   C. Tyrone does not like science
   D. Tyrone plays basketball at lunch

54. If Mr. Tower decided to tap Tyrone on the shoulder when his head is down, instead of ignoring his behavior, Mr. Tower is changing the

   A. antecedent of the behavior (1)
   B. behavior (2)
   C. reinforcement of the behavior (3)
   D. intervention plan

55. Mrs. Ludly, the school nurse, observes Tyrone's behavior. She reports that "Tyrone does not pay attention in science class." She tells Mr. Tower that this statement should be the problem behavior on the FBA. Mr. Tower disagrees.

   Do you agree with Mrs. Ludly or Mr. Tower?
   A. Mrs. Ludly because Tyrone is most likely sleeping when his head is down
   B. Mr. Tower because he has described an observable, measurable behavior
   C. Mrs. Ludly because she has pinpointed the behavior problem
   D. Mr. Tower because he has observed Tyrone more frequently

56. To begin his class, Mr. Deeds has his students read a list of questions that help to activate prior knowledge and encourage students to make predictions about what they will learn. Mr. Deeds is using a(n)

    A. graphic organizer
    B. anticipation guide
    C. a think sheet
    D. brainstorming strategy

57. Lydia has a chart on her desk and a short list of behaviors she is working on. Every fifteen minutes she looks at the behaviors and records her progress. This is an example of

    A. charting
    B. self-monitoring
    C. recording
    D. self-reinforcement

58. Gabby has an intellectual disability as well as an orthopedic impairment. In which category of disability should she be classified?

    A. intellectual disability
    B. multiple disabled
    C. orthopedic impairment
    D. other health impaired

59. Justin has a twelve-month IEP. Justin is unable to maintain developmental levels when he is away from school for long periods of time. The school developed and issued the twelve-month IEP to prohibit

    A. loss of memory
    B. substantial regression
    C. transition loss
    D. loss of vision

60. According to New York State Department of Educaion regulations, which of the following best represents the membership of the special education committee?

    A. the parents, regular education teacher, special education teacher, school psychologist
    B. special education teacher, school nurse, principal, school counselor
    C. assistant principal, regular education teacher, parent member, reading teacher
    D. the parents, reading teacher, principal, school social worker

61. Once a school district is in receipt of a request for an initial referral, the school district has

   A. forty days to request parent consent to imitate the evaluation
   B. ten days to provide the parent with a copy of the referral and to inform the parents of their rights
   C. forty days to begin the evaluation
   D. fifty days to implement the IEP

62. Can a district evaluate a student for an initial referral without the parents' consent?

   A. no, a district must have the parent's written consent
   B. yes, the district can at any time evaluate a student without parental consent.
   C. maybe, if the district has verbal consent.
   D. possibly, if the parents do not respond in 30 days

63. During a discrete trial, Emily is learning to make a request. Emily needs some help so Mr. Nigel, her teacher, models the behavior. Mr. Nigel is

   A. providing Emily a prompt through modeling
   B. showing Emily how to make the request
   C. reinforcing Emily's positive behavior
   D. withholding the reinforcer

64. Willow is not successful at manipulating the blending and segmentation of phonemes used in speech. Which is the *best next step* that her teacher could implement to address this specific need?

   A. work on activities to develop Willow's phonemic awareness.
   B. devise vocabulary study guides to increase word knowledge.
   C. orally read passages to Willow so she can develop her listening skills.
   D. provide Willow with a graphic organizer during reading instruction.

65. Courtney is an active and engaged reader, but often does not fully understand a passage. You observe that Courtney does not understand that word endings such as "-s" and "-ed" change the meaning of a word. You also observe that Courtney struggles with understanding prefixes such as "pre-" or "mis-." For example, Courtney explains a paragraph incorrectly because she defines *misfortune* as "something good that happens." The first strategy you will implement to address this need will be to

   A. color-code all of Courtney's spelling words before the next test
   B. provide direct instruction in word structure or morphology to Courtney
   C. give Courtney a dictionary and instruct her to use it while reading
   D. provide a behavior chart to keep Courtney on task while reading

66. Your next unit in science requires a mini-lecture, but you want your students to be engaged during the lecture. There are 30 children in your class and you want to assess that they are following along during the mini-lecture. Which strategy could you use for this purpose?

    A.   ask questions when the lecture is completed
    B.   have students write notes from the SMART board during the lecture
    C.   provide guided notes and as you circle the classroom to see the student's responses
    D.   use a PowerPoint presentation while giving the lecture

67. To enhance students' memory of various steps in a process, you could teach them to

    A.   create a mnemonic for the steps
    B.   study the information by reading it multiple times
    C.   research the steps and write a paragraph about each step
    D.   write the steps ten times each night

68. Ms. Golden provided oral multi-step directions to the class. When she instructed the students to begin the task, the students demonstrated varied interpretations of the oral directions. When giving oral directions, what is the best strategy Ms. Golden should employ?

    A.   Ms. Golden should ask the students to repeat the exact directions given
    B.   Ms. Golden should repeat the directions over and over again
    C.   Ms. Golden should ask the students to use their own words and orally retell the directions
    D.   Ms. Golden should speak in an overly loud voice so everyone can hear her

69. Behavioral Intervention Plans are required for all *except*

    A.   students that exhibit persistent behaviors that impede their learning or are disruptive to the class and impede the learning of others, despite school wide interventions such as Positive Behavioral Supports or class wide interventions such as behavioral contracts.
    B.   students who are in special education classes and are classified with a low-incidence disability or a learning disability
    C.   students whose behavior places themselves or others at risk of harm or injury
    D.   students being considered for more restrictive placement as a result of the students' behaviors

70. Keiko had an outburst in class and began to exhibit an out of control rage. His aide, Miss Chamblin, escorted him to a room down the hall so that he could de-escalate and regain control of himself. Keiko knows that once he is ready to return to the classroom, he may. This procedure is written in his Behavior Intervention Plan. Miss Chamblin most likely escorted Keiko to the

    A. empty classroom
    B. school suspension room
    C. time-out room
    D. teachers and staff cafeteria

71. In a brief conversation, the assistant principal has reported to you that your student, Isaac, is receiving a disciplinary change in placement. He tells you the details are forthcoming. From this information you can determine that Isaac

    A. must stay in your class for sixty days before a change in placement can occur
    B. will be suspended indefinitely
    C. must stay in your class for twenty days before a change in placement can occur
    D. will be suspended for a period of ten consecutive days or less

72. Tahira verbally and physically assaulted her teacher, Mrs. Cummings. The verbal assault is against district policy and is regarded as a grave infraction. Tahira's parents and a team of school personnel are meeting to determine: (1) the relationship of Tahira's disability and the circumstances of the attack and (2) the disciplinary action to follow. This meeting is called a

    A. manifestation review
    B. disciplinary meeting
    C. emergency CSE meeting
    D. school board review meeting

73. The manifestation review team can issue a *determination* if the behavior

    A. was not related to the disability
    B. was non-compliant with the school's code of conduct
    C. was only exhibited once
    D. was related to the disability

74. During a lesson, you observe Mr. Singh's students working on the same objective: one group is reading a play; another group is listening to a recording; a third group is cutting out pictures for a collage; and a fourth group is creating a song. You are sure that Mr. Singh has set up

    A. cooperative groups to achieve different goals
    B. cooperative groups based on learning style preferences
    C. groups based on the amount of time needed to complete the assignment
    D. groups based on academic need or tiers

75. Ms. James uses the Strategic Intervention Model (SIM) mnemonic PIRATES for test taking. She tells the students to write PIRATES on the top of the page. The first step "P" stands for "prepare to succeed." Ms. James knows that this is important because research advocates that

    A. having a positive mental attitude before taking a test may increase the student's accuracy rate
    B. writing something down before taking a test causes students with disabilities to become motivated
    C. thinking about this mnemonic will activate the student's prior knowledge on the subject matter
    D. engaging in the strategy will cause students to sustain attention for more than two hours

76. Victoria is severely disabled. You are working with Victoria and want her to tell you about what she did over the weekend. Which strategy could you use to get Victoria to share this information?

    A. instruct Victoria to write a paragraph
    B. provide precut pictures and have Victoria point to the picture that best shows what she did over the weekend
    C. ask Victoria to give a five minute oral speech about her weekend
    D. direct Victoria to write three sentences about her weekend

77. Emily suffered an accident and sustained memory and hearing loss. She was evaluated by a physician and also received an education evaluation that measured learning and adaptive behavior. As a result of a CSE meeting, Emily was classified with Traumatic Brain Injury. Emily is in your class and you have determined that she would benefit from curriculum overlapping in which she will participate in

    A. the same activities but have different goals from her classmates
    B. different activities and goals from her classmates
    C. the same activities and have the same goals as her classmates
    D. none of the class activities and use only IEP goals

78. Mrs. King has fifteen students in her class. Most have been classified with high-incidence disabilities. When planning instruction, Mrs. King uses strategies that will benefit all students in her class even though they have varying classifications. This approach to making instructional adjustments for her students is called a

    A. cross-categorical approach
    B. cross-classification approach
    C. category approach
    D. high-incidence approach

79. Which of the following is a skill that would be presented in a life skills curriculum?

    A. reading sentences
    B. calculating fractions
    C. ways to greet others
    D. elements from the periodic table

80. One essential skill taught in self-determination is

    A. setting goals
    B. counting
    C. recognizing the alphabet
    D. memorizing historical dates

81. Alex's mother reads a schools report that states Alex's comorbidity condition includes learning disabilities, personality disorders, and attention deficit hyperactivity disorder. Alex's mother asks that you explain the term *comorbidity*. Which is the best answer?

    A. Alex has learning disabilities that affect his personality
    B. Alex has a learning disability and will eventually develop a personality disorder followed by ADHD
    C. Alex has a learning disability but the personality and ADHD are assessed to be of more concern
    D. Alex has a learning disability, personality disorder, and ADHD all occurring together

82. Christopher's teacher says that he does not pay attention. Christopher says that he does pay attention . . . to everything, including the sounds of cars passing by, people talking in the hallway, and the hum of the overhead lights. Christopher may have a compromised

    A. visual field
    B. auditory sensation
    C. selective attention
    D. hyperactivity disorder

83. Madison was assessed and it was determined that she is unable to perceive the differences in vowel and consonant sounds. This is a problem with

    A. visual perception
    B. auditory discrimination
    C. hearing
    D. figure-ground discriminations

84. When reading, Xenia is unable to discriminate between the letters *b* and *d* and the letters *q* and *g*. For example she will read *dab* instead of *bad*. Xenia's visual discrimination impact hers reading. What is one strategy you could implement to help Xenia visually discriminate letters in a word?

    A. read the words to her
    B. encourage her to draw pictures of the word
    C. use different colors for writing each letter
    D. use blocks to sound out the words

85. Mr. Kensington is modeling how to sound out the word *sh-i-p*. He tells the students to orally "scoop" the sound together. Mr. Kensington is modeling

    A. tapping
    B. blends
    C. auditory blending
    D. auditory discrimination

86. Mrs. Kelly asks the class to repeat and recall sentences. Each day the sentences become longer. She does this every day as an exercise to improve the students'

    A. auditory skills
    B. auditory memory
    C. auditory blending
    D. auditory discrimination

87. Geneva has a central auditory processing deficit. During instruction and transition, what could her teacher provide?

    A. items in large print
    B. preferential seating in the rear of the room
    C. a classmate to be her scribe
    D. written directions and a schedule of activities

88. Writing in sand, tapping out sounds, using blending blocks, and skywriting are all activities that are _____.

    A. audio/visual
    B. auditory/sensory
    C. tactile/kinesthetic
    D. gross motor/visual

89. Claire's behavior in class is very disruptive. Claire blurts out an answer before being called on and before the speaker finishes asking the question. She can never wait for her turn and interrupts conversations and games as if she has no mediated thoughts. Ms. Simmons has used an ABC analysis to determine the function of her disruptive behavior. Ms. Simmons has determined that the negative peer attention that occurs after her disruptive behavior increases the frequency of Claire's disruptive behavior. In this analysis, negative peer attention

    A. is an antecedent of Claire's disruptive behavior
    B. is a consequence to Claire's disruptive behavior
    C. is a behavior that is disruptive
    D. has a negative effect on the frequency of Claire's disruptive behavior

90. Piper has severe hearing loss. When she communicates she uses a combination of oral speech and sign language. This method is referred to as cued speech. Why would using speech and sign language together benefit some students?

    A. some words look similar when they are spoken, so a sign helps differentiate similar words
    B. sign language benefits some students who have difficulty communicating
    C. using sign language and speech make communication more inefficient
    D. using speech and sign language together ensures that the student can remember what he is trying to communicate

Constructed Response

Use the information from the exhibits to answer each prompt in the question. Analyze all exhibits and use evidence from each to support your ideas. Write a 400- to 600-word essay in which you will:

- describe one of Michelle's academic needs.

- describe one of Michelle's management or non-academic needs.

- recommend one research-based strategy or intervention that you would implement to address the academic area you described in the first prompt. Explain why you would implement this strategy/intervention and how it will address Michelle's academic need.

- recommend one research-based strategy or intervention that you would use to address the management or non-academic need you described in the second prompt. Explain why you would implement this strategy and how it will address Michelle's management or non-academic need.

- explain how addressing the management or non-academic need could positively affect the academic need.

Exhibit 1—Excerpt from Teacher's Conference Notes

5th Period Science Class

Michelle is always on time to class, but she is always the last to have her materials ready for instruction. She seems very disorganized and is constantly losing items. Her homework is usually in the wrong section of the binder—her Social Studies notes were in the Science section. I have told her several times that she needs to make sure she is in the correct section of the binder. I have observed her writing Science notes in the Social Studies section of her binder as well. This disorganization slows her down and she seems frustrated. She disrupts the entire class with many questions concerning directions which are written on the board. She needs clarification for everything as if she cannot read from the board and listen to directions simultaneously.

Michelle does well on multiple-choice exams when she has extended time. In class, however, it is very difficult to read her lab reports due to her writing which looks like a long string of letters with no spaces. When she reads aloud she jumbles the words and reads them as if there are no spaces between the words. This has a negative impact on her reading the textbook, lab directions, and filling out the lab reports.

When given an opportunity to redo the lab assignments, Michelle's work looks the same. The writing is still incomprehensible. Her ability to read scientific text is lacking.

Exhibit 2—Assessment Data

Michelle's Scores for the Marking Period

Test Number	Type	Score
1	Multiple Choice	78% (Resource Room)
2	Lab Report 1	50%
3	Multiple Choice	75% (Resource Room)
4	Essay	40%
5	Lab Report 2	35%
6	Lab Report 3	53%
7	Lab Report 4	40%

Exhibit 3—Information taken from Michelle's IEP

TESTING

Woodcock Johnson III ACH Tests

Broad Math Cluster 87 (standard score)

Broad Reading Cluster 87 (standard score)

Broad Written Language 82 (standard score)

Wechsler Intelligence Scale for Children

Full Scale IQ 97 (Intelligence Quotient)

ACADEMIC ACHIEVEMENT, FUNCTIONAL PERFORMANCE, AND LEARNING CHARACTERISTICS

Reading

Michelle is functioning below grade level in decoding skills and reading comprehension. She demonstrates difficulty understanding concepts and benefits from graphic and visual organizers.

Writing

Michelle is functioning below grade level in written expression. She continues to demonstrate difficulty with the mechanics of writing.

Math

Michelle has difficulty with multi-step math equations. The visual spatial needs and organization of math problems are difficult for her.

Social Development

Michelle is excellent in social skills. She is very friendly and well accepted by her peers.

Student Strength

Michelle works well in small groups and is receptive to assistance.

Management Needs

Michelle requires additional support of Special Education services to be successful in the general education classroom.

ANNUAL GOALS

Study Skills

Michelle will arrive to class on time with the needed materials.
Michelle will use organizational strategies to study class notes and prepare for exams.

Reading

Michelle will use comprehension skills of root words, synonyms, antonyms, and multiple meanings to define 10 unknown words.

Writing

Michelle will use the process of prewriting, drafting, revising, and proofreading to produce a 5-paragraph essay.

Services

Resource Room—5:1 in the Resource Room
Organizational Strategies—Daily in the Classroom

NYSTCE STUDENTS WITH DISABILITIES TEST 1 GRID

Competency	Items
Competency 0001: Foundation of Special Education	11, 14, 26, 27, 28, 60, 61, 62, 71, 72, 73
Competency 0002: Knowledge of Students with Disabilities	1, 3, 22, 23, 24, 25, 50, 58, 81, 82, 83
Competency 0003: Assessment and Individual Program Planning	2, 4, 5, 6, 7, 8, 9, 12, 13, 15, 16, 17, 18, 19, 20, 21, 29, 37, 38, 39, 40, 41, 44
Competency 0004: Strategies for Planning and Managing the Learning Environment and for Providing Behavioral Interventions	42, 43, 53, 54, 55, 57, 59, 69, 70, 78, 89
Competency 0005: Instructional Planning and Delivery to Promote Students' Success in the General Curriculum	30, 31, 32, 33, 34, 35, 36, 45, 46, 56, 64, 65, 66, 67, 68, 74, 75, 77, 84, 85, 86, 87, 88
Competency 0006: Strategies for Teaching Communication Skills, Social Skills and Functional Living Skills	10, 47, 48, 49, 51, 52, 63, 76, 79, 80, 90
Competency 0007	Constructed response

ANSWER KEY

1. C	31. B	61. B
2. D	32. C	62. A
3. C	33. B	63. A
4. C	34. B	64. A
5. B	35. C	65. B
6. B	36. D	66. C
7. C	37. B	67. A
8. A	38. A	68. C
9. B	39. D	69. B
10. B	40. B	70. C
11. A	41. C	71. D
12. C	42. B	72. A
13. D	43. C	73. D
14. A	44. D	74. B
15. D	45. A	75. A
16. A	46. C	76. B
17. A	47. A	77. A
18. C	48. A	78. A
19. D	49. C	79. C
20. D	50. D	80. A
21. D	51. B	81. D
22. C	52. D	82. C
23. B	53. D	83. B
24. C	54. C	84. C
25. D	55. B	85. C
26. C	56. B	86. B
27. C	57. B	87. D
28. D	58. B	88. C
29. C	59. B	89. B
30. A	60. A	90. A

ANSWER EXPLANATIONS

1. **C**

   Mr. Graham is the occupational therapist. Some students with disabilities have fine motor issues. He is working on these skills including crossing midline.

2. **D**

   (A), (B), and (C) are actions that take place after the referral process and are not unmet needs. Helping Mario improve his attendance is a need that should be addressed prior to asking if his difficulty in school is related to a disability.

3. **C**

   Kelly's behavior is chronic and problematic because it impedes reading. The behaviors of Taylor, Sal, and Shawn are in response to a specific event and are not chronic.

4. **C**

   Meeting with the family or guardian is the first step because you can gain information concerning the need. Choices (A) and (B) would not be a first step. Meeting with the principal is a step that would happen prior to addressing the need. It would happen while in the process of identifying the need.

5. **B**

   As part of the IEP process, a justification statement must be made that explains the considerations of the students to participate in regular education. If a decision is made that the student will not participate in general education, the rationale must appear on the document.

6. **B**

   The annual goals and objectives state the projected learning which will be achieved by the end of the school year.

7. **C**

   A Post-Secondary Goal states the career-related goal and what the student aspires to do after high school.

8. **A**

   According to the NYS Department of Education and the recommended statewide IEP, an annual goal must contain four components

   1: a description of what the student will be expected to achieve by the end of the year.
   (Scott will solve math problems that involve addition and subtraction of three- and four-digit numbers)

   2: a criteria which is a measure to determine if the goal has been achieved (with 90% accuracy)

   3: The method how the progress will be measured (Scott will meet the criteria on no less that 7 out of the 10 tests)

   4: The schedule by which progress will be measured (Scott will be assessed weekly)

   Choice (A) is complete, whereas the other choices are missing a component.

9. **B**

   According to NYS policy and the recommended statewide IEP, service delivery must be reported to include: the type of service, the frequency, the duration, where the service will be provided, and the projected start date.

   Answer (B) is the only choice that fulfills the complete state criteria.

10. **B**

   Text to speech software and/or an iPad are technologies that will assist Maya's learning needs. Therefore, it is assistive technology.

11. **A**

   The question describes best the integrated co-teaching class setting. Choice (D) is not defined in part 200.

12. **C**

   This choice has all three components, whereas the others are missing at least one of the components.

13. **D**

   Transition activities/plans state the activities that will occur to help prepare the student for life after high school.

14. **A**

A self-contained class is a *program service* and not a placement recommendation location of where the IEP will take place. The IEP must state where the plan is to be executed. Choices (B), (C), and (D) are all probable locations.

15. **D**

Post-secondary goals are related to job readiness. Although an individual may need counseling, it is not a goal but rather a support service.

16. **A**

Testing modifications is a separate section of the IEP and not a part of the measurable annual goals. The annuals goals must have information on what the student will achieve, the criteria, an evaluation method, and an evaluation schedule of progress monitoring. Testing accommodations are not a part of that statement.

17. **A**

The program's location, frequency, and duration are all required and necessary information that Gloria needs.

18. **C**

Taken directly from NYS policy information, management needs is defined as, "environmental modifications, human resources and materials resources required to enable the student to benefit from instruction." The dimensions of definition are the specific components that are addressed when making statements about the student's management needs and documenting those needs on the IEP

19. **D**

Choices (A), (B), and (C) all define Social Development, whereas choice (D) does not.

20. **D**

Audio and visual stimulation does not address the information mandated in Physical Development. Information about audio and visual stimulation would appear in another section of the IEP if necessary. Choices (A), (B), and (C) must be addressed and documented so that the reader of the IEP can ascertain the student's level of physical health.

21. **D**

Related services and transition plans do not address the present levels of student performance.

22. **C**

A speech and language therapist helps students with verbal and auditory tasks. Mr. Johnson is a speech and language therapist.

23. **B**

Speech and language disabilities are characterized by a lack of age-appropriate development in communication. The fact that Kelly is developmentally appropriate in all other areas rules out choices (A) and (C). There is not enough information to indicate choice (D).

24. **C**

The characteristics exhibited by Joseph indicate that choice (C) is the best answer.

25. **D**

Based on the description of characteristics, choice (D) is the best answer.

26. **C**

According to IDEA, there are 13 federally defined categories of disability.

27. **C**

Although inclusion models vary across the state, LRE is linked to the amount of time spent in a special education service. Choice (C) is the least restrictive because the amount of special education service time would be far less than that of an inclusion class.

28. **D**

The ADA introduced universal design as a way for individuals with disabilities to gain physical access in the environment. For example, the legislation encouraged changes such as wider doorways, handicapped-equipped bathrooms, handicapped-equipped parking spaces, and ramps into the building. These features make access better for people with disabilities. Later, the term *universal design* became applicable to instruction.

29. **C**

Choices (A), (B), and (D) are components of an IEP but choice (C) is not. Instructional methods are not required for the IEP although a team may choose to include them in the document.

30. **A**

Mrs. Alverez is teaching while Mrs. Chen observes students and collects data.

31. **B**

In station teaching, the class is divided into groups that are teacher- and student-facilitated.

32. **C**

Parallel teaching is a collaborative teaching approach that allows for teaching the same topic to students in smaller groups and giving the students more opportunities to participate in the lesson.

33. **B**

Mr. Devon teaches and Mrs. Raymond assists students one on one with the order of operations.

34. **B**

Parent conferences allow an opportunity for teachers and parents to collaborate on the education of the student.

35. **C**

Inviting parents to be a part of the school increases parent involvement. Choice (C) is the best answer.

36. **D**

To collaborate, choices (A), (B), and (C) are all necessary. However, choice (D) does not support collaboration, which indicates partnership and not one person having power over another.

37. **B**

Universal screening is conducted on all students as a proactive measure in Tier 1.

38. **A**

    Norm-referenced tests are not recommended to be given as frequently as you would need to test for progress monitoring. In addition, norm reference tests are used to compare the student's performance against a sample of the population which is not the assessment question in progress monitoring. The desired data is to compare the student's performance against himself over time.

39. **D**

    Choices (A), (B), and (C) are testing accommodations. Collaborating with peers is not a testing accommodation.

40. **B**

    These types of tests compare students' performance on curriculum as defined by the New York State Learning Standards and Common Core Standards.

41. **C**

    Fluency is the rate at which a student can perform a skill or recall information.

42. **B**

    The four areas that make up instructional environments are organization, grouping, technology, and methods. Parts of the other choices would fall into one of the categories present in choice (B).

43. **C**

    Maria is having difficulty when moving from one activity to another. This indicates the need to manage transitions.

44. **D**

    Adaptive behavior assessments are used to evidence and measure the characteristics associated with intellectual disabilities.

45. **A**

    Mr. Tsu uses data to inform his planning of instruction. Using data to make these decisions is referred to as a data-based decision.

46. **C**

Ms. Canty is activating prior knowledge so that the students can make connections about what they know to the new topic. Although they will make some associations, choice (D) is too general and not as precise as choice (C).

47. **A**

Social stories are used to teach children with disabilities appropriate social expectations through reading examples of social situations.

48. **A**

This system uses pictures to elicit communication.

49. **C**

A visual schedule is used with students who have autism so that the student can see what will occur during the school day.

50. **D**

OHI stands for Other Health Impairments. Matthew, Peter, and Tanisha's conditions would be classified under OHI because they are not IDEA-defined disability categories. Jennifer has a cochlear implant, which indicates she has a hearing impairment which is an IDEA classification category.

51. **B**

Mrs. Tau is teaching the students how to demonstrate social skills that are valued in society. Social skills training is an evidenced-based practice that focuses on appropriate behaviors. Choices (A) and (D) are also evidenced-based practices, but are not social skills training as exampled by Mrs. Tau.

52. **D**

Choices (A), (B), and (C) are components of the core curriculum. Choice (D), orientation and mobility, is a part of the expanded curriculum which addresses functional living skills.

53. **D**

An antecedent defined is something that usually occurs just before the behavior. In this question, (D) is the best choice.

54. **C**

A reinforcement of a behavior is what occurs after the behavior. Mr. Tower would be changing the reinforcement of the behavior.

55. **B**

On the FBA, the behavior must be described in observable, measurable terms.

56. **B**

An anticipation guide activates prior knowledge and has been evidenced as an effective teaching strategy.

57. **B**

Self-monitoring involves that student taking ownership of their behavior through reflective practice. By charting her behaviors every fifteen minutes, Lydia can evaluate her performance to her actual goals.

58. **B**

Students who have characteristics of two or more federally defined categories of disability fall into the category of multiple disabilities.

59. **B**

Twelve-month programs are designed for students who would suffer substantial regression if they were out of school for the summer months. These students also require a higher intensity of individualized attention with high levels of management needs.

60. **A**

Although it is recommended to have any professionals who are knowledgeable about the student, their learning needs, and the services provided by the district, New York State policy mandates that certain professionals be a part of the committee. Choice (A) is the best representation of that membership.

61. **B**

According to New York State policy, districts must inform parents of the referral and their rights within ten days.

62. **A**

A New York State school district must have written parental permission to evaluate a student for an initial referral.

63. **A**

Mr. Nigel is modeling the behavior through prompting. Although he is showing her the behavior as he prompts, some aspects of the behavior will not be modeled so that Emily will need less prompting to engage in the behavior. Choice (A) is precise and accurate and a part of our academic vocabulary as Special Education Teachers.

64. **A**

Although all of the choices could be implemented, the *best* next step would be to work with Willow on developing her phonemic awareness.

65. **B**

By teaching word structure and morphology, Courtney will be able to detect prefixes, root words, and suffixes.

66. **C**

This response is the only choice that allows for immediate feedback. By providing guided notes you can observe the students writing in the correct or incorrect responses as you circle the class. Choice (A) happens after the lecture but you want to assess during the lecture. Choices (B) and (D) do not afford an opportunity to assess if the students are following along.

67. **A**

Research shows that teaching students to create mnemonic devices will aid in retention and also activate recall.

68. **C**

Although all of these choices have merit, the best strategy is to make sure the students understand the directions and can repeat them to you orally. By having the students restate the directions in their own words, you can assess if they know what is expected.

69. **B**

   Choices (A), (C), and (D) are based on New York State policy and reasons for mandating a Behavior Intervention Plan. Choice (C) does not apply and students are not mandated nor do they need a Behavior Intervention Plan based on the classification of their disability.

70. **C**

   A time-out room is an area for students to regain control and, as per New York State policy, has conditions and characteristics which distinguish a time out room from simply removing a student to another room. One of those conditions is that the student knows the purpose for removal and how this strategy relates to the overall Behavior Intervention Plan.

71. **D**

   Procedural safeguards for the discipline of students with disabilities states that a disciplinary change of placement indicates that a student will be suspended for ten consecutive days or less depending upon the particular factors of the suspension.

72. **A**

   (A) is the correct choice because a manifestation review deals specifically with the manifestation of the student's actions and how it relates to their disability. In addition, a disciplinary action will be considered. This distinguishes a manifestation review from choices (B), (C), and (D).

73. **D**

   The manifestation review team can issue a determination if the behavior was related to the student's disability.

74. **B**

   The activities described in the cooperative groups suggest planning based on different learning style preferences.

75. **A**

   This is the only choice that is supported by research or evidence.

76. **B**

   For students with severe disabilities, choice (B) is the most appropriate answer.

77. **A**

By definition, curriculum overlapping is defined as a strategy in which students with disabilities participate in the same activities as their classmates, but the goals and objectives may be different.

78. **A**

Choice (A) defines the approach that Mrs. King has implemented.

79. **C**

The goal of a life skills curriculum is to focus primarily on the non-academic skills that are essential for daily living. Choice (C) is the most appropriate choice.

80. **A**

Choice (A) is the only choice that is a component of self-determination.

81. **D**

Comorbidity is the condition in which multiple conditions occur together. One condition is not necessarily more prevalent or a precursor to another disorder.

82. **C**

Compromises to selective attention make it difficult for students to focus on tasks and ignore peripheral or less relevant stimuli.

83. **B**

Madison is unable to distinguish or discriminate the different phonemes.

84. **C**

By using different colors, this strategy will help Xenia with visual discrimination. The other choices do not address visual discrimination of letters.

85. **C**

Mr. Kensington is showing the action of scooping sound together (auditory blending). Choice (A) is not as precise as choice (C).

86. **B**

Mrs. Kelly is teaching students to remember longer sentences. Doing this orally taps into the skill of auditory memory. To improve upon the skill set needed for choices (C) and (D), memorizing sentences and adding length would not be the best exercise. Choice (A) is not precise because (B), (C), and (D) are all auditory skills. The precise auditory skill is choice (B), making it the best choice.

87. **D**

Auditory processing deficits manifests when the listener does not perceive exactly what the speaker is saying. Choices (A), (B) and (C) do not accommodate for this process. Choice (D), having written directions instead of oral instructions and a schedule of activities, are appropriate accommodations.

88. **C**

All four activities are tactile or kinesthetic.

89. **B**

A consequence is what happens following the behavior.

90. **A**

Sign language with speech helps students to identify words when they are reading lips. The signs cue the students to understand the spoken word.

Answering the Constructed-Response Prompt

When answering the constructed-response prompt, be sure to read the question completely. Precisely address each bullet. Exhibits will be available which you will use to derive evidence to support your ideas. Make sure you read each exhibit.

In the practice question, there are two possible academic needs that are evidenced in the exhibits—Michelle has a need in reading and Michelle has a need in writing. Selecting either would be correct. There are at least two management needs evidenced in the exhibits. First, Michelle has visual spatial deficits, and second, she is in need of organizational skills. Selecting either would be correct.

The strategies or interventions you select to address the problem will vary but you must explicitly explain why you chose that strategy and how it will address the *specific* need you described.

PRACTICE TEST 2

NYSTCE
Students with Disabilities

Also available at the REA Study Center (*www.rea.com/studycenter*)

This practice test is also available online at the REA Study Center. The NYSTCE Students with Disabilities test is only offered as a computer-based exam; therefore, we recommend that you take the online version of the practice test to receive these added benefits:

- **Timed testing conditions**—Gauge how much time you can spend on each question.

- **Automatic scoring**—Find out how you did on the test, instantly.

- **On-screen detailed explanations of answers**—Learn not just the correct answer, but also why the other answer choices are wrong.

- **Diagnostic score reports**—Pinpoint where you're strongest and where you need to focus your study.

TOTAL TIME: 195 minutes
90 selected-response questions
1 constructed-response question

Each question in the first section is a multiple-choice question with four answer choices. Read each question CAREFULLY and choose the ONE best answer.

1. What is considered to be the most important piece of legislation affecting the education of students with disabilities?

    A. The Children with Disabilities Act of 1969
    B. Public Law 94-142, The Education for All Handicapped Children Act (EHA), passed in 1975
    C. The Elementary and Secondary Education Act of 1965
    D. The Americans with Disabilities Act

2 . Which of the following is the best example of ongoing scaffolding?

    A. a teacher sits with a student who is working on a project and reiterates instructions and expectations, offers specific directives about what to do next, and provides corrective feedback
    B. a teacher periodically looks over the shoulder of a student who is working independently on a project and offers a brief comment or suggestion
    C. a teacher briefly summarizes the main theme of a passage before asking students to read the passage independently
    D. a teacher who sits with a student and periodically looks over the shoulder of a another student who is working independently on a project and offers a brief comment or suggestion or briefly summarizes the main theme of a passage before asking other students to read the passage independently

3. Throughout normal development, receptive language tends to be superior to expressive language. What does this statement mean? At any given age,

    A. children's ability to understand language is superior to their ability to express themselves
    B. children's ability to understand language is more important than their ability to express themselves

    C.   children understand more vocabulary, more grammar, more pragmatic rules, and so on, than may be evident in their speaking and writing

    D.   children's ability to understand language is superior to their ability to express themselves and they understand more vocabulary, more grammar, more pragmatic rules, and so on, than may be evident in their speaking and writing

4.   In the field of education, assessment is known as the collection and analysis of information (i.e., data) about students in order to make decisions. Select the two correct ways in which the word "assessment" can be used.

    A.   the test and the test period

    B.   the specific tool used to gather information and the process of gathering information

    C.   formative and summative

    D.   the subject of the assessment and the administrator of the assessment

5.   The assessment of students with disabilities is governed by federal as well as New York state laws and regulations. IDEA requires that the assessment of students who have, or who are suspected to have, disabilities must meet the following criteria:

    A.   School officials must notify parents prior to any assessments over and above those that are routinely administered to all students.

    B.   Parental permission is required prior to beginning these assessments.

    C.   Assessments must be carried out on an individual basis.

    D.   Parents must be notified, parental permission achieved, and an individualized assessment must be performed.

6.   For students who fall within the age range 3 to 21 years, IDEA lists 13 categories of disability, including

    A.   mental retardation

    B.   autism

    C.   epilepsy

    D.   mental illness

7.   An ecological assessment focuses on student functioning in different environments. The goal of the assessment is to

    A.   identify environments in which the student functions with greater or lesser difficulty

    B.   understand what contributes to these differences in functioning

    C.   draw useful implications for instructional planning

    D.   identify environments, understand what contributes to differences in functioning in these environments, and draw implications for instructional planning

8. Ms. Jones agrees that safety is a fundamental concern in any learning environment. Therefore, she is certain to

    A. call parents each time a child acts up in her classroom
    B. keep the room free from clutter and monitor student behavior
    C. not allow students to use scissors or other sharp objects in class
    D. do many things to ensure student safety everyday including, calling parents, keeping the room free from clutter, continually monitoring student behavior, not allowing students sharp objects in class

9. The Common Core Learning Standards, to which states voluntarily comply,

    A. supplement the former standards used in New York for these areas
    B. contradict the former standards used in New York for these areas
    C. replace the former standards used in New York for these areas
    D. build upon the former standards used in New York for these areas

10. Procedural safeguards are a set of rules and procedures designed to protect the rights and interests of

    A. parents and their children with disabilities
    B. all parents and their children
    C. teachers
    D. administrators

11. Semantics refers to the meanings of parts of words, words, sentences, and larger units. Identify the statement below that is TRUE.

    A. vocabulary acquisition is an important part of semantic development involving changes in both expressive and receptive language
    B. over time, children learn new words and gain a deeper understanding of the words they already know
    C. over time, children also develop knowledge of how a word's meaning may shift to a greater or lesser extent from context to context
    D. vocabulary acquisition is an important part of semantic development and over time, children learn new words, gain a deeper understanding of the words they already know and develop knowledge of how a word's meaning may shift from context to context

12. Although the terms *assessment* and *evaluation* are often used interchangeably, there is a distinction. Evaluation refers to the

    A.   test
    B.   outcome
    C.   determination of what students have already achieved
    D.   score

13. In order for teachers to achieve the most effective classroom management, they must focus on

    A.   communicating with administration, parents, and other teachers
    B.   collecting data on all student behavior
    C.   their use of time, student behavior, and classroom environment
    D.   overall classroom control

14. The purpose of assessment is to answer questions such as:

    A.   Is the extra support being provided to a particular student effective?
    B.   In what areas do particular students need extra support?
    C.   Which approaches to providing extra support are likely to benefit a particular student?
    D.   Does a student need support, and if so, what approaches might be effective in providing this support?

15. Teaching students with disabilities so that instruction is aligned with state learning standards depends on ensuring that these students access the

    A.   general education classroom
    B.   general education curriculum
    C.   general education textbooks
    D.   education tests

16. Ms. Smith has a child with an articulation disorder in her classroom. This means the child has

    A.   anatomical or physiological limitations in the physical mechanisms used to produce speech
    B.   difficulties producing certain speech sounds
    C.   difficulties with the rhythm and timing of speech
    D.   difficulties producing language sounds of appropriate quality, pitch, and/or loudness

17. You have been informed that you will have a student in your classroom with language impairments. This could include a student with a(n)

    A. phonological disorder
    B. expressive language disorder
    C. mixed receptive-expressive language disorder
    D. phonological disorder or expressive language disorder or mixed receptive-expressive language disorder

18. According to IDEA, a team approach to the identification and support of students who have, or may have, a disability is

    A. recommended
    B. required
    C. discouraged
    D. encouraged

19. Aspects of language development are rather predictable. Therefore, the more extreme the deviation from a typical time frame of development, the more likely the child has a disability that is related to language and communication. Which of the following statements is FALSE?

    A. atypical development is possible with respect to one, some, or all components of language (phonology, semantics, grammar, pragmatics, orthography)
    B. children must reach a specific level of language development before starting school
    C. children vary widely in rate of language development
    D. some extent of delay in the emergence of these abilities and behaviors is not necessarily indicative of a problem

20. Which one of the following assessments would be administered to individual students who may need extra support?

    A. screening assessment
    B. prereferral assessment
    C. diagnostic assessment
    D. progress monitoring assessment

21. Sally continues to exhibit inappropriate behavior. One cause may be that she

    A. is unaware of the behavioral expectations of the class
    B. is too closely watched
    C. does not like the teacher
    D. is not behaviorally ready to attend school

22. If Mr. Hall wishes to improve his classroom management, he may want to consider

    A. modeling desirable behaviors and responding positively to desirable behaviors
    B. structuring activities for individual students so that the students are appropriately challenged
    C. creating a sense of community by treating students positively, including students in decision-making processes, and enforcing the rules fairly and consistently
    D. designing a comprehensive classroom management system that includes modeling and responding positively to desirable behaviors, structuring challenging activities, and creating a sense of community in order to meet the various needs of individual students

23. As the parent of a child with a disability, your child is eligible for all of the following at no cost to you *except*

    A. child care
    B. program modification
    C. supplemental aids and service
    D. related services

24. You are informed that one of your students has an expressive language disorder, also known as a specific language impairment. An expressive language disorder refers to an impairment

    A. of language rather than speech
    B. in which both receptive and expressive language abilities are affected
    C. in which expressive language abilities are much lower than expected for the student's age, although mental functioning and receptive language skills fall within the normal range
    D. that is commonly overlooked

25. It is possible to prevent speech and language discords if a teacher is aware of signs such as

    A. a hearing impairment
    B. a family history of communication disorders
    C. a medical disorder such as cleft palate
    D. a family history of communication disorders with the identification of a hearing impairment or a medical disorder such as a cleft palate

26. P.L. 94-142 was later reauthorized as the

    A. No Child Left Behind Act
    B. Individuals with Disabilities Education Act, or IDEA
    C. The Education for All Handicapped Children's Act
    D. The Dignity for All Students Act

27. The purpose of prereferral is to help students who are struggling in the general education setting before referring them for

    A. disciplinary action
    B. special education services
    C. academic supports
    D. special education assessment

28. Which one of the following assessments is used to determine whether an individual student's progress is adequate?

    A. screening assessment
    B. prereferral assessment
    C. diagnostic assessment
    D. progress monitoring assessment

29. Which one of the following assessments is administered to all students in a particular group, such as a grade or a school?

    A. screening assessment
    B. prereferral assessment
    C. diagnostic assessment
    D. progress monitoring assessment

30. The third grade students are acting hostile toward one another. This could be caused by

    A. third graders being generally hostile to one another
    B. the students experiencing hostility in their homes
    C. diversity in the classroom
    D. the teacher's response to students' behavior being openly hostile

31. Children from birth to age 3 who are identified with a disability are eligible for early intervention services. IDEA requires that these services be provided in a

    A. school setting
    B. hospital setting
    C. therapeutic setting
    D. natural setting such as the home or a child care center

32. Communication supports consist of technologies that facilitate communication among students who are deaf or hearing-impaired. Which of the following is not an example of a communication support?

    A. hearing aids
    B. conventional cell phones (with texting capacity)
    C. closed captioning
    D. speech-to-text translators

33. A student in your class requires instruction in adaptive life skills. Instruction might include

    A. domestic living, self-care, health and safety
    B. social, communication, community use
    C. self direction, work and leisure
    D. domestic living, health and safety, social, community use, self-direction, and work and leisure

34. IDEA is grounded in a number of concepts that were innovative at the time of its initial passage, including

    A. mandated standardized assessments at all grade levels
    B. free and reduced lunch programs
    C. the granting of children with disabilities the right to a free, appropriate public education in the least restrictive environment
    D. extended-year programming

35. After presenting students with new information and skills, a teacher wishes to provide them with an opportunity for guided practice. Which of the following scenarios is an example of a guided practice activity?

    A. A chemistry teacher introduces a new formula and, using this formula, solves two problems on the board as students watch. While solving the problems, the teacher explicitly notes how each part of the formula is being applied.
    B. A math teacher who is introducing long division to students will review simple division problems, and then provide explanations and examples illustrating the need for long division.
    C. After a language arts teacher has recited a poem, students are given the opportunity to recite the poem while looking at the written text as little as possible. The teacher provides corrective feedback with respect to students' accuracy as well as their phrasing and expression
    D. After students in a social studies class have learned a new concept by observing and then participating in interactions with the teacher, they are asked to write a short essay paraphrasing and critically evaluating the idea

36. Which one of the following assessments is administered to individual students in some states before formally referring them for special education?

    A. screening assessment
    B. prereferral assessment
    C. diagnostic assessment
    D. progress monitoring assessment

37. Teachers who wish to establish and maintain rapport with students should try to

    A. get to know students as a group, rather than individually
    B. treat students warmly, with respect, and engage in active listening
    C. maintain professionalism and appropriate boundaries
    D. limit communication about students' feelings regarding classroom activities and others

38. Traditional educational assessments

    A. rely heavily on standardized tests such as the state-mandated group achievement tests
    B. are not standardized
    C. are not norm-referenced
    D. are based on short answer response formats

39. The least restrictive environment for students with disabilities is the

    A. special education classroom
    B. general education classroom
    C. age appropriate classroom
    D. classroom the parent determines is least restrictive

40. Rubrics and portfolios are examples of what type of assessment?

    A. ecological
    B. observational
    C. authentic
    D. traditional

41. Checklists, rating scales, and duration records are all examples of what type of assessment?

    A. ecological
    B. observational
    C. authentic
    D. traditional

42. As children acquire reading skills, their development can be divided into stages. Select the sequence below that accurately describes these stages.

    A. pre-reading; learning to read; transitional reading; reading to learn
    B. learning to read; pre-reading; transitional reading; reading to learn
    C. pre-reading; transitional reading; learning to read; reading to learn
    D. pre-reading; learning to read; reading to learn; transitional

43. A student's IEP includes community-based instruction. Community-based instruction includes all of the following elements *except*

    A. instructional activities that take place in community settings
    B. field trips
    C. repeated visits to a community setting in which instruction takes place and is cumulative over time
    D. opportunities to practice skills in the actual settings in which they will someday be applied

44. RTI is a school-level process that involves screening, monitoring, and responding appropriately to individual students based on their academic progress. Which of the elements below define the RTI process?

    A.   all students receive high-quality instruction
    B.   over time, students who struggle academically are provided increasingly intensive and individualized instruction
    C.   if a student reaches the final "tier" or level of individualized instruction and continues to struggle, the student will be referred for special education assessment
    D.   the RTI process includes high-quality instruction, increasing intensity in individualized instruction, and referral to special education assessment when a student reaches the final tier

45. Determine which of the statements about authentic assessment is TRUE.

    A.   authentic assessment provides descriptions of student performance
    B.   authentic assessment is based on the assumption that the purpose of learning is simply to do well on tests
    C.   the goal of authentic assessment is to determine how well a student performs when the knowledge and skills acquired in class are applied
    D.   the goal of authentic assessment is to determine how well a student performs when the knowledge and skills acquired in class are applied to meaningful tasks

46. A portfolio is a collection of work produced by a student over time. The goal of portfolio assessment is to

    A.   determine if a student has achieved a particular standard
    B.   determine if a student is ready to advance to the next grade level
    C.   gauge student effort, progress, and achievement through examination of many different kinds of work that the student has produced in a particular class or related to a specific theme
    D.   measure a limited number of benchmarks or objectives, usually two to six, across various content areas

47. When grouping students for the purpose of special education instruction, special education teachers must keep in mind that

    A.   students must be grouped by gender
    B.   teachers may use wide variability when grouping according to academic achievement, functional performance, and learning characteristics
    C.   teachers must limit variability when grouping according to academic achievement, functional performance, and learning characteristics
    D.   the more diverse the group, the better for all students

48. Which of the following statements is FALSE?

    A. alternative assessments are appropriate for use with general education students as well as with students with disabilities

    B. alternative assessments are appropriate only for use with students with disabilities

    C. alternative assessments can supplement the evaluation of student progress through traditional forms of assessment

    D. in some cases, alternative assessments should be used in place of traditional ones

49. As a teacher, you wish to differentiate instruction for your students. In order to meet the learning needs of individual students, you must

    A. differentiate process
    B. assess your learners' needs
    C. differentiate product
    D. differentiate content

50. A student in your class repeatedly talks out of turn because the work assigned to him is too easy. This student

    A. is a student with a disability
    B. is a student without a disability
    C. could be a student with or without a disability
    D. is a student with attention deficit disorder

51. Depending on the nature and severity of a student's disability, the student may have needs in one or more areas such as

    A. academic functioning
    B. behavioral functioning
    C. social functioning
    D. academic, behavioral, and social functioning

52. Social skills training focuses on providing students with a variety of skills that benefit their interpersonal relationships and communication with others. Examples of social skills training include all of the following *except* how to

    A. establish and maintain friendships
    B. recognize and respond to conflict with others
    C. ignore one's needs
    D. deal with being bullied or neglected

53. A student with a disability in academic functioning will need support in

    A.   mastering the general education curriculum at the same rate as peers
    B.   impulse control to sit quietly in class or concentrate on individual work
    C.   interacting effectively with teachers or peers
    D.   participating in physical activities with peers

54. In the New York State Testing Program, the alternative assessment is called the New York State Alternative Assessment (NYSAA). All of the following statements are TRUE *except*:

    A.   alternative assessments can also be used in place of state-mandated testing
    B.   eligibility to participate in the NYSAA is determined by the CSE team
    C.   the NYSAA is administered to students whom the CSE has designated as having severe cognitive disabilities
    D.   these students must be assessed by means of the NYSAA twice a year

55. In your classroom, you have several students with disabilities. You wish to differentiate their instructional materials. All of the examples below are minor adaptations to instructional materials *except*

    A.   the addition of arrows, underlining, or other graphics that demarcate key information in a text for a student with attention problems
    B.   a brief, simplified summary of the instructions and expectations associated with a particular task for a student with an intellectual disability
    C.   using different instructional materials from the general education students
    D.   oral instructions that are delivered to other students in writing for a student with vision problems

56. The No Child Left Behind Act (NCLB) of 2001 requires that instructional practices be based on scientifically-based research. What is an example of scientifically-based research?

    A.   educational theories
    B.   informal anecdotes about teaching and learning
    C.   common sense
    D.   clear, detailed reports of studies in peer-reviewed journals, books, and other sources

57. With respect to instructional and classroom management strategies, best practices in the general education classroom tend to be desirable for the education of students with disabilities. One example of a best practice in including students with disabilities in general education is:

   A. having students work in ability groupings to avoid frustration
   B. not requiring students to complete homework
   C. holding high expectations for students' academic performance and behavior
   D. allowing students with disabilities to take breaks throughout the day as needed

58. NYSAA performance is recorded in the form of observations, interviews, parent surveys, student work, and other materials gathered over a period of several months. Performance is then scored

   A. on a four-point rating scale, with a 1 indicating that the student requires extensive scaffolding, and a 4 indicating that the student can participate in the activity independently, in a variety of settings, and can evaluate his/her own performance
   B. on a three-point rating scale with 1 indicating that the student requires extensive scaffolding and a 3 indicating that the student can participate in the activity independently, in a variety of settings, and can evaluate his/her own performance
   C. the same four-point scale used to assess students on the standardized tests
   D. on a checklist of skills achieved at a level ranging from minimal achievement to mastery

59. Modifications to instruction and/or curriculum for students with disabilities include

   A. modifications to presentation
   B. modifications to response
   C. modifications to setting
   D. modifications to presentation, response, and setting

60. Teachers are now required to use research-based practices when teaching students with disabilities. Which of the practices below is NOT research based?

   A. practices that build speed reading
   B. practices that build phonological and phonemic awareness skills
   C. practices that build phonics skills
   D. practices that build reading fluency

61. You are required to teach an adolescent with disabilities skills of self-determination. You will know that they have acquired these skills when they

    A. have the ability to choose actions that will help achieve goals
    B. have an understanding of right and wrong
    C. have an ability to pay their bills
    D. can follow others' directions

62. Students with disabilities may take medication as one of several strategies to manage their disability. When a student is taking medication for a disability, teachers should

    A. monitor students' level of fatigue
    B. respond appropriately to signs that medication-related benefits are declining or the side effects are increasing
    C. be aware of increased absences
    D. be aware of students' dislike for taking medications

63. One important goal of instruction is generalization. Generalization is the

    A. recall of what has been learned
    B. application of what has been learned to new situations
    C. initial learning of new content or skills
    D. process of trial and error

64. The following groups of students (which are not completely exclusive of each other) have been found to be overrepresented in special education programs *except*

    A. students from certain racial or ethnic backgrounds (e.g., African-American and Hispanic students)
    B. students from low socioeconomic status backgrounds (i.e., poor students)
    C. students from non-majority linguistic backgrounds (e.g., students who speak a regional dialect)
    D. students from white middle class backgrounds

65. A primary concern about disproportionality is that it represents some degree of inaccuracy in the identification of students with disabilities. That is, disproportionality is assumed to result in part from a

    A. higher rate of mislabeling students from certain groups as having disabilities
    B. higher rate of discrimination against students from certain groups
    C. higher rate of mislabeling girls as having disabilities
    D. lower rate of mislabeling students from certain groups as having disabilities

66. IDEA requires that schools make adaptations to increase the accessibility of materials, facilities, activities, and other resources to students with disabilities. Which of the following examples is not an adaptation that promotes accessibility?

   A. a teaching assistant is assigned to provide one-on-one instruction throughout the day
   B. instructional activities and materials can be modified to increase accessibility for individual students
   C. desks and other furniture can be arranged to allow sufficient space for students with wheelchairs or crutches to move around
   D. technological devices can be used in the classroom to increase accessibility to instruction for individual students

67. Teachers wishing to increase the acquisition of high-frequency words should use which of the following strategies?

   A. a word wall, word banks, and word games
   B. repeated readings, timed readings
   C. read-alouds
   D. choral reading

68. Explicit vocabulary instruction is critical to literacy development. Which of the examples below is not an example of explicit vocabulary instruction?

   A. dictionary usage
   B. multiple exposures
   C. conversations with parents and teachers
   D. word analysis

69. This requirement within IDEA, commonly referred to as inclusion, was originally based on the concept of

   A. individualized educational program
   B. child find
   C. nondiscriminatory assessment
   D. the right to a free, appropriate public education in the least restrictive environment

70. Which of the following statements best describes why mislabeling students is problematic?

    A. Labeling a student with a disability can create social and academic stigmas for the student and for the group represented by the student.
    B. Once students have begun to receive special education services, they tend to remain in special education.
    C. Students in special education programs may have diminished opportunities for contact with peers, experience lower academic expectations, less rigorous curricula, and fewer opportunities both in and beyond school.
    D. Mislabeling will have multiple impacts on a student including academic and social stigma, lower academic expectations leading to fewer opportunities beyond school, and significant challenges in producing data to reverse the previously incorrect identification.

71. When working with students with disabilities who also exhibit cultural or linguistic differences, teachers should keep in mind that

    A. individuals from other cultures may have culturally specific concepts of disabilities that differ from those reflected in American educational practices
    B. students who exhibit cultural or linguistic differences are not eligible for special education services
    C. individuals from other cultures may not fully understand the American educational system
    D. individuals from other cultures may not be fluent in the English language

72. In contrast to traditional approaches, positive behavior support (PBS) is an evidence-based approach to promoting desirable behaviors

    A. while discouraging undesirable ones
    B. based on the assumption that problem behaviors cannot be effectively addressed unless their causes are understood
    C. which uses knowledge about the causes of problem behaviors to develop interventions
    D. through three key factors: the examination of root causes of problem behaviors, discouraging undesirable behaviors, and the development of positive interventions to improve behaviors

73. As children build reading skills, they increasingly rely on syntactic clues. Syntactic clues help readers to

    A. recognize familiar words
    B. anticipate upcoming words in a text
    C. infer the meanings of unfamiliar words
    D. recognize familiar words, anticipate upcoming words in a text, and infer the meanings of unfamiliar words

74. Comprehension monitoring

    A. refers to the meanings of parts of words, sentences, and larger units
    B. refers to the reader's ongoing awareness of whether the text makes sense
    C. pertains to rules governing the placement of words in phrases, clauses, and sentences
    D. refers to the meanings of parts of words, sentences, and larger units, the reader's ongoing awareness of whether the text makes sense, and the rules governing the placement of words in phrases, clauses, and sentences

75. Behavioral instruction, alone or as part of an intervention, often reflects the following sequence:

    A. prompts, task analysis, shaping, chaining, fading, transfer
    B. task analysis, chaining, shaping, prompts, fading, transfer
    C. shaping, chaining, task analysis, fading, transfer, prompts
    D. transfer, fading, prompts, shaping, chaining, task analysis

76. One point upon which all experts would agree is that there is much variability in reading difficulties from child to child. Therefore, it is more important to identify

    A. the reading level at which a particular child needs extra support than it is to agree on how to label the child
    B. the reading interest of a particular child who needs extra support than it is to agree on how to label the child
    C. the reading skills for which a particular child needs extra support than it is to agree on how to label the child
    D. the reading history of a particular child who needs extra support than it is to agree on how to label the child

77. Studies have shown that Curriculum Based Measurement (CBM) is a reliable and valid approach to progress monitoring with students who have, or who are suspected to have, disabilities. One advantage of CBM is that

    A. it does not require specialized training
    B. the quickness and ease of CBM administration and the nature of what is tested allows CBM to be readily used for the screening of all students as well as the progress monitoring of individual students with disabilities
    C. it can be administered by peers
    D. parents love it

78. You are teaching a student to use strategy comprehension monitoring. What are you teaching them to look for?

    A. elements of a text that are inconsistent with each other or with the reader's prior knowledge
    B. elements of a text that are unclear, ambiguous, or lacking in key information
    C. elements of a text that represent unwarranted conclusions or an unexpected event
    D. elements of a text that are inconsistent with each other or with the reader's prior knowledge, unclear, ambiguous, or lacking in key information, and represent unwarranted conclusions or an unexpected event

79. Which of the following is not considered a text feature?

    A. an author
    B. a timeline
    C. a table of contents
    D. an index

80. Inclusion refers to the practice of

    A. educating students with disabilities in the general education classroom, so that they may participate in day-to-day routines alongside students without disabilities to the greatest extent possible
    B. guaranteed participation in the general education classroom 100% of the time
    C. having students with disabilities included in the general education classroom only when their achievement would be near grade level without substantial support
    D. educating a student with disabilities outside the general classroom, or by other experts

81. If text features are elements added to a text that facilitate the reader's comprehension, text structures are the

    A. sequence of a text
    B. cause and effect elements of a text
    C. ways that information is organized in a text
    D. introduction of a problem followed by many solutions

82. Federal laws protect the confidentiality of assessment results and other educational records. Which of the following are some of the legal requirements pertaining to confidentiality?

    A. parents may request that the records be amended if they believe the records are inaccurate, misleading, or violate the child's privacy
    B. generally, the school must obtain parental consent before disclosing assessment results and other records containing personally identifiable information about the child
    C. the school must obtain parental consent before disclosing to those outside the school assessment results and other records containing personally identifiable information about the child, and parents may request that the records be amended if they feel the records are inaccurate, misleading, or violate the child's privacy
    D. a school has the right to share student assessment results with whomever they believe is appropriate

83. When teaching writing, a teacher should focus on the four main areas of

    A. good posture, location of paper, pencil grip, and letter formation
    B. mechanics, orthography, content, and process
    C. orientation of text, spelling, capitalization, and punctuation
    D. word choice, sentence construction, organization, and clarity

84. Teaching strategies that promote self-determination among students with disabilities, include

    A. maintaining positive expectations for students
    B. helping students identify their own strengths and interests
    C. teaching students about their own disabilities
    D. maintaining positive expectations, and teaching self-awareness and advocacy

85. In order to meet the requirements of the least restrictive environment, schools must make available a continuum of services to meet the needs of individual students with disabilities. As per New York State law, these services may include which of the following?

    A. consultant teacher
    B. resource room
    C. special classes
    D. consultant teacher, resource room, and/or special classes

86. A teacher wishing to implement strategies to teach effective writing may include which of the following strategies?

    A. explicit, systematic instruction in necessary skills
    B. opportunities to engage in meaningful writing
    C. integration of writing activities with content instruction
    D. explicit, systematic instruction in necessary skills, opportunities to engage in meaningful writing, and the integration of writing activities with content instruction

87. Some instructional practices that a teacher may use to teach mathematics include

    A. peer tutoring, authentic activities, and visual tools
    B. use of technology, audio books, and counting out loud
    C. enlarged print, graph paper, and colored pencils
    D. numerous activities including peer tutoring, authentic activities, and visual tools, enlarged print, graph paper, and colored pencils

88. Transitions may pose physical, cognitive, and/or emotional challenges for students with disabilities. Supports and services that are designed to help students with disabilities shift from life in a secondary school environment to adult life in the community include

    A. transition services
    B. group home opportunities
    C. social services
    D. transportation services

89. Related services consist of developmental, corrective, and other supportive services that help students with disabilities access

    A. community-based activities
    B. the general education curriculum
    C. the special education curriculum
    D. activities with peers

90. Assistive technology refers to any device that maintains or improves the functioning of individuals with disabilities. An example of assistive technology is

  A. a wheelchair
  B. large pencils
  C. graphic organizer software
  D. a wheelchair, large pencils, and/or graphic organizer software

Constructed Response

Write a 400- to 600-word essay on the following:

After several prereferral team meetings and multiple interventions implemented, it has been determined that Ann, a 3rd grader, may be eligible for a full psychological evaluation to determine if she may benefit from special education identification and services. In your role as the elementary special education teacher, please briefly explain to Ann's parents the process of referral, evaluation, determination, and program identification.

NYSTCE STUDENTS WITH DISABILITIES TEST 2 GRID

Competency	Items
Competency 0001: Foundation of Special Education	1, 5, 10, 18, 26, 27, 34, 44, 56, 69, 80
Competency 0002: Knowledge of Students with Disabilities	3, 6, 11, 19, 42, 51, 53, 57, 62, 71, 76
Competency 0003: Assessment and Individual Program Planning	4, 7, 12, 14, 20, 28, 29, 36, 38, 40, 41, 45, 46, 48, 54, 58, 64, 65, 70, 77, 82, 85, 89
Competency 0004: Strategies for Planning and Managing the Learning Environment and for Providing Behavioral Interventions	8, 13, 21, 22, 30, 37, 47, 50, 66, 72, 75
Competency 0005: Instructional Planning and Delivery to Promote Students' Success in the General Curriculum	2, 9, 15, 23, 31, 35, 39, 49, 55, 59, 60, 63, 67, 68, 73, 74, 78, 79, 81, 83, 86, 87, 90
Competency 0006: Strategies for Teaching Communication Skills, Social Skills and Functional Living Skills	16, 17, 24, 25, 32, 33, 43, 52, 61, 84, 88
Competency 0007	Constructed Response

ANSWER KEY

1.	B	31.	D	61.	A
2.	D	32.	A	62.	B
3.	D	33.	D	63.	B
4.	B	34.	C	64.	D
5.	D	35.	C	65.	A
6.	B	36.	B	66.	A
7.	D	37.	B	67.	A
8.	B	38.	A	68.	C
9.	C	39.	B	69.	D
10.	A	40.	C	70.	D
11.	D	41.	B	71.	A
12.	C	42.	A	72.	D
13.	C	43.	B	73.	D
14.	D	44.	D	74.	B
15.	B	45.	D	75.	B
16.	B	46.	C	76.	C
17.	D	47.	C	77.	B
18.	B	48.	B	78.	D
19.	B	49.	B	79.	A
20.	C	50.	C	80.	A
21.	A	51.	D	81.	C
22.	D	52.	C	82.	C
23.	A	53.	A	83.	B
24.	C	54.	D	84.	D
25.	D	55.	C	85.	D
26.	B	56.	D	86.	D
27.	D	57.	C	87.	A
28.	D	58.	A	88.	A
29.	A	59.	D	89.	B
30.	D	60.	A	90.	D

ANSWER EXPLANATIONS

1. **B**

    All other laws named either paved the foundation for this law, or followed this law in a broader application. This law was specific to the education of children with disabilities.

2. **D**

    This response is correct as it provides the most comprehensive response.

3. **D**

    This response is correct because it refers to children's ability to understand language as being stronger and develops earlier than children's ability to use language.

4. **B**

    This response provides the most comprehensive definition of assessment.

5. **D**

    Parents must be notified, parental permission achieved, and an individualized assessment must be performed—you must achieve *all* of these, not just some.

6. **B**

    Mental retardation, epilepsy, and mental illness are not the correct names of the categories of disability under which students with these needs would be identified.

7. **D**

    This response is correct as it refers to multiple steps in the process and the information gathered through an ecological assessment.

8. **B**

These overall strategies incorporate the smaller details named in the other choices.

9. **C**

The Common Core Learning Standards are not meant to build upon, supplement, or contradict the earlier NYS standards. They are intended to replace them.

10. **A**

The procedural safeguards in IDEA are available *only* for parents and their children with disabilities.

11. **D**

This is the correct response because it identifies the development of semantics, the importance of word meanings, and how vocabulary develops over time.

12. **C**

Evaluation refers to the determination of what students have already achieved. This is the distinct purpose of an evaluation, which then allows for instructional planning.

13. **C**

If a teacher focuses on their use of time, student behavior, and their classroom environment and becomes effective in monitoring these, all other details will follow.

14. **D**

Assessments provide data that offers answers to complex, multi-faceted questions rather than a simple response to a finite question.

15. **B**

Access to the classroom, textbooks, and tests is not sufficient. Students with disabilities need access to the entire curriculum.

16. **B**

A child with an articulation disorder has difficulties producing certain speech sounds. This is the definition of an articulation disorder.

17. **D**

A student with language impairments could exhibit phonological disorders, expressive language disorders, or receptive or expressive language disorders. This is a very broad category of identification and may include a combination of disorders.

18. **B**

A team approach is not a choice.

19. **B**

This statement is *false*, children may begin school at the age required by state law, regardless of language development. Statements (A), (C), and (D) are all true.

20. **C**

A diagnostic assessment is the most appropriate assessment as it will indicate the areas in which extra support may be needed.

21. **A**

Teachers often assume that students know what is expected of them; often this is not the case. To ensure that students know what is expected, be clear in stating the behavioral expectations and check for understanding.

22. **D**

This response provides the most comprehensive classroom management plan. Modeling desirable behaviors, structuring appropriate activities, and creating a sense of community are all effective classroom management strategies.

23. **A**

Your child is eligible for everything listed except child care, as it is not educationally relevant.

24. **C**

An expressive language disorder is an impairment in which expressive language abilities are much lower than expected for the student's age, although mental functioning and receptive language skills fall within the normal range. This provides a much more specific identification of the individual student's needs.

25. **D**

A teacher may help to prevent a speech and language disorder by addressing a student's needs early on if the teacher is aware of the student having a hearing impairment, a family history of communication disorders, and/or other medical disorders which affect speech and language. Knowledge of all of these elements of a student's life will help to implement early intervention to prevent further development of the disorder.

26. **B**

The other legislations named were either the original title of this law or legislation that developed after IDEA.

27. **D**

The prereferral team obtains information about the student's strengths and weakness, designs and oversees the implementation of interventions, and evaluates the results of the interventions. If the interventions are not successful, referral for special education assessment will be made.

28. **D**

A progress monitoring assessment allows a teacher to determine if the pace of a students' progress is adequate, or if the intervention may need to be revised.

29. **A**

A screening assessment is an assessment specific to group administration. The other choices are administered in an individual setting.

30. **D**

Students often model what they see. Teachers need to check their responses to make sure they are modeling what they wish to see in students' responses.

31. **D**

IDEA requires early intervention services be provided in a natural setting such as the home or a child care center. Schools, hospitals, or therapeutic settings are not considered natural settings for children from birth to age 3.

32. **A**

Hearing aids are not a communication support; they are a hearing device. Cell phones with texting, closed captioning, and speech-to-text translators all help with communication rather than specifically improving hearing.

33. **D**

Instruction in adaptive living skills includes instruction in all of the following areas: domestic living, social skills, and self-direction in work and leisure.

34. **C**

IDEA involved the granting of children with disabilities the right to a free, appropriate public education in the least restrictive environment. This concept was philosophically a new idea when first introduced.

35. **C**

Choice (C) is an example of guided practice because it offers practice on a skill recently taught, with the support of the text, as well as the teacher. It helps close the gap between new information being taught and being able to use that information independently.

36. **B**

A prereferral assessment, as the name suggests, is administered prior to referring students for a full evaluation for special education services. This data will support your referral.

37. **B**

Teachers should treat students warmly, with respect, and engage in active listening, which forms a positive bond with students as individuals. All the other answer choices create distance between the teacher and students.

38. **A**

Traditional educational assessments rely heavily on standardized tests such as the state-mandated group achievement tests. They are norm-referenced and generally rely on multiple-choice responses.

39. **B**

The general education classroom is identified as the least restrictive environment in IDEA.

40. **C**

Rubrics and portfolios are examples of authentic assessments. This type of assessment relies heavily on rubrics and portfolios to capture individualized student learning.

41. **B**

Checklists, rating scales, and duration records are all examples of observational assessments. They all allow you to collect the data/information you are observing.

42. **A**

Choices B, C, and D all have an error in the sequence. Notice the placement of transitional reading—the transitional time in which students gain independence in reading and are able to move from learning to read, to reading to learn.

43. **B**

Field trips are not considered community-based instruction as there may not be specific instructional activities that involve repeated visits and learning skills that may later be applied in this setting.

44. **D**

RTI includes high quality instruction, increasing intensity in individualized instruction, and referral to special education assessment when a student reaches the final tier and continues to struggle. The RTI model requires that all of these components be included—not just some.

45. **D**

This response provides the only true statement regarding authentic assessments.

46. **C**

A portfolio is used to gauge student effort, progress, and achievement through examination of many different kinds of work that the student has produced in a particular class or related to a specific theme. Portfolio assessments are not meant to determine if a student has achieved a particular standard or if they are ready to advance to the next grade level.

47. **C**

When grouping students for the purpose of special education instruction, teachers must limit variability when grouping according to academic achievement, functional performance, and learning characteristics. This focus on limited variability is specific to special education teachers for the purpose of special education instruction only. This supports the specialized instruction provided to groups.

48. **B**

Alternative assessments can be used for all students. It is a common misunderstanding that alternative assessments are only for students with disabilities when, in fact, alternate assessments may benefit all students and can be used as a supplement to other traditional forms of assessment.

49. **B**

In order to meet the learning needs of individual students, a teacher must assess the learners' needs. Step 1 is understanding your students' needs.

50. **C**

This student could be a student with or without a disability. There is nothing that identifies the student as a student with a disability. Any student could exhibit this behavior for a variety of reasons.

51. **D**

All three—academic, behavioral, and social functioning—may be part of a student's disability.

52. **C**

Ignoring someone's needs is not a social skill. Social skills include establishing and maintaining friendships, responding to conflict, and dealing with bullying.

53. **A**

Mastering the general education curriculum at the same rate as peers specifically refers to why a student with a disability will need support in academic functioning.

54. **D**

This answer is false because the NYSAA is administered once a year, not twice.

55. **C**

Using different instructional materials than for the general education students is not a minor adaptation. It is actually a modification because you are using different materials rather than the same materials as for other students.

56. **D**

    The definition of scientifically-based research is clear: detailed reports of studies in peer-reviewed journals, books, and other sources.

57. **C**

    The practice of having high expectations for students' academic performance and behavior has been supported through research as one which results in greater positive outcomes for students with disabilities within the general education classroom.

58. **A**

    The other responses indicate a three-point scale, checklists or the same scale used on the standardized tests, all of which are inaccurate.

59. **D**

    This is the best response, as all three types of modification can be made to the instruction and/or curriculum for students with disabilities.

60. **A**

    Practices that build phonological awareness, phonics, and reading fluency are all research-based practices. Speed reading is not a research-based practice.

61. **A**

    A student's ability to choose actions that will help them achieve their goals is key to having learned self-determination.

62. **B**

    The teacher should respond appropriately to signs that the medication-related benefits are declining or the side effects are increasing. This statement is the most important relative to the student's academic and behavioral performance in the classroom.

63. **B**

Generalization is the application of what has been learned to new situations. The key words in this response are application and new situations. This is the definition of generalization.

64. **D**

Generally, students from white middle class backgrounds are accurately represented in special education programs.

65. **A**

The other responses may be suspected or beliefs on the part of some individuals, but have not been proven.

66. **A**

A teaching assistant assigned to provide one-on-one instruction throughout the day does not support accessibility. The student does not experience independence and time with peers when supported one-on-one throughout the day. Other strategies are much more effective.

67. **A**

Teachers wishing to increase the acquisition of high-frequency words should use a word wall, word banks, and word games. The other answer choices are strategies to improve reading fluency.

68. **C**

Conversations with parents and teachers is not an example of explicit vocabulary instruction as it does not ensure that vocabulary will explicitly be identified. This is a subtle, implicit, uncertain strategy. It does not provide direct instruction.

69. **D**

Inclusion is grounded in the IDEA requirement of the right to a free, appropriate public education in the least restrictive environment.

70. **D**

This response is correct as it *best* describes the fact that labeling and mislabeling a student has multiple impacts on a child. Labeling can result in social or academic stigmas. Often students do not move out of special education services, and this label may limit opportunities both in and out of school for a number of reasons. Therefore, mislabeling can have a significant impact on an individual's life.

71. **A**

Individuals from other cultures may have culturally-specific concepts of disabilities that differ from those reflected in American educational practices. This response is the best response as it relates specially to students with disabilities and their families. The other responses may be true of students with or without disabilities.

72. **D**

This response is correct in that discouraging undesirable behaviors, understanding the cause of the behaviors, and developing interventions are all required components of PBS.

73. **D**

All of the answer choices allow children to build reading skills.

74. **B**

Comprehension monitoring refers to the reader's ongoing awareness of whether the text makes sense or not. The other choices relate to the use of syntax clues. Comprehension monitoring requires an ongoing awareness on the part of the reader.

75. **B**

Task analysis, chaining, shaping, prompts, fading, and transfer is the accurate sequence for behavioral instruction. All the other answer choices show items out of order.

76. **C**

It is important to identify the reading skills for which a particular child needs extra support than it is to agree on how to label the child. There has been much debate in the world of reading instruction; however, it has become clear that reading skills are the main focus of support.

77. **B**

This response is true; the other statements are false because you do need to know how to administer CBM, it cannot be administered by student peers, and often parents do not know much about it, much less love it.

78. **D**

This is the correct response, as there are a variety of strategies that teach students how to monitor their comprehension of a text.

79. **A**

An author is not considered a text feature. Text features include timelines, the table of contents, and an index.

80. **A**

Inclusion refers to the practice of educating students with disabilities in the general education classroom, so that they may participate to the greatest extent possible in day-to-day routines alongside students without disabilities. There is no requirement that this must happen 100% of the time, based on educational achievement or require removal from the general education classroom.

81. **C**

The key here is that text structure relates to organization. Although sequence is one example of an organization, there can be many ways how organization can be accomplished.

82. **C**

This response is correct in that parents can request that records be amended and a school must obtain permission before disclosing any personally identifiable information about the child.

83. **B**

Responses in (A), (C), and (D) may contribute specific details to these categories, but mechanics, orthography, content, and process are the main areas that must be focused on when teaching writing.

84. **D**

Teaching skills that lead to self-determination include maintaining positive expectations, helping students identify and advocate for their strengths and interests, and helping them to be more self-aware by teaching them about their own disabilities. Once equipped with these tools, they can make choices for themselves.

85. **D**

A consultant teacher, resource room, and special classes are all included in the continuum of services available to students with disabilities in New York State. The appropriate setting is determined by the student's needs.

86. **D**

This response is correct as all of the strategies named have been identified as effective, research-based strategies in teaching writing.

87. **A**

Peer tutoring, authentic activities, and visual tools are instructional practices that are research based and have been proven effective in teaching mathematics.

88. **A**

Although students experience many transitions, when specifically referring to transition services, IDEA refers to moving from the school environment to adult life in the community.

89. **B**

Related services focus on helping students with disabilities access the general education curriculum.

90. **D**

This response is correct, as wheelchairs, large pencils, and graphic organizer software are all examples of assistive technology because they improve the functioning of the student with disabilities.

◼ Constructed-Response Sample Answer

Thank you for meeting with me so I might explain the process of referral, evaluation, determination, and program identification for your daughter Ann.

Ann's teachers have shared some concerns regarding her academic progress, and have been meeting to recommend and implement various interventions. However, even with these additional interventions, it seems that Ann continues to struggle and has not made the progress we would expect from her in 3rd grade. Therefore, the team would like to refer her for a psychological evaluation.

When teachers make a referral, the referral must include the concerns the teachers have, any data such as classroom assessment and standardized assessments that support this concern, a description of the interventions previously implemented, and the results of these interventions. If it is determined by the team of teachers and you the parent that an evaluation is justified, then you will need to provide permission for the evaluation. An evaluation will then be scheduled and completed.

The evaluation process looks at multiple aspects of a child's academic life and includes information about the child's school and home environment as well as the child's medical history. Tests are an important part of the evaluation, but the family's input is also very important. A complete evaluation will include (1) a physical examination; (2) an individual psychological evaluation by the school psychologist or an outside evaluator; (3) a complete social history usually provided by the parents; (4) a written observation of the student in the classroom setting; and (5) appropriate educational evaluations and assessments relating to the areas of suspected disabilities.

After the evaluation is completed, the team, including teachers, you the parent, and the evaluators, review all the evaluation materials that have been gathered. After a thorough review and discussion of the data, the team determines if your child is eligible for special education services. If so, the team will then, along with your input, develop an Individualized Educational Program (IEP) for your child.

INDEX

T

U

V

NOTES

NOTES

NOTES

NOTES

NOTES

NOTES